LESSONS
FROM THE
LETTERS

Living the Abundant Life

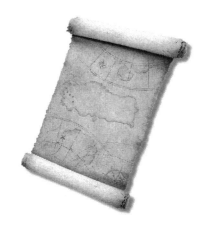

LEIGH W. YOUNG

DEDICATION

I dedicate this book to my wonderful family. Your care and devotion give me a glimpse of the beautiful love of God.

To Lucretia, my nurturing firstborn. You have taught me many lessons and have brought such joy to my life. You, Nate, Carolina, and Bella have prayed me through the research and the writing of this book. Those sweet innocent toddler prayers inspire me! Your thoughtful and kind love and attention brighten my life.

To Kathryn, my editor and advisor. You lovingly read each and every word and then read them again…and again. Baby Jude refused to be born until you put the finishing touches on the manuscript. You and Scott inspire me to excellence with your brilliance and tenacity. Your edits are invaluable. We birthed this book alongside your precious baby.

To Mary Victoria, my true and constant companion. You have devotedly hung with me through this entire process. Your laughter made the hours of research fly by. Your forced study breaks helped me to keep perspective. Your encouragement is invaluable. Your heart is pure. Your wit is sharp. Your wisdom is well beyond your years.

To David, the great romance of my life. You bring the wisdom of King Solomon and the heart of King David into our lives. You make my heart soar.

ACKNOWLEDGMENTS

To my Bible study gals, our journey together has been on holy ground, worshiping and studying the Word. Our lives are intertwined with the love of the Lord and the love of each other. Your feedback and encouragement are invaluable. I cannot express my gratitude for your insight and vision.

To my prayer warriors, I appreciate your loving care more than I can express. We have covered each other in prayer. It is a privilege and honor to join with you in prayer. Our unique bond of friendship truly divides our sorrow and multiplies our joy.

To Rob, thank you for mentoring and pastoring me. Your wisdom has opened my eyes to see the Word in a different context. You gently nudged me out of my comfort zone to experience God's plan. Your support has encouraged me to "say yes to God's yes."

Dear Lord, I am an empty vessel seeking the filling of the Holy Spirit. May these words be yours. May this journey be less of me and more of You. Thank you for amazing me, loving me, and saving me. Amen.

TO THE READER

Thank you for journeying with us. Sharing a voyage with you is a great honor and privilege. Your time is one of your most precious assets, and I appreciate your investing it in this expedition.

In the Bible in the book of Acts, the early church members gathered together amid threats of persecution and prayed to the Lord for the strength and perseverance to continue studying and spreading His word. God answered their prayer: "After they prayed, the place where they were meeting was shaken. And they were all filled with the Holy Spirit and spoke the word of God boldly" (Acts 4:31). God rocked the house.

The letters we are studying rocked their recipients as well. Each letter was custom designed to be specific for that congregation. My prayer is that you will allow these words from our Lord to rock your world just as they rocked the worlds of those early church members.

We have intentionally left much white space so that you can make notes in the margin. As you read the stories and the scripture, listen for the Holy Spirit to help you see how these words apply in your world and can help you live your most abundant life.

I prayed for you, my fellow sojourner, as I was writing these words. I will continue my prayers that these lessons will lead you to the abundant life that Christ has intended for you.

The Lessons written to the churches of Revelation over two thousand years ago are as relevant today as they were then. So, grab your bags and let's journey to these seven churches to find the Lessons from the Letters.

Please let me know what lessons you learned from the letters and how the Word has changed you at LessonsfromtheLetters@gmail.com. You can also follow us at our website, LessonsfromtheLetters.com or on Instagram @leighw.young.

If you would like to host a weekend journey for your church or other group using *Lessons from the Letters*, contact me at the Gmail address above.

Many thanks again for joining me on this adventure.

Bon voyage!

In His love,
Leigh

CONTENTS

FOREWORD

In her introductory remarks, Leigh Young notes how the author of Revelation "propels us into God's future." What she doesn't mention is how masterfully she leads the reader to understand how that future vision calls us to live in new ways right here, right now. One might call this the Christian way of living in the future present.

Back to the Future is a highly imaginative motion picture which prospered at the box office several years ago. The film features a madcap scientist who perfects a machine capable of achieving the human dream of traveling through time. A teenaged boy uses the machine to journey to his hometown as it was in the 1950s before the boy was born. What happens in the movie from that point on is, of course, ludicrously good fun. The boy meets his parents and discovers what they were like in their awkward teenage years. He dazzles the populace with the unknown sport of skateboarding, and he even manages to introduce Chuck Barry to the throbbing guitar licks of the as-yet-unwritten "Johnny B. Goode." Signs of 50's quaintness abound, from soda bottles whose caps will *not* twist off to a service station with a platoon of crisply uniformed attendants who swarm each car to check the oil, clean the windshield, and sweep off the floor mats.

For all of its warm frivolity, however, this movie does ponder one serious theme: how possessing knowledge of the future would create an awesome responsibility in the present. Before moving back into time, the boy has been warned not to attempt to alter the future in any way. Indeed, as the plot unfolds, the boy has to work vigorously to ensure that the further he has already seen and lived does, in fact, develop. His mother and father, for example, are having difficulty, as teenagers, developing a romantic relationship, and the boy has to employ every ounce of his inventiveness to ensure that the conditions are created which will lead to their mutual attraction, eventual marriage, and paradoxically, the boy's own birth. Because the boy knows the future, he bears its burden and is compelled to work for its fulfillment.

The movie is playful, but the insight is a serious one. Knowledge of the future creates momentous responsibility in the present. The book of Revelation clearly states that we have seen what God's future is like, and so we live today in the light of that tomorrow, even if that means at times "going against the flow."

Leigh Young, in *Lessons from the Letters-Living the Abundant Life*, captures the breadth and depth of eschatological hope and call. By the time you get to the end of her work, you will see that we have seen the future in which Jesus is Lord and that we are called to serve him in a time when his Lordship seems hidden and in doubt.

It is quite a responsibility to have seen the future, but the future we have seen is God's future. In that day, says John, the Evangelist:

> "Look! God's dwelling place is now among the people, and he will dwell with them. They will be his people, and God himself will be with them and be their God. 'He will wipe every tear from their eyes. There will be no more death' or mourning or crying or pain, for the old order of things has passed away." (Rv 21:3-4)

As a pastor, I have used the "core" words of Christianity time and time again. Good words like "faith" and "hope." What helps me to keep using those words is that someone like Leigh Young comes along, and suddenly these words are no longer an abstraction. I see them wrapped up in the flesh of a friend, and they become powerful and useful once more. I am so grateful for my twenty years as Leigh's pastor and for my experience of her winsome witness in our midst.

Leigh Young has a rare constellation of gifts: intellectual carefulness coupled with remarkable relationship sensibilities. As a teacher and writer, she will catch your imagination with a riveting phrase as she leads you down pathways where you will discover new truths about yourself, your world, and your faith.

Dr. Rob Blackburn
Pastor and Author

OVERVIEW

I s there more to life than just going through the daily motions and routines?
Do you want a life that is deeper, more fulfilling, more meaningful?

What if you discovered letters that promise to bless you if you read them?

What if you found writings that reveal the way to your most abundant life?

Would you take the time to read and to study them?

These texts exist. They are contained in seven letters tucked away in a book written by Jesus Christ, the Son of God, and dictated to the apostle John. We call this book Revelation.

These letters, found in the second and third chapters of the book of Revelation, are addressed to the believers in seven churches in the area called Asia Minor in New Testament times. Today, we call this land Turkey.

Although penned to actual congregations centuries ago, the words of advice and counsel in the letters are as relevant to us today as they were to the seven churches in the first century.

Join us as we journey to these ancient cities and the churches within them and discover the *Lessons from the Letters-Living the Abundant Life.*

LIVING THE ABUNDANT LIFE

Before we embark on our journey to the seven churches, we need to make two quick but important stops. The first place we will visit will provide a deeper knowledge and greater understanding of exactly what it means to live the abundant life.

Our stopover is not the court of a king who rules vast kingdoms. The venue is not a boardroom touting graphs denoting soaring profit margins. The location does not include pricey cars, vogue clothes, or buff bodies.

We will not be learning about the abundant life from movie stars, wealthy entrepreneurs, fit athletes, or powerful executives.

Our stop is in a sheep pen. Jesus is meeting us there to educate us on the subject of the abundant life. You can read his words in the Gospel of John.

> "Truly, truly, I say to you, he who does not enter the sheepfold by the door but climbs in by another way, that man is a thief and a robber. But he who enters by the door is the shepherd of the sheep. To him the gatekeeper opens. The sheep hear his voice, and he calls his own sheep by name and leads them out. When he has brought out all his own, he goes before them, and the sheep follow him, for they know his voice. A stranger they will not follow, but they will flee from him, for they do not know the voice of strangers." This figure of speech Jesus used with them, but they did not understand what he was saying to them.

> So Jesus again said to them, "Truly, truly, I say to you, I am the door of the sheep. All who came before me are thieves and robbers, but the sheep did not listen to them. I am the door. If anyone enters by me, he will be saved and will go in and out and find pasture. The thief comes only to steal and kill and destroy. I came that they may have life and have it abundantly. I am the good shepherd." (Jn 10:1-11 ESV) [1]

Jesus is the "good shepherd," the one willing to give his life for his sheep. Good shepherds are willing to fight wild animals who want lambs for their evening meal. He will give his life to save the life of the sheep.

Jesus did the same for us. He sacrificed his life for our lives so that we can live forever in heaven with Him. This gift demonstrates the first characteristic of the abundant life.

The abundant life holds the promise of an eternity in heaven.

Jesus describes Himself as the "gate" (Jn 10:9). The shepherd would guide the sheep into a pen which was secured on three sides. When the animals were safely inside, the shepherd would lie down, creating the fourth side of the pen with his body. He formed a living gate to keep the sheep in and other animals out. The protection of the pen provided the sheep the security and space they needed to relax and settle down.

Sheep, more than other animals, have bodies which require adequate rest to be healthy. They belong to a group of animals called ruminants who eat their food and swallow it. Later, they regurgitate this food. When they are calmly resting, they will reprocess the partially digested food. This chewing of the cud is what gives the sheep the nutrients required to make milk, grow thick wool, and maintain their overall health. Therefore, the shepherd has to lead them to a place where they can find peaceful respite.

Jesus leads us into "the paths of righteousness" (Ps 23:3) and makes us "lie down in green pastures" (Ps 23:2). He shows us the boundaries in which we will thrive. He helps us establish these parameters in two ways. First, He teaches us in the Word. Second, He is the Word and shows us the way by His example. The security of clear boundaries helps us to enjoy an abundance of peace and security.

—

The abundant life holds the promise of clear boundaries.

The good shepherd "leads [the sheep] out" (Jn 10:3). He "goes ahead of them," encountering the dangers and challenges before the sheep arrive (Jn 10:4) God and His word are the "lamp unto our feet, and the light unto our path" (Ps 119:105).

The abundant life holds the promise of a Lord who will lead you.

The good shepherd remains with the sheep; "he calls his own sheep by name and leads them out. When he has brought out all his own, he goes before them" (Jn 10:3-4). Phillip Keller tells of the importance of the shepherd's constant vigilance. A fatal danger for sheep is to become cast. Casting occurs when the animal is on its back and unable to get back on its feet. In the cast position, a sheep is helpless and vulnerable to the attack of a predator.[2] The observant shepherd is there to help the cast sheep when it is in trouble.

**The abundant life holds the promise of a Lord
who will never leave or forsake you.**

The good shepherd "calls his own sheep by name" (Jn 10:3). The shepherd does not see a mass of white wooly, stinky beasts. He lovingly views each individual as unique with his or her own name. Jesus invites us to bask in his love: "As the Father has loved me, so have I loved you. Now remain in my love" (Jn 15:9).

**The abundant life holds the promise of a God who
knows your name and has a special love for you.**

While we are still on our break at the sheep pen, let's notice what Jesus did *not* say about the abundant life. He never promises good health, great wealth, or an easy ride. God is not a genie in a bottle granting wishes.

Jesus is very clear on this point. "In this world you will have trouble" (Jn 16:33). Yet, His next statement speaks to the abundant life: "But take heart! I have overcome the world" (Jn 16:33).

Tell the sheep goodbye and come along to our next stop, an island in the Mediterranean Sea.

THE BOOK OF THE REVELATION OF JESUS CHRIST

You may be thinking that this island vacay sounds much more appealing than the sheep pen excursion. Unfortunately, the island jaunt is not as attractive as it sounds.

Our Mediterranean destination, the island of Patmos, is the Alcatraz of the Med. This treeless, rocky island served as a prison work camp. The letters in the book of Revelation were penned on this small island. We will stop here long enough to uncover the background of the letters and their author.

Throughout this study, we will use historical and cultural facts to help us contextually. Scholars disagree on the exact details and dates of some of these occurrences. Knowing that we gain more from focusing on eternal truths than we do from debating worldly minutiae, we will concentrate on the larger lessons in lieu of discussing dates and details.

No one knows the particulars of the apostle John's final years. However, many historians and scholars agree on these facts: John was one of the original twelve disciples of Christ. He wrote the Gospel of John and the Epistles, 1 John, 2 John, and 3 John. He also wrote the book of Revelation as a prisoner on the island of Patmos. This beloved follower of Jesus was banished to this brutal work camp by Emperor Domitian because of his insistent desire to share the love and good news of Jesus with the Roman world. This sentencing would have occurred around the time of the mass persecutions ordered by Domitian in 81 AD. Tertullian, the Christian Latin author from the first and second centuries, tells a story about John in his work, *On Prescription Against Heretics*.[3] His account claims that John was punished for his faith by being placed in a cauldron of boiling oil. John emerged from the oil unscathed. The emperor, shaken by this incident, exiled John to the work camps of Patmos to quarry stone.

While on the island, John received a revelation from Jesus.

I, John, your brother and companion in the suffering and kingdom and patient endurance that are ours in Jesus, was on the island of Patmos because of the word of God and the testimony of Jesus. On the Lord's Day I was in the Spirit, and I heard behind me a loud voice like a trumpet, which said: "Write on a scroll what you see and send it to the seven churches: to Ephesus, Smyrna, Pergamum, Thyatira, Sardis, Philadelphia and Laodicea." (Rv 1:9–11)

The voice behind John was the voice of Jesus dictating the letters to him. Since John was merely the scribe writing down the words, I will refer to Jesus as the author.

The book of Revelation begins with these words.

The revelation from Jesus Christ, which God gave him to show his servants what must soon take place. He made it known by sending his angel to his servant John, who testifies to everything he saw—that is, the word of God and the testimony of Jesus Christ. (Rv 1:1-2)

Jesus is part of the trinity of God. He came down from heaven to live among us. The Apostle, Paul, describes the heavens from which Jesus descended in this way.

"What no eye has seen, what no ear has heard, and what no human mind has conceived"-- the things God has prepared for those who love him. (I Cor 2:9)

Jesus left streets of gold to walk the dusty roads of Palestine. He traded the sounds of angelic praise for the cry of a hungry baby, the plea of a hopeless beggar, and the tirade of a disgruntled shopper in a crowded marketplace. He went from sitting on the throne of heaven next to God the Father Almighty to reclining at a boisterous celebration hosted by a tax collector.

After thirty-three years of experiencing the aches and pains of daily life, the harsh abuse of jealous enemies, and the lonely heartache of misunderstanding, Jesus gave us the greatest gift. He sacrificed his life for us on this globe so that we can live with him in the glory of heaven. He availed himself to scorn, to shame, and to the physical abuse of a shameful crucifixion on a cross. At the pinnacle of his suffering, when "with a loud cry, Jesus breathed his last," something remarkable happened (Mk 15:37). "The curtain of the temple was torn in two from top to bottom" (Mk 27:51).

God meticulously and specifically designed this curtain himself. "Make a curtain of blue, purple, and scarlet yarn and finely twisted linen with cherubim worked into it by a skilled craftsman. The curtain will separate the Holy Place from the Most Holy Place" (Ex 26:31). This veil separated man from God. At the very moment of Jesus's death and sacrifice for us, the veil split in two, and God revealed his plan of salvation to us. The barrier between sinful people and a perfect God was removed by the atoning sacrifice of God's own son, and the plan for salvation was "unveiled."

In the book of Revelation, the Lord describes this "revelation" with vivid imagery to the apostle, John. While serving his prison sentence on Patmos, John sees Jesus in a graphic vision that stretched his imagination to its outer limits. He is afforded the miraculous opportunity to see another veil discarded.

In a stanza of "Hark the Herald Angels Sing," Charles Wesley paints a picture of Jesus coming to earth, "veiled in flesh, the Godhead see; hail the incarnate Deity."[4] Jesus was swaddled in his humanity like a baby wrapped in a blanket. His Deity was "incarnate." This word derives from the Latin word *carn,* meaning meat or flesh. Jesus literally came to earth with flesh wrapped around Him. He was fully man while also being fully God. In the book of Revelation, Jesus is without "carn." Jesus was "de-carnate," rolling back the flesh to reveal supernatural knowledge and wisdom to His apostle, John.

In 1895 H. G. Wells published *The Time Machine,* in which he introduced a vehicle able to transport its riders back and forth in time. If the Bible had a "time machine," John would be the conductor writing about a longer period of time than any other writer of the Bible. He carries us back to the beginning of time in the Gospel of John writing, "in the beginning was the Word and the Word was with God and the Word was God" (Jn 1:1). He carries us forward in time, chronicling Jesus Christ's time on earth. In his three Epistles, 1 John, 2 John, and 3 John, he advances us to the time of the early church, giving guidance to these believers and to the church today. In Revelation, he propels us into the future, recording the end of this world as testified by Jesus.

———

SEVEN CHURCHES

Jesus addresses letters to seven churches in seven cities. Why not six churches or eight cities? Is the number seven significant?

Numbers are important in the Bible, and particularly in the book of Revelation. The Lord loves numbers. He even named one of the books in the Bible "Numbers."

The divine number three represents the triune nature of God as the Father, the Son, and the Holy Spirit. Jesus refers to this as He gives the Great Commission. "Therefore: go and make disciples of all nations, baptizing them in the name of the Father and of the Son and of the Holy Spirit" (Mt 28:19).

Time reflects the trinity: past, present, and future.

The nature of the Lord reflects the trinity. The book of Revelation opens with the Lord introducing Himself as the One "who is, and who was, and who is to come, the Almighty" (Rev 1:8).

The body reflects the trinity. "May your whole spirit, soul, and body be kept blameless at the coming of our Lord Jesus Christ" (I Th 5:23).

The Resurrection of Jesus reflects the trinity. "The Son of Man must be delivered over to the hands of sinners, be crucified and on the third day be raised again" (Lk 24:7).

The number four represents the completeness of the Earth: "The end has come upon the four corners of the land!" (Ez 7:2). The four corners represent north, south, east, and west. Today we still use the phrase "four corners of the earth" to generalize the entire world.

Another example of the use of four comes from the book of Isaiah: "He will raise a banner for the nations and gather the exiles of Israel; he will assemble the scattered people of Judah from the four quarters of the earth" (Is 11:12).

Seven represents completeness and perfection. Three (the number of divinity) plus four (the number of the earth) equals seven (the number of perfection). When the divinity of the Lord permeates the four corners of the earth, there will be perfection. This precision materializes in the seven days of creation and the seven days of the week. The word seven is used fifty-four times in the book of Revelation, numbering the seven seals, the seven angels, the seven thunders, the seven plagues, and the seven churches.

Sending letters to seven churches implies completeness. The churches represent a full range of characteristics and challenges. Thus, the letters to these churches address a comprehensive series of praises, exhortations, and consequences for any church and its believers in any time period.

THE IMPORTANCE OF CONTEXT

As a child, I remember watching my dad's secretary insert two pieces of paper in the typewriter with a blue sheet of carbon paper between them. As the steel arm struck the top page of the packet, the carbon from the middle sheet rubbed off onto the back page producing a "carbon copy" of the document she was typing. Therefore, when I see the "Cc" (carbon copy) or "Bcc" (blind carbon copy) on the distribution lines of an email, I understand the meaning of this. Many who have never seen carbon paper will not grasp this connection and, therefore, may not fully understand why an email copied to someone is called a carbon copy. Explaining the process of copying a letter using a carbon sheet insert would give greater understanding to the derivation and meaning of this phrase.

My grandmother had a black, sturdy-looking telephone that took up the majority of the top of an end table. To place a call, you would put your finger in the correct numbered hole of the circular dial, guide it around the circle to the endpoint, and then let it go. To this day, I can hear the grating sound it made as it returned to its original place. Today, we still say that we are going to "dial" a phone number even though we are no longer using the old-fashioned round dialing mechanism. Describing this to someone who has never seen a rotary phone would provide context for the phrase "dialing the phone."

One might roll his eyes at an individual "getting on his soapbox" again. The nuance is that this person is inclined to give lengthy, repetitive speeches to convey their view. But, why would we relate this to a cleaning product container? This phrase was coined over one hundred years ago when people would physically step on wooden crates designed to ship and store soaps to make themselves tall enough to be seen by a crowd of onlookers and listeners. Again, portraying the history of the phrase enables a better understanding of it.

In scripture, no word is carelessly placed. Every word is selected for a specific purpose and meaning. In His letters to the churches in Revelation, Jesus chose specific phrases and word pictures that were relevant to that church. On our journey, we will explore the seven cities and the churches within these cities so that we can fully comprehend and capture the true meaning of these passages. The more we ascertain about these locations and their churches, the better we can appreciate the nuances of their correspondences.

Therefore, we will venture to each of these cities to assess the deeper meaning of Jesus's words. We will explore the characteristics, assets, and liabilities of the cities to determine how they affected the Christian churches within. In some of the cities, such as Laodicea, the city influenced the church. In other cities, such as Smyrna, the church survived despite the city. Some churches mirrored their hometown. Some were the opposite. In situations where the church rebelled against the city's unscrupulous morals, the believers were subjected to intense persecution. In those cities in which the church melded into the culture, little or no persecution is recorded. The congregation did not make a meaningful impact on its environment and presented no threat to the existing state of affairs. The leaders of those cities had no reason to notice and harass the believers.

After we explore the city, we will seek out the church within it. We can plant ourselves on the pews to hear the reading of the words to the congregation and catch the subtle meanings implied by the author. As we slide in between two parishioners, we can apply the context of the location to gain greater understanding of His words.

These cities and their churches are filled with interesting stories that will make their letter from Jesus come alive with meaning for the church of that day and time, for the church today, and for us personally.

THE PATTERN OF THE LETTERS

The US Constitution mandates that the president "shall from time to time give to the Congress Information of the State of the Union, and recommend to their Consideration such measures as he shall judge necessary and expedient" in Article II, Section 3, Clause 1.[5]

On Friday, January 8, 1790, President George Washington delivered the first State of the Union address in New York City. His address was said to have lasted no more than ten minutes. This short speech greatly contrasts with the longest address which was given by President Bill Clinton in one hour, twenty-eight minutes, and forty-nine seconds.[6]

In the letters to these churches in Asia Minor, Jesus gives information and recommends measures that he judges necessary and expedient for these believers. These seven letters are similar to a State of the Union address for each location. Each letter follows the same model.

First, Jesus begins by introducing himself in a way that is relevant to that particular congregation. He selects the most appropriate and fitting features of himself, which are articulated in the first chapter of Revelation. Jesus selects a phrase that will have a special meaning to that particular church.

The next section of each letter starts with the words "I know" (see Rv 2:2, 2:9, 2:13, 2:19, 3:1, 3:7, and 3:15). Jesus assures the churches, their parishioners, and us today that He knows. Our omniscient Lord is aware of all situations and sees through to their heart.

Christ then complements the church and its congregation on the things they are doing well. The only exception to this is the letter to the church at Laodicea, in which Jesus finds no positive traits.

Following the encouraging words of commendation are condemnations citing ways the church needs to improve. There are no words of exhortation for the martyred church in Smyrna or the missionary church in Philadelphia.

The letter concludes with a warning revealing the negative outcomes of not heeding the suggestions for improvement and the positive consequences of following the prescribed actions.

The pattern works well for analyzing and advising these particular churches and their members. Additionally, this practical analysis and well-ordered procedure is a concise and workable technique for anyone charged with giving constructive criticism to another. This model would be effective for other situations as well. For example, a boss could use this model during a performance review with an employee. A teacher could use this model when conducting a quarterly grade report with a student. A parent could use this model when disciplining a child.

Here is an example. Let's say you are a boss in a department store charged with giving a performance review to an employee who works the sales floor in men's suits. Following the pattern of the letters, you would first need to establish who you are and why it is appropriate for you to be the judge: "I have worked in this company for over ten years now. I started in the men's department doing a similar job to yours and now manage these areas."

This preface helps the employee realize the value of your experience. Although no validation is required, the employee may be more willing to accept criticism and advice, knowing that you once faced similar situations and challenges.

Next, you would commend the employee for the wise and effective strategies they have utilized. These positive words recognize and reward outstanding work and lift confidence levels: "You are doing well greeting the customers coming in the door. Your smile and personable manner are welcoming."

The next stage of the process—the exhortations—is not as easy for either party. This section of the review highlights the subpar aspects of job performance. Here is an example: "You are not helping customers navigate the racks to select items to try. We have received feedback that customers are unable to locate the desired style and size and leave the store without purchasing anything."

To wrap up the meeting, you would give the ramifications and consequences of taking and applying the advice given: "If you sell more, you will receive a raise. If not, we will need to relocate you."

—

This process is a logical and useful blueprint. Jesus repeats this format in all seven letters.

Our stay on Patmos has given us the background necessary to start visiting the congregations in the seven cities. Let's continue our expedition to Ephesus to explore the *Lessons from the Letters.*

THE LOVELESS CHURCH IN THE OPULENT CITY: EPHESUS

W elcome to Ephesus! This city, called the "Crown Jewel of Asia Minor," was home to nearly a quarter million people in the first century AD. Even the name, Ephesus, means "desirable."

This culturally rich and fashionable city boasted a theater that seated over twenty thousand people. Their ancient theater is close in capacity to today's Staples Center in downtown Los Angeles (home to the Lakers, Clippers, Kings, and Sparks) and Madison Square Garden in New York City (home to the Knicks and the Rangers). Considering the population of New York City is a tenth of the entire ancient world, this is quite the comparison! It was the largest and most prestigious theater of its time in the Roman Empire.[7]

The banking system of Ephesus was the predecessor of modern banking today. Institutions based in the city set the exchange rates for and dominated the banking centers of this region.

Ephesus was also an influential political city. The Roman governor would hold court there periodically, initiating a time of celebrated pageantry in which the city would put forth its finest to welcome him.

As the "Harbor to the World," it was a mecca for the erudite and urbane. Ephesus lured the rich and the famous with her mild climate, beautiful waterfront, and sophisticated city life. Among the notable frequent guests were Antony and Cleopatra.

Imagine a scene set in 100 AD. A wealthy, vibrant couple sail their yacht to a reserved slip in the port of Ephesus. As a crew is unpacking their vessel, the pair disembark and stroll hand-in-hand along the wide, column-lined Harbor Boulevard. Their sandals click along the pure white street paved with prized Parian marble mined from Paros Island in the Aegean Sea. Along the way, the travelers stop to peruse the items in the stylish shops selling the hottest and most sought-after treasures from around the world. At last, they arrive at their ornately decorated terrace home filled with sculpture, artwork, and intricate mosaic tiles, eager to enjoy all this multifaceted city has to offer.

As we continue to get to know this opulent city, let's explore another of the features that made Ephesus such a popular destination.

THE TEMPLE OF ARTEMIS

We have all heard of the Seven Wonders of the World.

Have you ever wondered who earned the right to pick the wonders? If so, wonder no more.

The Seven Wonders of the World are a collection of structures that were heralded by the poets of ancient Greece. Antipater of Sidon summarized and recorded them in a poem in the second century AD.

> I have set eyes on the wall of lofty Babylon on which is a road for chariots, and the statue of Zeus by the Alpheus, and the hanging gardens, and the Colossus of the Sun, and the huge labor of the high pyramids, and the vast tomb of Mausolus; but when I saw the house of Artemis that mounted to the clouds, those other marvels lost their brilliancy, and I said, "Lo, apart from Olympus, the Sun never looked on aught so grand."[8]

In Antipater's estimation, the most wondrous of the wonders was the Temple (or as he calls it, the house) of Artemis.

What made it so "wonder" full?

The size was impressive. With dimensions of 450 feet long by 225 feet wide and a height of approximately six stories high, this temple was the largest in the ancient world, boasting an area four times larger than the Parthenon. [9]

The temple was considered valuable enough to be rebuilt after it was burned down. In 356 BC, a man named Herostratus set the temple on fire in an attempt to gain fame. Unfortunately for him, his scheme was unsuccessful. His actions sparked the ire of government officials who made speaking his name an offense punishable by death. [10] The Temple of Artemis was a magnificent sight as it sparkled in the sun. It was the first temple to be built entirely of marble. The altar was a treasure itself sculpted from prized and beautiful limestone. Paintings and sculptures from the most prominent artists of the day adorned the walls.

The myth of Artemis and her brother, Apollo, begins with a tragic tale. Leto, the twins' mother, had an affair with the king of the gods, Zeus, and became pregnant. Zeus, fearing the wrath of his wife, Hera, for his unfaithfulness, abandoned his lover and their unborn children. No country or island wanted to rise the ire of the vengeful Hera. Therefore, no one would allow Leto to have her babies on their shores. Finally, Leto stepped on the small floating island of Delos, asked for refuge, and had her babies on the island.[11]

Although Artemis was of Greek origin, the goddess had similar stories but different names in other cultures. The Romans referred to Artemis as Diana and emphasized her hunting skills and wilderness acumen. The Ephesians took the story of Artemis and transformed the image of her body by adding many appendages. Some scholars refer to these as breasts representing life-giving milk, fertility, and prosperity.[12] Other researchers identify these as bull testicles signifying the animal sacrifices offered to her.[13] Legend maintains that a statue of Artemis fell from the heavens on to the ground in Ephesus. The city leaders claimed that this was a gift from the gods which "fell down from Zeus," causing the Ephesians to believe that she was the patron goddess of their city. (Acts 19:35)

This temple and countless other shrines in the ancient world were built and set apart to appease and please the fictional gods and goddesses created in the imaginations of people throughout the centuries. People were obsessed with pacifying the deities to get something for themselves. Therefore, worshipers would follow the prescribed religious practices to appease the god who would then, supposedly, grant a gift and blessing to the participant. These religious rites, which were created in the human mind, were often carnal and sensual.

Some gods were thought to require a grain or animal sacrifice in return for the promise of good health or prosperity. Other gods required the death of a child in return for the gift of success. The gods and goddesses of fertility often required sexual acts to be watched by or performed with priests or priestesses in exchange for the hope of bountiful harvests and fruitful families.

The worship of Artemis in the temple in Ephesus was fever-pitched debauchery in which hundreds of temple prostitutes, dancers, musicians, and eunuchs engaged the participants in sexual revelry, mutilation, and other debasing activities. Heraclitus, a Greek philosopher, wrote, "The morals of the temples were worse than the morals of animals because even dogs do not mutilate each other."[14]

Pilgrims from across the ancient world trekked to Ephesus to worship Artemis and reap the benefits promised by serving her. Her worship was central to the life of the pagan followers. Michael Sprague describes it this way in his book *Disaster.*

> If you got a pay raise, thank Artemis. If you had a baby, it was a gift from Artemis. If you had bumper crops and good health, it was Artemis. If you had bad crops, people wondered what you did to tick off Artemis. If you didn't give thanks to Artemis or didn't attend the dinner party at her temple, you might lose your job, your friends, your family, your honored positions.[15]

Pagan worship was so vastly different from the worship of the real God that the pagans had a difficult time understanding and relating to it. When Jesus came to earth, he proclaimed radical ideas that were countercultural to the worshipers of this host of human-made gods. His proclamations must have seemed unbelievable to this polytheistic audience.

Although their vulgar worship routines were at the center of the idolators' activity, the followers did not connect their worship and their gods with their moral conscience or their everyday deeds and actions. They did not view their gods as an example of the correct way to live. The raucous behavior of these invented deities was not worthy of their imitation.

Conversely, Christ was a perfect example for believers to emulate. "The Word became flesh and made his dwelling among us" (Jn 1:14). Jesus descended to earth to show His disciples the way of the abundant life. He patterned a godly life for believers to follow. The gods of the pagans were terrible role models and horrible examples. Therefore, the pagan believer's religion did not affect how they lived their life.Jesus also revealed that he was the son of God and that he was sent to earth to suffer and die for us. The apostle, John, records this in John 3:16: "For God so loved the world that he gave his one and only son that whoever believes in him should not perish but have eternal life." For a moment, place yourself into the mind of a resident of the city of Ephesus. Think about how Jesus's claims would compare to the stories of the gods which you had heard since you were a child. The Greek gods who would trick, abuse, and kill humans out of jealousy or rage existed to please and promote themselves. They had little concern for the humans whom they considered lowly beings. The pagans had heard the stories of these fickle gods all their lives. Their mindset was that the mighty gods lived selfishly, carelessly meddling in the lives of helpless humans. This preconceived notion of gods would have made it difficult to accept the truth that the true God would send his Son to earth to suffer and die for humanity's benefit. Believing that God's son would then rise from the dead to go and prepare a place for believers in heaven would have been a major paradigm shift.

This amazing truth is as real today as it was over two thousand years ago in the ancient cities of Asia Minor. Christianity is the only religion where God pursues and chooses us. "We love because he first loved us" (1 Jn 4:19). Being a Christian does not mean pandering to a god or a multitude of gods in hopes of getting what we want and need. The Lord assures us that "everyone who calls on the name of the Lord will be saved" (Rom 10:13).

For those worshiping Artemis and the scores of other false gods, this truth would have been difficult to accept and believe. The members of the church in Ephesus faced this challenge as they interacted with their neighbors and tried to evangelize them into the faith.

Now that you have settled into the city and have some background material, let's dive into our first letter.

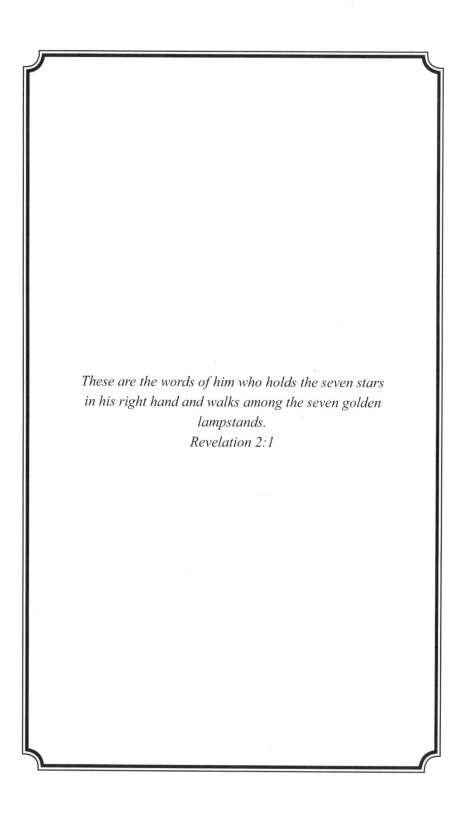

These are the words of him who holds the seven stars in his right hand and walks among the seven golden lampstands.
Revelation 2:1

SEVEN STARS

In each of the seven letters, Jesus introduces himself using an attribute listed in the first chapter of Revelation. The characteristic pertains to the church to which he is writing. His self-description in the letter to the congregation at Ephesus is as the "one who holds the seven stars in his right hand and walks among the seven golden lampstands" (Rv 2:1).

Why did Jesus introduce himself to the Ephesian church in this way? What is the significance of the seven stars and the seven lampstands, and how do they relate to this particular congregation? The first chapter of Revelation answers these questions.

Jesus reveals the identity of the seven stars and lampstands:

> "The mystery of the seven stars that you saw in my right hand and of the seven golden lampstands is this: The seven stars are the angels of the seven churches, and the seven lampstands are the seven churches" (Rv 1:20).

The stars represent angels. The Greek word for angel means "messenger," probably referring to the leader of the church. In his commentary of Revelation, Bible teacher, J. Vernon McGee, quips that this refers to the pastor of the church: "I like to hear a pastor called an angel because sometimes they are called other things. So, if you don't mind, I'll hold to that interpretation."[16]

The church I have attended for the better part of half a century has a hallway lined on both sides with pictures of the ministers from years past. Having known many of these preachers, walking through this portrait gallery is a walk down memory lane for me. As I focus on the people whose portraits are displayed, memories of their words, mannerisms, and theology reverberate in my mind. Sound bites of sermons and scenes from stories stream through my mind as I view one portrait and then the next.

I remember one minister who served our church during my elementary school years. He compared life to a mixture of peanut butter and jelly; we must accept the sticky, challenging situations along with the sweet, joyful ones. His words would echo in my mind during my PB and J lunch in the cafeteria. Another preacher from my childhood years captured my attention with his spiritual insights from the Peanuts cartoon characters.

As an adult, I valued the comparison made by our wise preacher who demonstrated the similarities between Barabbas and us, all sinners freed by Christ. Another preacher challenged us to focus more on our attitudes and less on our circumstances. Another preacher's smiling face reminds me of a man who motivated, encouraged, and inspired us to say yes to God's yes.

Gazing at our church's portraits of ministers, I realize that our church has thrived under the tutelage and care of a succession of talented and faithful servants of God. These giants of the faith have shepherded us and led us on a journey to move closer to our Lord and Savior.

If photography had been a reality in the first century, the church at Ephesus would have designated several passageways as portrait galleries. Pictures would have lined these halls of fame. This congregation rubbed shoulders with many heroes of the early church. They shared their pews with men and women who made "the Way" of Christ, a way of life for many believers throughout the centuries.

Who were the champions of the faith who ministered in Ephesus? The book of Acts tells us that Paul did some of his greatest missionary work there. Paul reached out to the Gentiles by preaching in the Hall of Tyrannus every day for two years (Acts 19:9-10). Did you get that last fact? Paul preached every day for two years. He possibly delivered over seven hundred sermons in Ephesus!

In addition to Paul, Barnabus, the encourager, taught in Ephesus. Timothy, the young protégé of Paul who has two books of the Bible bearing his name, ministered there. Apollos, Priscilla, and Aquilla were also elders rubbing shoulders with the parishioners. Even Mary, the mother of Jesus, attended services here.

The apostle John, the beloved disciple, who recorded these letters from Jesus, was an elder in this church. Tradition says that when he was too old to walk, he was carried down the aisle to participate in the service.

The church at Ephesus was similar to today's megachurch with an all-star cast of leaders. By human standards, they had every right to be a bit smug and self-satisfied. However, Jesus is not going to let pride permeate the pews.

He reminds them that He alone is the heart of the church and introduces himself as the one who "holds the seven stars in his right hand and walks among the seven golden lampstands" (Rv 2:1). The Almighty One is omnipotent. Although the church leaders were powerful, godly, and inspirational, Jesus is supreme. The church must center on Him, the Lord of lords. This lesson is as relevant today as it was in the first century.

What individuals have impacted your life and led you to a deeper faith? How have these mentors shaped your beliefs? There is a delicate balance between a strong leader in a ministry and a ministry centered around a strong leader. How can a church guard against a ministry being marketed or sustained on the personality of an individual?

How do we, as a church, emphasize a relationship with Christ instead of with an individual?

How do we, as a church, emphasize a relationship with Christ instead of organized religion?

How do we, as individuals, value the relationship more than the religion?

SEVEN LAMPSTANDS

John goes on to explain that the lampstands represent the church. Since there are seven churches, this signifies the church as a whole. As we discovered in the overview, the number seven is significant as it represents completion and perfection. Jesus is letting this church know that in his omnipotence, he flawlessly embraces the entire church--every church of every age.

The grammar surrounding the Greek verb *"kratein,"* meaning "to hold," indicates that Jesus holds the stars in His hands in the way that one could hold the entirety of a coin versus merely the handle of a pitcher. William Barclay summarizes it this way: "The meaning is that Jesus Christ holds the whole of the church within his hand. He holds all the churches in his hand, for all the churches are his, and all belong to him." [17]

Chapter 31 in the book of Exodus first describes lampstands. In this passage, the Lord has rescued his people, the children of Israel, from slavery in Egypt. They are journeying to the Promised Land through the desert. He is articulating very specific details for a portable house of worship for their trek. This tabernacle is only to contain one source of human-made light—the lampstand: "Make a lampstand of pure gold. Hammer out its base and shaft, and make its flowerlike cups, buds and blossoms of one piece with them" (Ex 25:31).

It is no coincidence that the lampstand was to be made from gold. Gold represents purity. The Lord was challenging the church to be pure. John A. Dutton, professor emeritus at Penn State, says, "It is not surprising that gold was the first metal processed by the Egyptians. Very few metals exist in their native state, i.e., not bound to other elements in a compound such as a mineral. Gold, although rare, can be found as flakes or nuggets." [18]

Another symbolic benefit of gold that the children of Israel would have immediately recognized was in the purification procedures. In the ancient world, gold was further purified by a process called smelting. Illustrations found in tombs dating as early as 2500 BC depict goldsmiths heating gold with charcoals and using blowpipes to increase its temperature. This extreme heating process caused the impurities, or slag, to rise to the top where they were skimmed off and discarded.

This process bears a striking resemblance to the church as well. Situations can "heat up" in churches or in the lives of those involved in these churches. Sometimes this heat comes from internal strife and discord. At other times, the heat comes from external sources like persecution. This heat can cause impurities to rise to the surface in the form of jealousy, conflict, and divisive actions. The hope is that as the slag in our churches and in our lives becomes evident, then we, as believers, will take the initiative to skim it off and get rid of it.

God continues with the instructions and gives further detail about the light from the lampstand: "Then make its seven lamps and set them up on it so that they light the space in front of it" (Ex 25:37). The lampstand was never intended to be the light. Its purpose is to reflect the light. The same is true for the church in that it is intended to reflect the light of the Lord. Jesus said in John 8:12, "I am the light of the world." He then challenged the believers to take that light and reflect it to the world.

> "A town built on a hill cannot be hidden. Neither do people light a lamp and put it under a bowl. Instead, they put it on its stand, and it gives light to everyone in the house. In the same way, let your light shine before others, that they may see your good deeds and glorify your Father in heaven." (Mt 5:14–16).

From the time of the Tabernacle, God has intended for his church and the individuals in his church to illuminate a dark world. The symbolism of the golden lampstands reminds the Ephesian believers and us today to ensure that we remain pure and that we shine our light to the glory of the Father.

How can you brighten the light from your church?

How can your lampstand be a better reflector of the light?

What impurities surface in your life when the heat is turned up?

What does it say about Jesus's love for us that He goes to extremes to refine us?

HIM WHO HOLDS

In 1955, Jim Jones founded the Peoples Temple of the Disciples of Christ. His ardent speeches and dynamic personality attracted followers and persuaded them to believe him to be the messiah of the Peoples Temple. Jones used his convincing rhetoric, staged faith healings, and meticulously planned and orchestrated conventions to lead as many as twenty thousand into his "church."

Jones relocated the temple to Guyana, a small South American country. He named their settlement Jonestown after, well, himself. His stated reason for relocating was to escape the evil influences of the United States. However, as the atmosphere of this supposed utopia became more restrictive, his ulterior motives for the move became apparent. Members were not allowed to leave the compound. The great distance from family and home combined with the remote location made it difficult, if not impossible, for those who wished to leave to do so. In November 1978, US Congressman Leo Ryan and a delegation of journalists flew in to investigate the claims of the disenfranchised members and to rescue those wanting freedom. Congressman Ryan and many journalists were killed.

With the temple's end imminent, Jones convinced the followers in the camp and their children to drink cyanide-laced punch. More than nine hundred people died a senseless death under the leadership of a man claiming the role of messiah. Rolling Stone stated that "until the September 11th attacks, the tragedy in Jonestown on November 18th, 1978, represented the largest number of American civilian casualties in a single non-natural event."[19]

Although the example of Jim Jones and the Jonestown Massacre is extreme, the premise remains the same. Jesus is *the* one "who holds" (Rv 2:1). He is the head of the church. He alone is the one who holds the seven stars in his right hand. He alone is the one who walks among the seven lampstands. No matter how gifted, dynamic, and convincing a leader becomes, Jesus must always be the head.

Fortunately, the horror of a heretic leading a church and claiming the place reserved for Jesus alone does not often escalate to this level. However, many churches have seen membership rising due to the vibrant personality of a minister. Youth programs have flourished because they were built around a dynamic leader only to falter when that person leaves. Churches built around individuals instead of God can show immediate incredible gains in attendance and money. However, these successes will be temporary without the rock of the Lord. Knowing our propensity to cling to a person, Jesus reminds the church then and now of "him who holds" (Rv 2:1).

Have you been involved in an organization which centered around an individual?

What were the positives and negatives?

Is it possible for a person to center his or her faith around a person other than Jesus?

What are the downfalls when this happens?

I know your deeds,
your hard work and your perseverance.
Revelation 2:2

YOUR DEEDS, YOUR HARD WORK,
AND YOUR PERSEVERANCE

In August 1896, three prospectors on Bonanza Creek, a small branch of the Klondike River, found their dream in the form of glowing nuggets that were bigger than they ever expected or imagined. With this event, the Gold Rush of 1896 began.

> A whopping one hundred thousand people journeyed to the harsh environment of Alaska in search of riches. The Seattle Post-Intelligencer ran this sensational headline on July 17, 1897: "GOLD! GOLD! GOLD! GOLD! Sixty-Eight rich men on the Steamer Portland. Stacks of yellow metal! Some have $5000. Many have more, and a few bring out $100,000 each. The steamer carries $700,000. Special tug chained to the Post-Intelligencer to get the news."[20]

Families, wealthy entrepreneurs, preachers, and business people left their homes and lives behind to seek fortune. The young, the old, and every aged person in between ventured out on the adventure. There were plenty of schemes and dreams for all who sought them.

Most of the prospectors journeyed to Seattle to catch a boat north on the inside passage of what is now Southeast Alaska. After a ten-day sail, the miners arrived in Skagway or Dyea, where they found hotel rooms, supplies, and food to be in high demand, limited, and very expensive, often ten times their normal cost.

The Mounties, Canada's border patrol, not wanting to have to rescue countless starving miners, would not allow entry into Canada without food and supplies for one year. Each person was required to purchase and carry to the border checkpoint provisions of food, shelter, equipment, and clothing.

—

This bundle of necessities often weighed over two thousand pounds, coining the term the "one-ton rule" of entry.

Once outfitted, the prospectors took the next leg of the journey up one of two passes into the mountains of gold country. The most common path was the thirty-three-mile Chilkoot Trail linking the tidewater area with the Yukon River. A seemingly endless stream of men and some women and children climbed the "golden stairs," an icy progression of footholds up into the mountains of Canada. Due to the one-ton rule, many miners had to make several trips up the mountain with supplies, storing them at the top and returning to a base camp for multiple other loads.

The determined speculators made their way in temperatures sometimes falling under 50 degrees below zero, with the ice and snow cutting their faces. Reaching the Yukon River, still 550 miles away from the goldfields, the miners were disappointed to realize that the waters were frozen and impassible. They passed the time in the winter cutting wood and making vessels to use for passage. Finally, in May 1898, a flotilla of 7,124 crude handmade boats set sail. The Whitehorse rapids claimed 150 boats and five lives. The miners dealt with scurvy, twenty-two hours of sunlight, bugs, hunger, and cold. Finally, in the early summer of 1898, many of them reached Dawson and the goldfields.

Dawson must have been a huge surprise and horrendous disappointment to the weary sojourners, as it was a thriving city with a population of over thirty thousand people. Thousands had arrived before them and staked their claims along the golden river. Imagine the miners' frustration when they realized that prospectors had already laid claim on the prime land. No vacant parcels remained on which they could search for gold.

Of the approximately one hundred thousand people who attempted the journey, only around thirty thousand reached the goldfields, and less than fifty people made their fortune in gold. The real riches for many, however, were not measured financially. The miners' true wealth was the growth and development they garnered from the experience. The difficulty and persever-ance molded many of these individuals into strong and determined people. The hardships challenged and changed them. They persisted and became better and stronger people because of the struggle. One man describes his journey in this way:

I had thirty-five cents in my pocket when I set foot in Alaska, but I gave that to a mission church at Dutch Harbor. I did not have so much when I left the country more than two years later. I made exactly nothing, but if I could turn time back, I would do it over again for less than that.[21]

Pierre Burton summarized the effects of the prospectors' perseverance and hard work in his book, *The Klondike Fever, the: The Life and Death of the Last Great Goldrush.*

The stampede resembled a great war. It was impossible to emerge from it unchanged, and those who survived it were never quite the same again....Their characters were tempered in the hot flame of an experience...In the brief span of the gold rush they learned more about life, more about their fellows, and more about themselves than many mortals absorb in threescore years and ten. "Do unto others as you would be done by," came to have a real meaning for each of them. [22]

God did not design us for a life of ease and comfort. Spoiling us would literally spoil us. He loves us too much to allow us to have spiritual atrophy.

We often learn our best and hardest lessons when we are operating in a difficult environment. As we examined before, Jesus warned us: "In this world you will have trouble. But take heart! I have overcome the world" (Jn 16:33).

Notice he does not say "if" you have times of trouble. Instead, he assures us that we will, and that this adversity will make us stronger as we seek to be holy more than we seek to be happy.

The apostle Paul names his adversity "a thorn in the flesh" in his letter to the Corinthians.

Therefore, in order to keep me from becoming conceited, I was given a thorn in my flesh, a messenger of Satan, to torment me. Three times I pleaded with the Lord to take it away from me. But he said to me, "My grace is sufficient for you, for my power is made perfect in weakness." Therefore I will boast all the more gladly about my weaknesses, so that Christ's power may rest on me. That is why, for Christ's sake, I delight in weaknesses, in

insults, in hardships, in persecutions, in difficulties. For when
I am weak, then I am strong. (2 Cor 12:7-10)

Paul laments that he was given this thorn in the flesh and admits that,
at first, he asked the Lord to remove it. God assures him that he will have
his most powerful and abundant life when he is weak in his own strength
and reliant on the Lord. Paul goes beyond accepting and merely persevering through his trials to boasting about them. He rejoices in his struggles,
knowing that God is beside Him, giving him strength.

Jesus opens the letter to the Ephesian church with commendations
on their deeds, hard work, and perseverance. Operating a church in a city
consumed with pagan worship and the evil that accompanies it was tough.
The Greek word for hard work is *"kopos,"* meaning "that which exhausts."
The word used for "perseverance" is *"hupomone,"* meaning "triumphant
fortitude." By using these superlative nouns, Christ recognizes the difficulty
of their ministry. To take a stand for Christ and to invite others to do the same
was a challenge anywhere in Asia Minor. However, Ephesus was particularly difficult because of the temple to Artemis's overwhelming influence.

As discussed previously, the worship of Artemis was blatantly sexual.
However, the allure of Artemis was not only one of base physical pleasure,
but also one of economic strategy. Worshiping Artemis was supposed to
bless a person with prosperity. A farmer would come hoping to ensure an
abundant harvest. A motherless child would come to ask for her barren
womb to bear a child. A struggling businessman would come pleading for
a profitable year.

To have their prayers answered, the visitors would not only participate
in the sexual rites, but they would also financially invest in the cult. Priests
sacrificed hundreds of animals to Artemis. The meat from these animals
was then used to feed the temple priests and priestesses, with the remainder
sold for profit.

Cult followers would bring their money to the temple to "invest" it with
Artemis. The temple financiers then lent that money back out at high-interest
rates, making the temple a cash machine.

The Temple of Artemis was designated as a safe haven for criminals. If
someone accused of a crime could reach the temple, he or she was immune
from prosecution. Thus, the temple was a haven for some of the most

notorious felons of the ancient world. Although it sounds counterintuitive, the temple was a depository for both money and for criminals.

Artemis appeared to be tough competition for the followers of the Way. Note the words the Lord has for this church, as recorded in Paul's letter to the Ephesians.

Artemis called followers to wild and unabashed orgies; Christ calls followers to "be holy and blameless" (Eph 1:3).

Artemis promised immediate riches and prosperity; Christ promises "the riches of his glorious inheritance in the saints" (Eph 1:18).

Artemis's followers believed they were created to have fun and fulfill their personal desires; Christ's followers believe they are "created in Christ Jesus to do good works" (Eph 2:10).

These exhortations are difficult even in pure and wholesome environments. They must have been exponentially challenging in the promiscuous city of Ephesus. Perhaps that is why the letter to this church begins with such elaborate praise.

Jesus starts with the words "I know" (Rv 2:2). They must have been comforted to know that He knew their challenges. He assures us today that he knows our trials as well. If we let him, he will use these trials to mold and shape us. Just as the Klondike gold miners' perseverance in their harsh environment brought the best out in some, the Lord can redeem our trials as well.

What do you imagine to be some of the most difficult challenges for the church in Ephesus?

Have you had challenges at your church which resemble these?

Was your church able to persevere?

What difficult personal challenges have you faced?

How have these situations ultimately strengthened you?

How did you grow from your perseverance?

We don't hope for hardship. However, we can readjust how we think about our difficulty. What are ways we can change our perspective?

What are the advantages of changing your attitude?

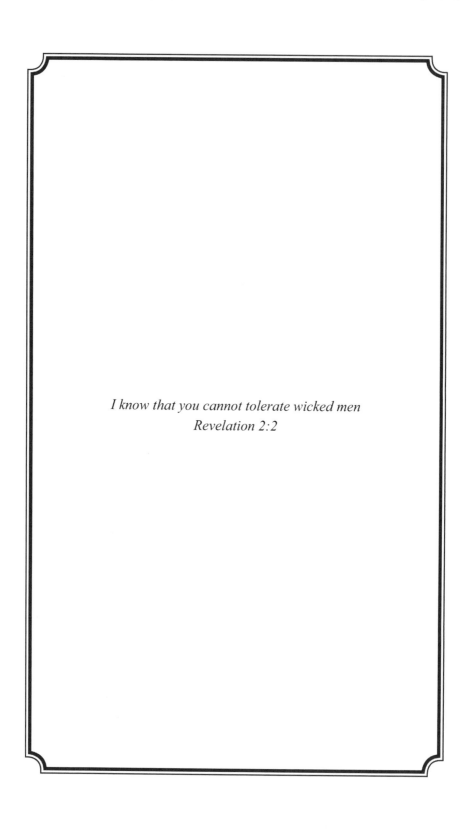

I know that you cannot tolerate wicked men
Revelation 2:2

A TASTE OF HIS OWN MEDICINE

In Aesop's fable, *The Cobbler Turned Doctor,* a deceitful man got "a taste of his own medicine."

> A cobbler unable to make a living by his trade and made desperate by poverty, began to practice medicine in a town in which he was not known. He sold a drug, pretending that it was an antidote to all poisons, and obtained a great name for himself by long-winded puffs and advertisements. When the Cobbler happened to fall sick himself of a serious illness, the Governor of the town determined to test his skill. For this purpose, he called for a cup, and while filling it with water, pretended to mix poison with the Cobbler's antidote, commanding him to drink it on the promise of a reward. The Cobbler, under the fear of death, confessed that he had no knowledge of medicine, and was only made famous by the stupid clamors of the crowd.[23]

The Cobbler in the fable "tasted" his own medicine of deceit as the Governor tricked him by suggesting that he drink poison with his concocted antidote. The Governor gave the cobbler a taste of his own medicine. Similarly, God gave the people of Ephesus a taste of their own medicine to show them that He is the one true God.

The city of Ephesus was a menacing environment with wicked people and a strong presence of the occult. William Barclay said that "into Ephesus, there flowed a torrent of credulous, superstitious people, for in a superstitious world Ephesus was well-nigh the most superstitious city in the world."[24] God knew that this town needed extraordinary miracles and signs to break away from the forces of evil. God beat them at their own game by giving them a taste of their own medicine.

> God did extraordinary miracles [in Ephesus] though Paul, so that even handkerchiefs and aprons that had touched him were taken to the sick, and their illnesses were cured and the evil spirits left them. (Acts 19:11-12)

Some men who were not genuine believers in Jesus attempted to profit from pretending to drive out evil spirits. The demons exposed these false prophets and attacked them.

> Some Jews who went around driving out evil spirits tried to invoke the name of the Lord Jesus over those who were demon-possessed. They would say, "In the name of the Jesus whom Paul preaches, I command you to come out." Seven sons of Sceva, a Jewish chief priest, were doing this. One day the evil spirit answered them, "Jesus I know, and Paul I know about, but who are you?" Then the man who had the evil spirit jumped on them and overpowered them all. He gave them such a beating that they ran out of the house naked and bleeding. (Acts 19:13-16)

This event did not go unnoticed by the people or by the church in Ephesus.

> When this became known to the Jews and Greeks living in Ephesus, they were all seized with fear, and the name of the Lord Jesus was held in high honor. Many of those who believed now came and openly confessed what they had done. A number who had practiced sorcery brought their scrolls together and burned them publicly. When they calculated the value of the scrolls, the total came to fifty thousand drachmas. In this way the word of the Lord spread widely and grew in power. (Acts19:17-20)

Paul had spent two years in Ephesus. He understood the prevalence of evil in this city, which prompted him under the inspiration of the Holy Spirit to write his own letter to the Ephesian church with this strong warning:

> Put on the full armor of God so that you can take your stand against the devil's schemes. For our struggle is not against flesh

and blood, but against the rulers, against the authorities, against
the powers of this dark world and against the spiritual forces
of evil in the heavenly realms. (Eph 6:11-12)

Paul knew that the only way for the church members to conquer the
great wickedness of the men coming into the church was to recognize that
they were actually fighting against the devil himself. The only chance they
had to defeat these wicked men was to fully arm themselves against the
evil of the enemy with the power of the Lord. He cautioned them that they
were not strong enough in their own strength to succeed.

Paul continues his advice to the church in Corinth. He warns them to
be wary of being in the presence of evil people:

Do not be misled: "Bad company corrupts good character."
Come back to your senses as you ought, and stop sinning; for
there are some who are ignorant of God—I say this to your
shame. (1 Cor 15:33-34)

The church members in Ephesus seemingly heeded this advice and
did not tolerate the wicked men who came into their congregation. Jesus
commends them for recognizing the schemes of the enemy and disassoci-
ating themselves. This lesson from this letter is as relevant today as it was
two thousand years ago.

*What does Paul's letter to the Ephesians tell us about the spiritual forces
of evil? (Eph 6:12)*

*How can we continue to walk with the Lord when we are surrounded by
bad influences?*

What are the dangers of getting too close to wickedness?

How can these truths help you battle the forces of evil?

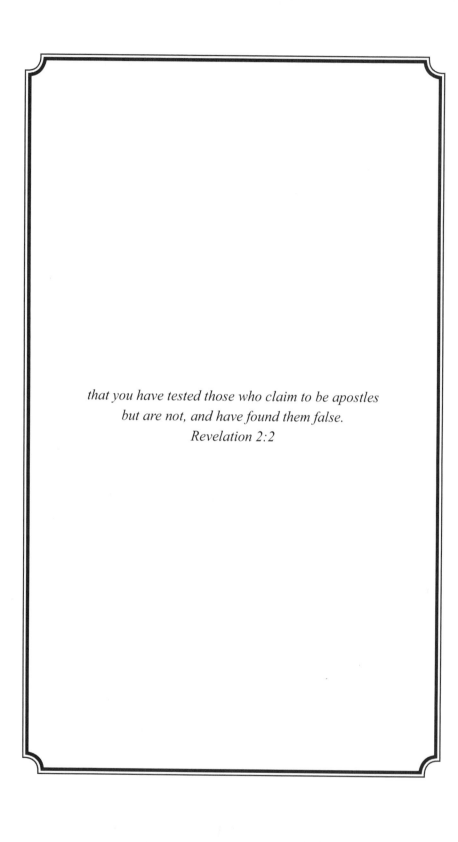

that you have tested those who claim to be apostles
but are not, and have found them false.
Revelation 2:2

COUNTERFEIT

After naptime, a young mother embarks on her errands. As the mother of three children under the age of seven, she frequents businesses with drive-through service to avoid getting everyone in and out of the car seats. With the children buckled in the back, she heads to the bank to cash a refund check of $51. The teller gives the mom an envelope with money inside and lollipops for the children.

Mom buys treats for the kids from the drive-through lane of their favorite fast-food restaurant. After ordering their treats, mom pulls out the money from the bank to pay. In the envelope are a $50 bill and a $1 bill. She pays with the fifty and puts the change back in the envelope.

The next stop is the dry cleaners. While the attendant loads her clothes in the trunk, she pays at the window with two $20 bills she received from the restaurant. The cashier disappears from the window to get her change.

The children start to get restless. Mom wonders why no one is coming back. This transaction should not take this long. Finally, the manager comes to her car with a distressed look on his face. "We are unable to accept your money. These bills are counterfeit."

Seventy-eight million dollars in counterfeit currency circulated in the United States in 2015.[25] Persons accept these bills, not realizing that they are not authentic. This currency is worthless, and the victims are not reimbursed for their loss. If a business or an individual takes currency and later finds out that it is not authentic, the victim has no recourse.

In 1865, after the Civil War, as much as 30 percent of the money in circulation was counterfeit. President Abraham Lincoln created the Secret Service to eradicate counterfeit currency. The agency is still fighting this battle. It recently released a detailed, ten-step guide entitled "Know Your Money."[26] Its purpose is to educate individuals, businesses, and banks on the components of legitimate dollar bills. The underlying premise suggests the best way to identify fraudulent bills is a systematic and detailed knowledge of genuine currency. The goal is to study and know the true currency thoroughly enough that any variances are easily recognizable.

The church at Ephesus had to combat counterfeiters of a different kind. Their frauds were ones "who claim to be apostles but are not" (Rv 2:2). The same premise holds true for recognizing counterfeit apostles as it does for discovering counterfeit money. The church had to thoroughly know and examine the genuine message. Its goal was to study the teaching of Christ meticulously so that they knew it in detail. When a false apostle presented incorrect doctrine, the parishioners would recognize and stop it before it could infiltrate the congregation.

Examining the paper, holographs, and images on a dollar bill is straightforward. But how do Christians know what is real and genuine? How do we live the truth that Christ lived? In some ways, it seems easier for John and the other disciples. They could physically watch to see what Jesus did. They saw the truth in action every day. This type of experiential learning and mentoring was prevalent in that culture.

In the time of Jesus, the best and the brightest students would hold the prestigious honor of being selected by a rabbi to study under him. These outstanding students, or talmidim, left their homes to travel with him. Their goal was not only to learn what the rabbi knew but also to be an extension of him.

A talmid would know and learn from the rabbi by walking the way he walked, talking the way he talked, believing the way he believed, and interpreting scripture the way he interpreted it. The rabbi called the student to take on the "yoke of the Torah" of the rabbi. This phrase comes from a farming analogy of their day. A yoke was a wooden bar placed across the shoulders of two or more animals. By physically joining the animals together, they were forced to walk and work in tandem. The yoke represented the talmidim's link to their rabbi. The students would follow and imitate this rabbi just as if they were yoked to him. At the age of thirty, the talmidim were experienced enough to become rabbis and teachers themselves.

Jesus, at the age of thirty, placed his "yoke" on twelve men whom we refer to as the disciples. He, however, did not pick the best and the brightest by the standards of the day. He called men who were overlooked by the other rabbis. These men were already at work in the family business. He called them to follow Him, to be yoked to Him. The disciples were with Jesus continuously. They knew what would make Him laugh. They recognized his snore. They knew His favorite foods. They saw genuine godly living in action. They were so familiar with Him that they could identify actions and beliefs that were not like Christ.

Jesus extends this call to us. He invites us to "yoke" ourselves to him. He doesn't discriminate with an exclusive offer. Instead, he gives this open invitation:

> Come to me, all you who are weary and burdened, and I will give you rest. Take my yoke upon you and learn from me, for I am gentle and humble in heart, and you will find rest for your souls. For my yoke is easy and my burden is light. (Mt 11:28-30)

Without possessing the advantage of being able to watch Jesus's actions, how do we become like the disciples and discern the genuine Christian lifestyle? How do we learn to recognize counterfeit lifestyles?

Jesus tells us that one way is to read and know the Bible and to live by the Word: "If you hold to my teaching, you are really my disciples. Then you will know the truth, and the truth will set you free" (Jn 8:31). By studying the Bible, we can learn to walk the way Jesus walked and talk the way Jesus talked. We learn how Jesus, God as a man, lived his life. As we learn the truth from scripture, we will be able to distinguish counterfeit teachers and fake doctrine.

The writer of this Psalm advises us to go beyond reading scripture to internalizing it: "I have hidden your word in my heart that I might not sin against you" (Ps 119:11). Knowing the word in the head and the heart enables us to identify counterfeits.

A third way to identify the genuine is through prayer. Ask God for spiritual discernment. Ask to be kept from evil deceptions. Ask for a hedge to be placed around you and your family to keep you from counterfeits. Jeremiah, an Old Testament prophet, assures us that God will hear us: "Then you will call on me and come and pray to me, and I will listen to you" (Jer 29:12). In the New Testament Gospel of Mark, we read, "Therefore I tell you, whatever you ask for in prayer, believe that you have received it, and it will be yours" (Mk 11:24).

Paul gives us another way in his inspired letter to the Galatians. He reminds them and us of the importance of being in a community of believers. "Carry each other's burdens, and in this way, you will fulfill the law of Christ" (Gal 6:2).

Through the practices of Bible study and obedience, scripture memorization, prayer, and involvement with other Christians, we will begin to recognize the true path that leads to the abundant life.

Jesus used the analogy of sheep to make this point. In his day, several shepherds would often bring their sheep to the same field, watering hole, or holding area. When a shepherd was ready to leave, he would call his sheep. Amazingly, the sheep, not particularly smart animals, would immediately recognize the voice of their shepherd. They would not follow the call of a different voice. They would only follow their shepherd's call.

> Very truly I tell you Pharisees, anyone who does not enter the sheep pen by the gate, but climbs in by some other way, is a thief and a robber. The one who enters by the gate is the shepherd of the sheep. The gatekeeper opens the gate for him, and the sheep listen to his voice. He calls his own sheep by name and leads them out. When he has brought out all his own, he goes on ahead of them, and his sheep follow him because they know his voice. But they will never follow a stranger; in fact, they will run away from him because they do not recognize a stranger's voice. (Jn 10:1-5)

A lesson we can learn from the letter to the Ephesian church is to know the genuine truth of Christ. This knowledge and familiarity protect the believer from the counterfeit.

Have you ever been deceived by something or by someone who seemed genuine?

What voices, other than the Lord's, have the ability to lead you or others astray?

The passage mentioned four ways to learn what is true: Bible study, scripture memorization, prayer, and involvement in a Christian community. What is your experience and practice in each of these areas?

In which area would you like to focus?

How does this lesson from this letter inspire you?

You have persevered
and have endured hardships for my name,
and have not grown weary.
Revelation 2:3

PERSEVERING IN PERSEVERANCE

In the early morning hours of April 14, Second Officer Herbert Stone stood watch on the deck of the battleship *California*, fifteen hundred miles off the coast of Boston. Large amounts of oceanic ice challenged the voyage. In the distance, Officer Stone observed white flashes of light. He radioed the captain, who asked him to communicate using Morse code. No response came from the elusive ship located less than ten miles off the bow. As Officer Stone watched, a white emergency streamer sailed into the air. Mysteriously, the steamer's cabin lights vanished into the darkness.

These lights were calls for help, desperate signals from a sinking ship. The ship had radioed multiple messages asking for assistance, but the young radio operator on the *California* had not reported to his shift and was sleeping soundly in his bunk, therefore, missing the radio calls for help and the opportunity to assist this neighbor in need. Meanwhile, the mighty *Titanic* was slowly disappearing into the depths while the *California* turned a blind eye.

By contrast, the Ephesian church did not make the same mistake. They were alert to the signs of distress from their pagan friends and acquaintances. The parishioners observed a culture investing its time, money, and life into a religion that served false gods. They witnessed their neighbors sinking into a shallow and meaningless existence in this life and, more importantly, passing up the opportunity to live in eternity with the one true God.

The Ephesian Christians, like the crew on the *California,* were near to people in need. They saw the false worship around them and were unwilling to ignore the warning signs. They did try to intercede and make a rescue effort. Jesus commended them as they "persevered," "endured hardships," and did not grow "weary."

Rescues are not without risk. To save a drowning person from a body of water is particularly perilous and can end up endangering the rescuer. The AVIR syndrome, Aquatic Victim Instead of Rescuer, occurs when a drowning victim panics and instinctively pushes up, often pinning their rescuer down. The Red Cross introduced a program with the slogan "Rescue, Don't Go, Throw." This initiative encourages people who see others in need to throw a lifeline to them instead of diving into the water and endangering themselves.

The Ephesian Christians were concerned enough about their neighbors to "dive in" and attempt to rescue those drowning in sin and perishing in that wicked culture. Many of these rescuers, however, become victims of AVIR syndrome, suffering for their evangelism and being harmed by the very people they were attempting to save.

Dr. Luke writes a history of the early church in the Bible book of Acts. He describes an incident that resembles AVIR syndrome, in which the ones trying to save people were harmed by those they were trying to save.

> About that time there arose a great disturbance about the Way. A silversmith named Demetrius, who made silver shrines of Artemis, brought in a lot of business for the craftsmen there. He called them together, along with the workers in related trades, and said: "You know, my friends, that we receive a good income from this business. And you see and hear how this fellow Paul has convinced and led astray large numbers of people here in Ephesus and in practically the whole province of Asia. He says that gods made by human hands are no gods at all. There is danger not only that our trade will lose its good name, but also that the temple of the great goddess Artemis will be discredited; and the goddess herself, who is worshiped throughout the province of Asia and the world, will be robbed of her divine majesty."

> When they heard this, they were furious and began shouting: "Great is Artemis of the Ephesians!" Soon the whole city was in an uproar. The people seized Gaius and Aristarchus, Paul's traveling companions from Macedonia, and all of them rushed into the theater together. Paul wanted to appear before the crowd, but the disciples would not let him. Even some of the officials of the province, friends of Paul, sent him a message begging him not to venture into the theater.

The assembly was in confusion: Some were shouting one thing, some another. Most of the people did not even know why they were there. The Jews in the crowd pushed Alexander to the front, and they shouted instructions to him. He motioned for silence in order to make a defense before the people. But when they realized he was a Jew, they all shouted in unison for about two hours: "Great is Artemis of the Ephesians!" (Acts19:23-34)

This incident ignited hate and suspicion against the Christians. Demetrius orchestrated a plan to mobilize the labor unions to band together under the guise of defending Artemis from her detractors. He used national pride and religious indignation as noble themes to mask their true motive of selfish profit. Demetrius organized this attack on the Christians realizing that if Artemis were not revered as a goddess, the stream of income produced from the tourists and the local visitors would dry up. The Temple of Artemis was a huge economic benefit to the businesses in the city.

Attractions still draw visitors and revenue to cities today just as the Temple of Artemis did in its day. These sites entice tourists and locals to part with their money. This spending impacts the pocketbooks of the local merchants. The Mall of America is a modern example of a facility luring tourists and their dollars to an area. Located near Minneapolis, Minnesota, the Mall has 5.4 million square feet of retail and restaurant space. Thirty-two Boeing 747s, 258 Statues of Liberty, or seven Yankee Stadiums could fit inside this shopping and entertainment mecca. The amount of steel used to construct the mall was twice the amount used to construct the Eiffel Tower. The Magic Kingdom at Disney World in Orlando is the largest attended amusement park in the world. The Mall of America hosts twice as many people each year as Disney. The total of those hosted is a whopping 40 million people annually. To put this in perspective, the mall hosts more visitors than the combined populations of North Dakota, South Dakota, Iowa, and Canada. Sixty percent of the visitors are tourists who come with their wallets open, spend the night in hotels, eat at local restaurants, and buy essentials (and some not-so-essentials) from stores in and around the mall. The tourist spending combined with local dollars generates almost $2 billion in annual revenue for the state of Minnesota.

If the mall were to close, over thirteen thousand individuals would immediately lose their jobs, and thousands of others operating hotels and services related to the mall and its visitors would see their income substantially diminished.

This situation is what the merchants of Ephesus feared. The revenue from the Temple of Artemis fed their families. They saw the Christians as a threat to their livelihood. As the early Christians reached more of the Ephesian citizens, they discredited the power of idolatrous worship. They challenged the credibility of the state's pagan religion.

Miraculously, in this evil city, this band of Christians was able to convert a substantial number of pagan worshipers to Christianity. It is evident that the believers were winning lives for the Lord and, at the same time, distressing the city officials and shaking up the status quo. Pliny, a Roman governor, wrote to Emperor Trajan lamenting that the Christians were converting the Ephesians and leaving the temples deserted. The locals felt a sting where it hurt, in their pocketbooks, and they fought back.

The Ephesians fought back by discriminating against the Christians. They were not allowed to be in the trade guilds unless they bowed to false gods. Excluding Christians from the guilds not only barred them from buying materials but also made it more difficult for them to sell their goods. Friends and family shunned believers. The government persecuted them. Their willingness to "jump in" and save the "drowning" pagans of Ephesus cost them dearly. As in the case of AVIR, the rescuers became victims.

Jesus recognized this and commended them, not once but twice, for their sacrifice. He assured them that they were rescuing souls for the omnipotent one who holds the seven stars. Although they were angering local officials, they were persevering for the almighty. In this very concise letter, he repeated his praise for their hard work, making it evident that this was important to him.

How willing are you to "dive in" to an uncomfortable situation to show others the way to Christ, even if your boldness might cost you in some way?

Have you ever been a victim of AVIR syndrome, helping someone who, then, hurt you?

What situations come to mind in which you could take a stand for the Lord?

Many Christians around the world are martyred because of their faith in God. What can you do to help and support these heroes?

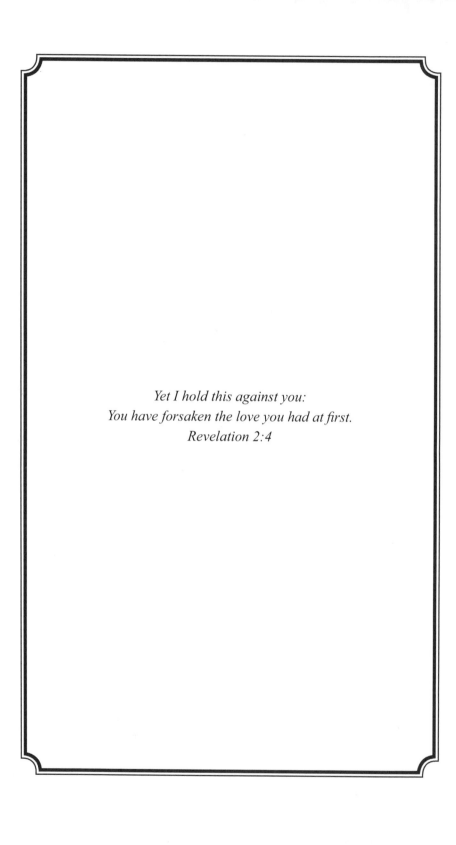

Yet I hold this against you:
You have forsaken the love you had at first.
Revelation 2:4

"YOU'VE LOST THAT LOVIN' FEELIN'."

Shah Jahan married several women, as was the custom of his day. However, he only had one true love—Mumtaz. He adored her. Tragically, in their nineteenth year of marriage, Mumtaz died from complications delivering their fourteenth (yes, fourteenth) child. She was only thirty-nine years old. The shah was so devastated by the loss of his love that he became melancholy and listless. Advisors suggested that he build a spectacular tomb to memorialize his love. The project was designed to help the shah deal with his grief.

In 1632 the project commenced. The box containing the remains of his beloved wife lay in the lower portion of the building as the construction progressed around it.

For two decades, the shah tirelessly directed the progress of this beautiful shrine. Over twenty thousand skilled artisans and over one thousand elephants participated in the project. The shah's intense desire for perfection grew with each passing year. On one particularly stressful period in the construction, the shah himself was walking around the site and bumped into the box. Angrily, he demanded that the box be removed from the shrine. Workers hesitated to obey his orders, making him even angrier. Finally, to quell his tirade, a senior official relocated the box—the box that contained the remains of his dearly beloved wife. The shah was so deeply engrossed in the project, that he forgot the purpose of honoring his beloved. He lost his passion for his first love.

The Taj Mahal, initiated as a labor of love, became just a labor.

The church at Ephesus experienced this same trial. They worked hard and persevered because of their love for the community of believers, their love for the unsaved, and, most importantly, their love for God. After years of persecution, false apostles, and attacks from within and without, the church had lost its first love.

In a nightclub in the 1960s, a singing duo crooned the words "if you would only love me like you used to do." A marine from the back of the club yelled out, "That was righteous, brothers." The name stuck, and the Righteous Brothers hit the top of the pop charts with their celebrated ballad, "You Lost That Lovin' Feelin'."

Jesus saw that this church and its members had lost that "lovin' feelin'." Furthermore, he knew that this love was what they needed to fuel the perseverance required to reach a pagan community like Ephesus. The difficult challenges in that city were surmountable only when armed with a vibrant love for God.

Jesus gave us the greatest commandment:

> "The most important one," answered Jesus, "is this: 'Hear, O Israel: The Lord our God, the Lord is one. Love the Lord your God with all your heart and with all your soul and with all your mind and with all your strength.' The second is this: 'Love your neighbor as yourself.' There is no commandment greater than these." (Mk 12:29-31)

Jesus says to love the Lord with "all" our heart. To give him any less is to break this commandment.

A similar loss of love can happen in a marriage. Some have said that the honeymoon period is over when "I do" turns into "you better."

Last week, I noticed two couples dining in a restaurant. The woman at the first table was looking intently into her man's eyes. She nodded as he spoke and giggled at his jokes. As he spoke, he would reach out and occasionally touch her arm for emphasis.

The table next to them seemed to have a cold breeze blowing around it. The woman was berating her husband for a myriad of things. He, in response, opened a newspaper forming a physical barrier in between them. They had "lost that lovin' feelin'."

This loss of passion can happen to our faith. Our first love, our sacred romance, should be with our Lord and Savior, Jesus Christ. How do we keep the relationship fresh and reignite the sparks of passion?

Let's explore the answer by comparing our relationship with the Lord to a relationship in marriage. If you were questioning someone who felt their marriage was becoming stale, what problems and solutions would this conversation reveal?

"Our marriage seems stale."

"Communication is key. Do you take time to have a real conversation with each other?"

"We try to say a few words to each other before a meal. But it is very one-sided. I have stopped even expecting him to respond."

"Hmmm. So how does he talk to you?"

"He has written me several letters. They are on my bedside table. I keep meaning to read them before I go to bed at night. You know how it is, I get so tired at night that I can't keep my eyes open to read them."

"Do you ever initiate a conversation with him?"

"When I desperately need something or if I am in a bad situation, I reach out to him."

"Do you spend special time together?"

"He asks me to set aside Sundays for him. So, I try to spend time with him on Sunday morning. I am so busy on the weekends that I am often distracted if we do get together. Some Sundays, I sleep in or spend the time getting caught up on things. I have not been able to make it very often."

"Do you eat meals together?"

"He has some bread and wine he wants to share. But again, I have been very busy. Perhaps I can make time for that soon."

You would not be surprised to learn that this relationship lacked excitement and depth. Similar issues arise in relationships with the Lord. He longs for us to talk with Him, to listen to Him, to read His word, to worship, to be in community with believers, and to invest the time to pursue a deeper relationship with Him. Time and energy must be invested to reap the return of a vibrant relationship and rekindled love.

Ministry without the love of Christ is ineffective. The apostle Paul reminds us in the letter to the church at Corinth that our service to the Lord is empty without our love.

> If I speak in the tongues of men or of angels, but do not have love, I am only a resounding gong or a clanging cymbal. If I have the gift of prophecy and can fathom all mysteries and all knowledge, and if I have a faith that can move mountains, but

do not have love, I am nothing. If I give all I possess to the poor and give over my body to hardship that I may boast, but do not have love, I gain nothing. (1 Cor 13:1-3)

Love is essential for an effective walk with the Lord and for a vibrant ministry. Evaluate these words as your Ephesian brothers and sisters did. In your relationship with the Lord, have you "lost that lovin' feelin'?"

How can a church lose the passion for serving Christ?

Can a church continue its programming even without the love of the Lord?

What are the results of this?

What are some of the reasons people lose their desire for a closer walk with the Lord?

What causes you to lose that "lovin' feelin'?"

Do you need to reignite your passion for the Lord?

What steps can you take to accomplish this?

—

Consider how far you have fallen! Repent and do the things you did at first... Revelation 2:5

TRUE FREEDOM

Picture yourself walking in the marketplace or agora in first-century Ephesus, around the time this letter was written. Possibly one out of every three people you see could be a slave. The percentage of slaves in the Roman Empire could have been as high as 40 percent. Even the poorest of the artisans generally owned one or two slaves. Emperor Nero was said to have owned over four hundred slaves.[27]

Historian Niall McKeown suggested that 90 percent of free people living in first-century Italy descended from slaves. They were not easily recognized because they were of different cultural and racial backgrounds and blended with the natives of the region. They were often citizens of lands surrounding the empire that were conquered by the Roman legions.[28] Poor citizens would sometimes sell themselves or their children into slavery to provide them with food and shelter.

The Greek philosopher Seneca wrote this warning to Emperor Nero regarding the dangerously high proportion of slaves to free men in the empire: "It was once proposed in the Senate that slaves should be distinguished from free people by their dress, but then it was realized how great a danger this would be, if our slaves began to count us."[29]

A majority of the slaves held menial jobs laboring in places such as mines, farms, and on the sea. However, citizens from a defeated foe who were conquered and captured to be sold into slavery and who possessed desirable skills, such as doctors or educators, were often put to work as slaves in their former trade. Others became slaves to pay off debts. Some voluntarily committed themselves to service under a master in exchange for the promise of food and shelter.

Slaves were a valuable commodity in the Roman Empire and were considered property. Runaway slaves were pursued, and a reward was offered for their capture and return. The punishment for recovered slaves was brutal. They were branded on their face or hands with the letters FGV, short for the Latin word "fugitivus," meaning "one who flees."

Onesimus was a runaway slave. We do not know how he became a slave or why he ran away. But we can see the hand of the Lord working in his life. Onesimus successfully escaped from his master, Philemon, in Colossae, a city about 125 miles west of Ephesus. Onesimus's best strategy for freedom was to venture to a faraway big city and get lost in the crowd. Onesimus somehow accomplished this mammoth task. He journeyed across Asia Minor to the sea and set sail for Rome and a life of freedom and anonymity. When he, at last, reached Rome, Onesimus stopped running. He thought that he was free from the chains of slavery.

At the same time, in the same city, another man was in chains. This man, however, had full citizenship rights. Paul's chains were not forced upon him. He chose to continue to preach and teach about his Lord, Jesus Christ, knowing that this meant he would be repeatedly bound and imprisoned. He forfeited his freedom and petitioned to be taken to Rome with the words, "I appeal to Caesar!" (Acts 25:11). Paul focused on the positive aspect of his chains: "As a result, it has become clear throughout the whole palace guard and to everyone else that I am in chains for Christ. Because of my chains, most of the brothers in the Lord have been encouraged to speak the word of God more courageously and fearlessly" (Phil 1:13-14).

One man ran from chains. Another embraced them.

The "free" man visited the imprisoned one. Onesimus studied under Paul and soon accepted the Gospel. Paul says he "became my son while I was in chains" (Phlm 1:10). Paul learned that Onesimus was the slave of a prominent church member in Colosse, Philemon, whom Paul may have met while serving the church in Ephesus, a town close to Colosse. Paul refers to Philemon as "our dear friend and fellow worker" (Phlm 1:1). Although free from the chains of slavery, Onesimus was still bound by the chains of guilt and deceit for cheating his master. The fear of discovery bound him. Onesimus, the man who seemed free, was in bondage, while the prisoner in chains, Paul, rejoiced in his liberty in Christ. Which man was truly free?

Paul convinced Onesimus that to be truly free, he must return to Philemon and repent. He sent him back with a letter imploring forgiveness. "I am sending him – who is my very heart – back to you. So if you consider me a partner welcome him as you would welcome me" (Phlm 1:12, 1:17). Paul a played on the name "Onesimus," which means helpful or useful, saying, "Formerly he was useless to you, but now he has become useful both to you and to me" (Phlm 11).

Although Paul would have liked to have kept Onesimus with him to help him and comfort him during his house arrest in Rome, he sent him back to Philemon. Paul knew that Onesimus had to forfeit his freedom and repent to be truly free.

Onesimus returned and repented. In the second century, a bishop named Onesimus served the church at Ephesus. Many scholars believe that this is the same runaway slave who was first bound by chains and later bound by guilt. His repentance set him free.

The Lord calls us to true freedom by repentance as well.

Jesus exhorted the Ephesian church members to regain their love for God and to repent. How are these two related?

Do you connect more with Paul or Onesimus?

How can unrepented sin keep us from a relationship with Christ?

Are there areas in your life that could benefit from the freedom which comes with repentance?

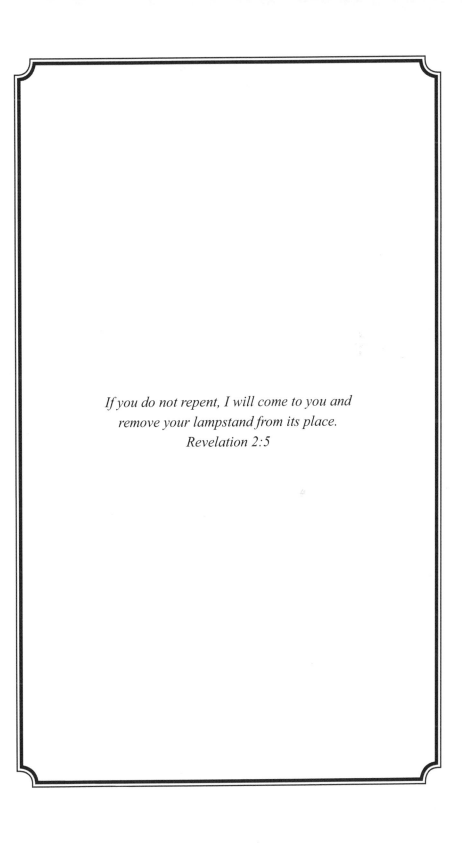

If you do not repent, I will come to you and
remove your lampstand from its place.
Revelation 2:5

A HEART OF REPENTANCE

He was an unlikely king. He felt that his humble background made him unworthy to be the leader of his nation.

It wasn't that his appearance was not royal. To the contrary, he was "an impressive young man without equal among the Israelites—a head taller than any of the others" (I Sm 9:2).

In the beginning, however, he modestly doubted that he should be the king.

The revered prophet Samuel was getting older and preparing to pass the cloak of the prophet to his sons. However, his boys "did not follow his ways. They turned aside after dishonest gain and accepted bribes and perverted justice" (I Sm 8:3). The leaders of the country came together and demanded a king. They were not impressed with the morality of the heirs apparent. They saw the other nations around them ruled by kings. Peer pressure nudged the Israelites to ask for a monarchy instead of the theocracy they had lived under for centuries.

Reluctantly, Samuel acquiesced. The Lord selected Saul as the first king of the nation, Israel.

On the appointed day, Samuel assembled the twelve tribes of Israel to announce and present the new king to his nation. The excitement and anticipation built as Samuel spoke to the crowd. All eyes were fixed on the prophet. The people eagerly waited for him to bring out the new king. The Bible doesn't tell us exactly how it happened, but imagine this: The trumpets played a regal melody. The drums rolled. Samuel ceremoniously and regally opened his arms to present the new king. However, the stage was empty. Saul was not there. Samuel urgently whispered, "Somebody find Saul!" The Bible account takes the action from here:

> But when they looked for him, he was not to be found. So they inquired further of the Lord, "Has the man come here yet?"

And the Lord said, "Yes, he has hidden himself among the supplies."
They ran and brought him out. (1 Sm 10:21-23)

This unlikely king is hiding. One of the most powerful nations in the world had a new king, and he is nervously hiding out between the toilet paper and the paper towels in the storage room.

Unfortunately, however, this humility did not last. Saul repeatedly disobeyed God and began to think of himself more highly than the Lord. He even "set up a monument in his own honor" (1 Sm 15:12).

The Lord gave Saul great victories over his enemies. After the Israelites defeated the Amalekites, Saul disobeyed God's order to destroy everything, including their sheep and cattle. When Samuel confronted him, Saul lied.

"The Lord bless you! I have carried out the Lord's instructions"
But Samuel said, "What then is this bleating of sheep in my ears?
What is this lowing of cattle that I hear?" (1 Sm 15:13-14)

Saul repeatedly disobeyed without true repentance.

Does the Lord delight in burnt offerings and sacrifices as much as in obeying the Lord?
To obey is better than sacrifice, and to heed is better than the fat of rams.
For rebellion is like the sin of divination, and arrogance like the evil of idolatry.
Because you have rejected the word of the Lord, he has rejected you as king. (1 Sm 15:22-23)

Saul's disobedience led to one of the saddest verses in the Bible. "The Spirit of the Lord departed from Saul" (1 Sm 16:14).

A sincere heart of repentance is important to the Lord. In ancient Israel, to show remorse and grief, a person would publicly "rend" or tear their garments in a dramatic outward symbol of penitence. God makes it clear that He prefers a broken heart over a theatrical action to showcase repentance:

Rend your heart and not your garments.

Return to the Lord your God, for he is gracious and compassionate, slow to anger and abounding in love, and he relents from sending calamity. (Jl 2:13)

Jesus warned the Ephesians that if they did not have a heart for true repentance, He would remove their lampstand. We, as Christians, are supposed to be the "light of the world" (Mt 5:14). If we are not repentant, our light will not shine. Just as a burned-out lightbulb is removed from a lamp, Christ will remove a lampstand that no longer produces light.

What areas of your life need examination and repentance?

In what ways can we allow our light to shine individually?

How can we allow our light to shine as a church?

What is keeping your lampstand from giving off the light and love of Christ?

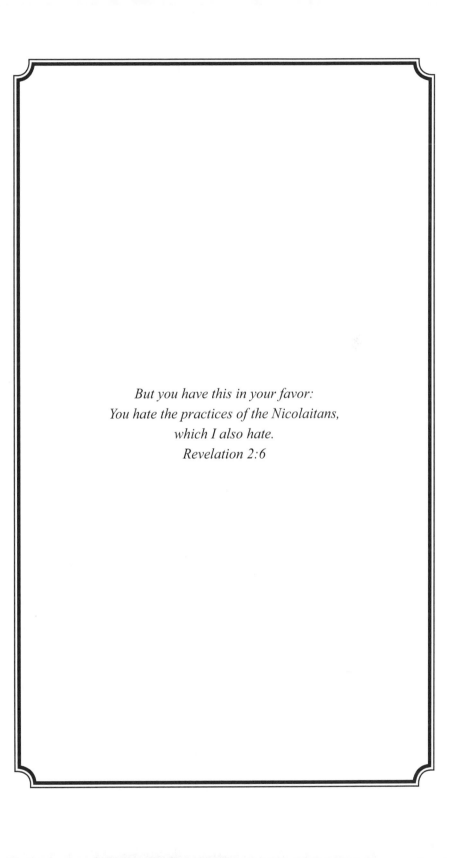

But you have this in your favor:
You hate the practices of the Nicolaitans,
which I also hate.
Revelation 2:6

FREEDOM THROUGH CHRIST

Have you ever looked at the church of today and nostalgically yearned for the churches of the past and their seemingly simpler times?

Dr. Luke gives us insight into a situation in the early church involving alleged prejudicial treatment. It appears that the early church was not immune to problems and controversy any more than the modern church.

> In those days when the number of disciples was increasing, the Hellenistic Jews among them complained against the Hebraic Jews because their widows were being overlooked in the daily distribution of food. So the Twelve gathered all the disciples together and said, "It would not be right for us to neglect the ministry of the word of God in order to wait on tables. Brothers and sisters, choose seven men from among you who are known to be full of the Spirit and wisdom. We will turn this responsibility over to them and will give our attention to prayer and the ministry of the word." This proposal pleased the whole group. They chose Stephen, a man full of faith and of the Holy Spirit; also Philip, Procorus, Nicanor, Timon, Parmenas, and Nicolas from Antioch, a convert to Judaism. They presented these men to the apostles, who prayed and laid their hands on them. (Acts 6:1-6)

Church membership grew to numbers as large as twenty-five thousand, and the scope of work became more than twelve disciples could handle. James, the brother of Jesus, described a church that was pleasing to God:

> Religion that God our Father accepts as pure and faultless is this: to look after orphans and widows in their distress and to keep oneself from being polluted by the world. (Jas 1:27).

The church was commissioned to care for widows and orphans. In this culture, it was difficult for a woman to financially support herself in a reputable way, and it was impossible for children. The government had no system to provide monetarily for widows or orphans. The church was their only safety net.

A riff was brewing in the church. Widows of a Greek pagan background felt that they were not treated as well as the Jewish widows and were airing their grievances. The disciples wisely appointed seven men to be leaders in this outreach ministry.

Two of these seven names are easily recognizable from other sections in the book of Acts. Stephen was the Christian martyr whose story appears in Acts chapter 7. Philip was an evangelist to the Samaritans, as is told in Acts chapter 8. The third name of interest is Nicolas of Antioch. Although there are differing schools of thought, some scholars believe that he may have been the leader of the Nicolaitans referred to by Christ in the letters in Revelation. Jesus commends the church in Ephesus for "hating the practices of the Nicolaitans, which I also hate" (Rv 2:6). Nicolas, who started as one of the chosen seven, ended up as a heretic who justified sinning on the grounds that the experience would deepen the believer's walk.[30]

The root words forming "Nicolaitans" also gives insight into Christ's ire. The root *"nico"* means "to rule." The root *"lait"* means "the people." We derive the word "laity" from this root. This word could have described a clerical group of people who took power away from the congregation or laypeople of the church.[31]

The Nicolaitans advocated freedom of actions. The Talmud, the legal code for Jewish people which interpreted biblical laws and commandments, contained over six hundred laws governing every hour of every day. These laws addressed dietary restrictions. They spelled out Sabbath day prohibitions, including the number of steps allowed on the Sabbath. Christians who had formerly been Jews were liberated from the pharisaical law. This independence was overwhelming to some who would take their newfound freedom to unhealthy extremes. Some new Christians formed a cult advocating sinful ways of exercising their freedom, including participating in sinful pagan practices for the supposed purpose of understanding the sin. Paul addressed the freedom of Christians as it related to eating meat that had been sacrificed to idols.

Be careful, however, that the exercise of your rights does not become a stumbling block to the weak. For if someone with a weak conscience sees you, with all your knowledge, eating in an idol's temple, won't that person be emboldened to eat what is sacrificed to idols? So this weak brother or sister, for whom Christ died, is destroyed by your knowledge. When you sin against them in this way and wound their weak conscience, you sin against Christ. Therefore, if what I eat causes my brother or sister to fall into sin, I will never eat meat again, so that I will not cause them to fall. (1 Cor 8:9-13)

The Nicolaitans advocated pushing the boundaries of sin for the supposed, selfish excitement of freedom. Jesus says in this letter that He hates this self-seeking lifestyle. The genuine believer finds the abundant life by putting the needs of others in front of his egotistical desires. True freedom is liberty from sin and self-centeredness.

How could actions which are not harmful to one person be detrimental to others?

What are some examples of these?

How can you change your patterns to keep a brother or sister from falling into sin?

Whoever has ears,
let them hear what the Spirit says to the churches.
To the one who is victorious,
I will give the right to eat from the tree of life,
which is in the paradise of God.
Revelation 2:7

THE TREE OF LIFE

What fast-food restaurant comes to mind when you see golden arches? Which retailer do you associate with a red dot encircled by a white circle which is surrounded by a red circle? Which sporting-goods company brings to mind a swoosh? What technology company pops to mind when you see an apple? Company logos identify businesses and their products. These images can elicit opinions and attitudes.

For the Greek polytheistic citizens of Ephesus, the phrase "tree of life" and the image of a date palm tree would have evoked the image of Artemis. This tree was the "logo" for the Temple of Artemis. Archeological excavations have uncovered a simple tree-shrine, which was probably the humble beginning of the grand structure known in their day. Therefore, the symbol of the tree was used to represent the temple and the city. It was the inscription on their coinage.

The Temple of Artemis was literally the tree *of life* for criminals and others seeking asylum. A political exile running from government officials could find safe harbor if he made it to the temple. A felon escaping law enforcement would also be protected once he arrived. This peace and security lasted only as long as the refugee remained in the physical building.

Jesus uses the phrase "tree of life" in his letter to incorporate a symbol representing the city and its evil worship. However, Jesus refers to the true meaning of the tree of life and a feeling of peace and security that is eternal.

The term "Garden of Eden" is synonymous with paradise. That is exactly what the Garden of Eden was for Adam and Eve. The garden was a shalom of perfect harmony. The story of humankind begins in paradise with trees.

> The Lord God made all kinds of trees grow out of the ground—trees that were pleasing to the eye and good for food. In the middle of the garden were the tree of life and the tree of the knowledge of good and evil. (Gn 2:9)

This oasis was so beautiful that it pleased even the creator himself: "And God saw that it was good" (Gn 1:25). Adam and Eve were allowed to enjoy the fullness of this lovely place. They had only one stipulation: "You must not eat from the tree of the knowledge of good and evil, for when you eat of it," you will surely die" (Gn 2:17). The Lord was referring to one of the two trees in the middle of the garden.

As humans are prone to do, Adam and Eve did the one thing that they were not supposed to do. They ate from the tree of the knowledge of good and evil. Their punishment included leaving this paradise: "So the Lord God banished him from the Garden of Eden . . . He placed on the east side of the Garden of Eden cherubim and a flaming sword flashing back and forth to guard the way to the tree of life" (Gn 3:24).

The decision to eat from the forbidden tree began a succession of wrong choices made by people throughout the ages. God gave humans the Ten Commandments to guide their actions. However, the law did not help them to obey. It merely showed the vast deviation of their choices from the way of God.

Then one day, by the grace of God, another tree entered the lives of humans. This tree had been cut and made into a cross, the Roman instrument of torture and death to punish and vilify the most heinous of criminals. In an outrageous and undeserved act of love and devotion, God sacrificed his son on this tree so that the humans could be restored to the garden. "For God so loved the world that he gave his one and only Son, that whoever believes in him shall not perish but have eternal life" (John 3:16). God did for the people what they were unable to do for themselves. He used this tree to redeem them and allow them to reenter the paradise of God.

Christ used the analogy of the tree because it was familiar to believers of Jewish heritage and those with a Greek background. The story of humankind began with a tree in the paradise of the Garden of Eden, and it will end with a tree in the paradise of heaven. The paradise we lost by one man, Adam, has been reclaimed by another man, Jesus.

Jesus offers the overcomers the amazing gift of eternal life in the presence of God in heaven. The prize has been won by Jesus's death on a tree. The believers can be victorious by repenting and by reclaiming their first love. They will then have the right and privilege of eating from the tree of life described later in the revelation. "On each side of the river stood the

---

tree of life, bearing twelve crops of fruit, yielding its fruit every month" (Rev 22:2).

Jesus is redeeming the tree of life for these believers.

What comes to your mind when you hear the term "tree of life?"

Do you feel that you have "the right to eat from the tree of life?" Explain.

What is one takeaway or insight from the letter to the Ephesian church that resonates with you?

In what way might that insight be calling you to a new way of being and doing?

THE SUFFERING CHURCH IN THE SUPERLATIVE CITY: SMYRNA

D o you know which US state is called the Sunshine State? How about the Tar Heel State, the Golden State, the Peach State, or the Grand Canyon State? Those slogans are easily identifiable and represent the states of Florida, North Carolina, California, Georgia, and Arizona.

Let's look at some of the more challenging ones. Do you know the SayWa! State? Which is the state of Great Faces, Great Places? Which one is the Keystone State? Which state is Full of Surprises? These superlatives of Washington, South Dakota, Pennsylvania, and Connecticut are not quite as familiar.

Jesus wrote the second letter in the book of Revelation to the church in a city that had many slogans, superlatives, and nicknames—Smyrna. This proud city boasted of its history, accomplishments, and citizens, earning it the title "a paradise of municipal vanity." It claimed to be the first in many categories. It produced coins claiming the title, "the First City of Asia." The citizens touted themselves as the first in loyalty to the Roman Empire by erecting a temple to the goddess Roma. They bragged that Homer, author of the epic poems the *Iliad* and the *Odyssey*, was a citizen of their city.

Smyrna was located approximately thirty-five miles north of Ephesus and only six miles from Greece, making it an important merchant city. Trade routes from the second-largest river in Asia Minor, the Hermus River, ended in Smyrna. Merchants sold their goods in the city or transported them to Greece and beyond from its large and impressive commercial harbor.[32]

Smyrna is still occupied and is a part of the modern city of Izmir. It's one of the two cities that received letters in Revelation that are still inhabited from Bible times until today. The other city is Philadelphia. Notably, these two churches are also the only ones for which the Lord had no negative remarks in his letters.

Another self-imposed superlative was the "First in Beauty." Writers compared the city to many lovely objects, including a flower, a statue, and a crown. Smyrna had the double blessing of being a city of great natural beauty as well as sophisticated and exquisite development. Alexander the Great designed the city with wide boulevards and impressive buildings. Magnificently built temples to Zeus, Aphrodite, Cybele, Asclepius, and Apollo lined the famous Golden Street. Colin Hemer, author of *The Letters to the Seven Churches of Asia*, explains, "The ancient sense of beauty extolled the buildings and their arrangement rather than the natural scenery." [33]

The arts and entertainment flourished in this "Glory of Asia." Its famous music center, the Odeum, held competitions for vocal and instrumental talent. The roof was specially designed for outstanding acoustics. Their stadium hosted sporting events and theatrical performances. This arena was the venue in which Polycarp, the bishop of Smyrna and a student of the apostle John, was burned at the stake.

Smyrna was a dichotomy for the early Christians. Its great beauty contrasted with the terrible persecution of these believers. The city's excessive wealth was juxtaposed with the poverty of the Christians, who were marginalized and impoverished by their exclusion from the city's pagan trade guilds. The polytheistic merchants made it impossible for the believers to make a living.

The city, which had seemingly unlimited resources, gave nothing to the followers of "the Way." This utopia was no paradise for persecuted Christians.

In his letter to this church, Jesus encourages this stalwart band of believers. Let's read on to find out His lessons for them and for us.

To the angel of the church in Smyrna write:
These are the words of him
who is the First and the Last.
Revelation 2:8

THE FIRST AND THE LAST

Four men from diverse backgrounds banded together in service to God and country. George Fox was an ordained Methodist minister from Vermont. He had lied about his age to serve in World War I and later enlisted in the Army Chaplain Service for World War II.

Alexander Goode, the son of a Brooklyn Rabbi, held degrees from the University of Cincinnati and the Hebrew Union College, as well as a Ph.D. from Johns Hopkins University. He married the niece of singer and actor Al Jolson and started his family in York, Pennsylvania. Rabbi Goode was appointed an Army chaplain in 1942.

Clark Poling, a Yale Divinity School graduate, served as the pastor of the First Reformed Church in Schenectady, New York. Clark enlisted during World War II, following in the footsteps of his father, a chaplain in World War I, despite his father's warning that chaplains suffered the highest mortality rate in the First World War.

John P. Washington was from a poor immigrant family in New Jersey. He felt the calling to enter the priesthood early in his life. Father Washington received his appointment as a US Army Chaplain after the attack on Pearl Harbor.[34]

These four men studied together at the Chaplains School at Harvard, taking classes in subjects such as chemical warfare, law, map reading, and first aid. They were reunited on the Army transport ship, *The Dorchester,* and headed to Greenland with nine hundred fellow Americans.

A mere 150 miles from their destination, a German submarine U-223 fired a torpedo, decisively damaging the ship's starboard side. Many were injured or killed from the impact. The ship fell into chaos as the survivors tried to navigate the dark hallways to the lifeboats.[35]

One website describes the bedlam of the incident in this way.

Quickly and quietly, the four chaplains spread out among the soldiers. There they tried to calm the frightened, tend the wounded, and guide the disoriented toward safety.

"Witnesses of that terrible night remember hearing the four men offer prayers for the dying and encouragement for those who would live," says Wyatt R. Fox, son of Reverend Fox.

One witness, Private William B. Bednar, found himself floating in oil-smeared water surrounded by dead bodies and debris. "I could hear men crying, pleading, praying," Bednar recalls. "I could also hear the chaplains preaching courage. Their voices were the only thing that kept me going."

Another sailor, Petty Officer John J. Mahoney, tried to reenter his cabin but Rabbi Goode stopped him. Mahoney, concerned about the cold Arctic air, explained he had forgotten his gloves.

"Never mind," Goode responded. "I have two pairs." The rabbi then gave the petty officer his own gloves. In retrospect, Mahoney realized that Rabbi Goode was not conveniently carrying two pairs of gloves and that the rabbi had decided not to leave *The Dorchester.*[36]

A Department of Defense article recounted the incident.

The chaplains tended to the soldiers' wounds, helped them toward lifeboats and distributed life jackets, even giving up their own when the supply ran out. Surviving soldiers said they were amazed because the recipients' faith didn't matter to the chaplains – they gave without discrimination in a world that was seemingly filled with it.[37]

After physically, emotionally, and spiritually ministering to those onboard, "all four chaplains were last seen with linked arms, bracing against the slanted deck, offering prayers and singing hymns. They were four of the more than 670 men who died in the attack."

These brave men from different backgrounds banded together to serve and to die for the Lord. They could have been the first ones off the sinking ship and into the lifeboats. They could have justified their actions by pointing to the Army's need for them. Instead, they chose to serve others and to serve God.

As He often did, Jesus turned the thoughts about being first upside down. Christ warned that, "the last will be first, and the first will be last'" (Mt 20:16). His teaching echoed the sentiments in Proverbs chastising a person who tries to push forcibly ahead for his own gain: "It's better to wait for an invitation to the head table than to be sent away in public disgrace" (Prv 25:7). The chaplains practiced Jesus's definition of first and last.

Conversely, the city of Smyrna took a world view of "first and last," putting great value on the temporal pleasures, benefits, and enticements of this life. The city leaders made sure that they were known and recognized as the "first" in loyalty to Rome. This designation was crucially important to the city's commerce, protection, and prosperity. The Roman Empire ruled most of the known world at this time. Being subjugated to Rome had many advantages. Pax Romana, literally "the peace of Rome," maintained an equilibrium that differed from previous periods in history.

Gone were the constant worries that a raiding party from a neighboring country would charge through the city, pillage your possessions, and capture your family. Rome protected its favored provinces from outside violence. Rome also maintained internal law and order. Fear of the empire's strong judicial hand kept crime rates low.

The Roman road system, developed for the ease of transporting troops, also served to facilitate trade. Delicacies from all corners of the world were now accessible, available, and, at least for some, affordable. Farmers supplying raw materials, artisans producing goods, and merchants selling both products used these roads and enjoyed their safety and convenience.

Cities demonstrating their loyalty to the empire received additional benefits, including the right to be a "free" or self-governing city and tax dollars for public projects. To prove their loyalty, the political leaders of Smyrna were the first to create and build a temple to the goddess Roma, who represented the Roman Empire. Smyrna then went a step further and instituted Emperor Worship. Each citizen was required to burn incense and recite "Caesar is Lord" in front of a government official. The official would then present the person with a certificate proving their faithfulness to Caesar. Those who refused were imprisoned on charges of atheism and treason and condemned to a torturous death.

Due to Smyrna's strategic and politically adept ploys to become a favored city of Rome, the citizens were afforded the best that Rome had to offer. The inhabitants had many opportunities for a life of ease, wealth, and prosperity. The members of the church in Smyrna could have been the "first and last" to grab these riches and opportunities. However, they refused to worship the goddess Roma and burn incense to Caesar.

In His letter, Christ reassures them and gives them the strength to withstand their upcoming persecution by reminding them of the words from Isaiah:

This is what the Lord says—
Israel's King and Redeemer, the Lord Almighty:
"I am the first and I am the last;
apart from me there is no God." (Is 44:6)

Being a believer in the early church was difficult in any city. However, the Christians in Smyrna faced the most dangerous and treacherous challenges of any believers in the region. Christ reassures these believers that He, indeed, is the First and the Last. His love will surround them from the first days until the bitter end. This acknowledgment of Christ's power must have given them great comfort and hope amid tremendous suffering.

Just as the four chaplains could have been the first to save themselves from the sinking ship, the early Christians could have taken the first and best the world had to offer if they had acquiesced to worshiping the goddess, Roma, and the emperor, Caesar. Both the chaplains and the Christians of Smyrna could have made excuses, lowered their standards, and saved their lives. Commendably, they did not. They remembered the Lord, who could have easily saved Himself from a horrible death on a cross but loved us so much that He chose to give His life as a sacrifice so that we could have eternal life.

The four chaplains and the faithful followers in Smyrna followed the example of Christ, the true "First and Last."

Both groups of believers faced horrible deaths with linked arms, offering prayers, and singing hymns.

What are some ways you can get caught up in the world's ideas of "first and last?"

In what areas of your life do find it difficult not to rush to be first?

What does the great love of Christ inspire in you?

Do you think you could have withstood the pressure to remain loyal to Jesus and not offer homage to Caesar?

What are some of the excuses we make in an attempt to fit into our world?

Jesus reassures and reminds us that He is the First and the Last. How does that comfort and strengthen you?

...who died and came to life again
Revelation 2:8

THE CITY WHICH DIED AND CAME TO LIFE AGAIN

Approximately six hundred years before the birth of Christ, the Lydians lived in an area that they called Anatolia and that we know today as Western Turkey. Their ruler, King Alyattes, attacked the city of Smyrna. He annihilated the city, leaving nothing but a trail of destruction.

For the next four hundred years, there was no life in Smyrna.

In 334 BC, Alexander the Great conquered Anatolia, making it part of the Greek Empire. Tradition holds that he was hunting on Mount Pagos on the southeastern side of Smyrna. Exhausted from the hunt, he fell asleep under a tree in the sanctuary of the goddess called Nemesis. Alexander dreamed that she directed him to found a city in the ruins of Smyrna. He designed an elaborate plan to rebuild the city in a grand style. As biographer Peter Green explains, "Alexander, with his superb natural eye for terrain, found a first-class site for a new city, some two and a half miles south of the old one."[38] The long and wide boulevards led from the magnificently large harbor into the heart of the city. The spacious agora, the name for their marketplace, was lined with stately columns. Opulent temples, built to honor the various gods, added to the stunning landscape. People in the area flocked to this beautiful city to repopulate it. This story of Alexander is recounted and validated by Romans coins from the era.

Smyrna literally died after King Alyattes's attack and came back to life through Alexander's vision. It was a resurrected city.

Smyrna was additionally associated with dying and coming to life again because of its name. Smyrna means "myrrh" and was synonymous with death and suffering to the readers of that day and time. Myrrh is an aromatic resin which comes from a thorny tree. Smyrna exported this valuable asset all over the world. Egypt was one of its best customers, buying large amounts of myrrh. Egyptians believed that a person continued to live in his earthly body in the afterlife. Therefore, they felt compelled to use large amounts of myrrh to properly embalm, prepare, and preserve their deceased loved ones' physical bodies for the eternal journey to come. Some scholars believe that the Egyptians learned these burial procedures from the children of Israel when they were slaves in that country.

The church at Smyrna experienced great tribulation and persecution. Jesus describes this in the next verse with the Greek word thlipsis, which means pressure. William Barclay describes the action depicted by this word: "It is always used in its literal sense. It is, for instance, used of a man who was tortured to death by being slowly crushed by a great boulder laid upon him." [39]

Jesus compares the suffering of the church in Smyrna to the breaking of the myrrh. Just as the myrrh must be crushed to release its aromatic scents, the believers' livelihoods, reputations, and very bodies were crushed by extreme persecution. As the weight of persecution fell on these believers, the sweet scents of faithfulness and perseverance rose to the Lord.

The Bible mentions myrrh three times in conjunction with Jesus. Matthew tells us in his Gospel that the wisemen brought myrrh to Jesus as a birthday gift.

> When (the wisemen) saw the star, they were overjoyed. On coming to the house, they saw the child with his mother Mary, and they bowed down and worshiped him. Then they opened their treasures and presented him with gifts of gold, frankincense and myrrh. (Mt 2:10-11)

The wise men presented Jesus with three gifts. The gold symbolized his status as a king. The frankincense, a form of incense, represented his deity. Although it was a gift to commemorate his birth, the myrrh denoted the significance of his death. [40]

The next time myrrh is mentioned is after Jesus was crucified. While he is dying on the cross, the soldiers offer him a tonic to ease his suffering. "Then they offered him wine mixed with myrrh, but he did not take it" (Mk 15:23). Myrrh was thought to be a pain reliever.

Smithsonian Magazine recently ran an article on the medicinal value of myrrh, proving the ancient mindset to be correct. In "There's More to Frankincense and Myrrh Than Meets the Eye,"[41] Colin Schultz reports, "From tests on mice, chemists at the University of Florence have found that molecules in myrrh act on the brain's opioid receptors, explaining its painkilling action."

The last time myrrh is cited in the Bible is after Jesus's death.

> Later, Joseph of Arimathea asked Pilate for the body of Jesus. Now Joseph was a disciple of Jesus, but secretly because he feared the Jewish leaders. With Pilate's permission, he came and took the body away. He was accompanied by Nicodemus, the man who earlier had visited Jesus at night. Nicodemus brought a mixture of myrrh and aloes, about seventy-five pounds. Taking Jesus' body, the two of them wrapped it, with the spices, in strips of linen. (Jn 19:38-40)

Two believers who had followed at a distance were empowered after the resurrection to serve their Savior in a very personal way. Joseph of Arimathea and Nicodemus prepared our Lord's body for death. The normal amount of spices required was a little less than half the body's weight. Seventy-five pounds of spices would have been used for a man weighing between 160 and 200 pounds. J. Vernon McGee describes it this way in his Bible commentary.

> They would prepare the body by rubbing it with myrrh and aloes, then wrapping it with linen strips. That would seal it and keep out the air. They would begin with a finger then wrap all the fingers that way, then the hand, the arm, and the whole body. On the Resurrection morning, when John saw the linen lying there and the body not in it, he understood that the Resurrection had taken place, and he believed. [42]

Isaiah prophesizes Jesus's second coming. Notice the two gifts which are relevant to the second coming.

> Arise, shine, for your light has come, and the glory of the Lord rises upon you. See, darkness covers the earth and thick darkness is over the peoples,
> but the Lord rises upon you and his glory appears over you.
> Herds of camels will cover your land, young camels of Midian and Ephah.

And all from Sheba will come bearing gold and incense and
proclaiming the praise of the Lord. (Is 60:1, 2, 6)

In the second coming, gold and incense, comparable to frankincense,
are brought as a praise offering. No myrrh is mentioned. No myrrh is
required. The resurrection of Christ defeated death eliminating the need
for this burial spice.

Jesus compares His resurrection to the rebirth and rebuilding of the city
of Smyrna. This association must have been a comfort to those believers who
could be arrested and killed at any moment. Their only crime was following
Jesus, and yet they were stalked and persecuted by the state. Knowing that
their Lord had endured unjust torture and death and remained firm in His
faith gave them strength. Jesus felt their pain and provided them an example
of godly perseverance amid unfair circumstances.

> For it is commendable if someone bears up under the pain of
> unjust suffering because they are conscious of God. But how
> is it to your credit if you receive a beating for doing wrong
> and endure it? But if you suffer for doing good and you endure
> it, this is commendable before God. To this you were called,
> because Christ suffered for you, leaving you an example, that
> you should follow in his steps.
> "He committed no sin,
> and no deceit was found in his mouth."
> When they hurled their insults at him, he did not retaliate;
> when he suffered, he made no threats. Instead, he entrusted
> himself to him who judges justly. "He himself bore our sins"
> in his body on the cross, so that we might die to sins and live
> for righteousness; "by his wounds you have been healed."
> (1 Pt 2:19-24)

With his words, Jesus also comforts those who are facing death, reassuring them that He has conquered it:

> He will wipe every tear from their eyes. There will be no more
> death or mourning or crying or pain, for the old order of things
> has passed away. (Rv 21:4).

Jesus writes to those in the church in this resurrected city whom He cherishes and commends for their perseverance. He assures them that He suffered and died so that believers throughout the ages may have eternal life.

Why do you think the wisemen were inspired to bring the myrrh to baby Jesus?

Why do you think that Jesus did not drink the myrrh while He was on the cross?

Jesus sacrificed His life so that we could live for eternity with Him. What comfort does that bring you?

Does Jesus's ultimate sacrifice make your daily trials easier to endure?

Although we may not face persecution, there are costs to following the way of Christ. In what areas do you feel these costs?

How do you handle these challenges?

How does the recognition of Jesus's great love and sacrifice change the way you are going to live your life?

—

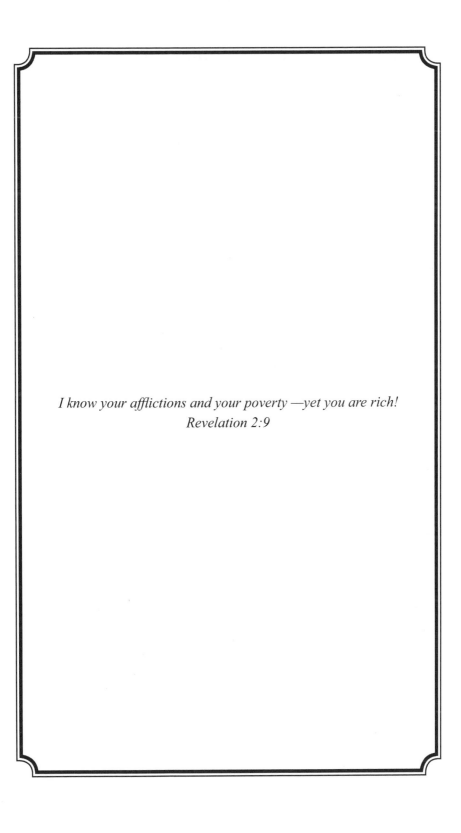

I know your afflictions and your poverty —yet you are rich!
Revelation 2:9

AFFLICTIONS AND POVERTY OF THE RICH

Two kings lived less than ten miles apart.

Although they were on this earth over two thousand years ago, they both impacted their world in ways that are still evident today. They both had people who paid homage and bent their knee to them. They both had much ink expended to tell their stories. These men never met face-to-face, but their paths are forever intertwined in history.

Herod the Great was crowned King of Judea in 40 BC by the Roman Senate. His appointment was due to his cunning political acumen. Herod had befriended and assisted Mark Antony, Cleopatra, and Caesar Augustus. His diplomatic skills kept the peace between Judea and Rome, enabling the Hebrew people a high degree of autonomy in their worship and their lifestyle.

Herod was a brilliant developer. He created the city of Caesarea as a harbor by sinking ship hulls. He named this beautiful and functional port after Caesar Augustus, earning additional political capital.[43]

Herod built several homes for himself. These palaces also served as protective fortresses for his family. One of the most beautiful of these was called Masada, a word meaning stronghold. Josephus, a Jewish historian, tells us that Herod incorporated living quarters and storehouses to sustain a battalion of soldiers for several months, as well as cisterns holding millions of gallons of water. In addition to being secure, Masada was lavishly appointed with breathtaking views, hot and cold bathhouses, and intricately designed mosaics.

His crowning achievement was the rebuilding of the Temple. Herod imported the best building materials. The fifteen-story columns were fashioned out of marble. The stones were imbedded with gold to cast a glow of brilliance in the sun. Even the disciples marveled at the splendor of the physical temple. "As Jesus was leaving the temple, one of his disciples said to him, 'Look, Teacher! What massive stones! What magnificent build-ings!' " (Mk 13:1). Herod had an abundance of resources available to him due to the generosity of the Romans to whom he pandered and the heavy taxes he levied on the Jews.

By all earthly measures, King Herod was one of the richest people in the world in his day.

During Herod's ostentatious reign, another king was born.

This king, however, did not have an abundance of money and resources. He did not have the trappings of royalty. His ignoble birth occurred in a cave or a stable. His peasant mother wore no crown and had no regal garments in which to wrap him. No servants assisted or attended his birth.

This king's name was Jesus.

By all earthly measures, Jesus was one of the poorest people in the world in his day. He had few possessions. In contrast to Herod's many palatial residences, by his admission, Jesus did not have a home at all. "Foxes have dens and birds have nests, but the Son of Man has no place to lay his head" (Lk 9:58).

For all his material wealth and success, Herod was paranoid. He slaugh-tered anyone he saw as a threat, including his favorite wife, three of his sons, his mother-in-law, and the High Priest of Jericho. The Roman Emperor, Caesar Augustus, is attributed as saying, "I would rather be Herod's pig than his son." Augustus made his point using two similar words. "*Hus*" is the Greek word for a pig, and "*huios*" is the word for son. The Jews did not kill pigs for food, as their dietary laws deemed pork an unclean food. For this reason, Augustus made the point that a pig has a better chance of escaping death at the hand of Herod, the king of the Jews, than one of his sons.[44]

The Bible gives us this account of Herod's suspicions:

> After Jesus was born in Bethlehem in Judea, during the time of
> King Herod, Magi from the east came to Jerusalem and asked,
> "Where is the one who has been born king of the Jews? We
> saw his star when it rose and have come to worship him."
> When King Herod heard this, he was disturbed...
> When Herod realized that he had been outwitted by the Magi,
> he was furious, and he gave orders to kill all the boys in

Bethlehem and its vicinity who were two years old and under. (Mt 2:1-3,16)

When Herod felt threatened, he relied on his riches and his power to rectify the situation. He manipulated to get his way. As he died, he issued a cruel edict to gather all the Jewish leaders in Jerusalem and kill them so that the city would mourn at the time of his death. Sadly, he knew that no one would grieve his passing.

A closer examination of the two kings reveals that the one who appeared to be wealthy was, in fact, a poor, miserable soul. He missed the real riches which were greater than even he could fathom:

> However, as it is written:
> "What no eye has seen, what no ear has heard, and what no human mind has conceived"—the things God has prepared for those who love him. (1 Cor 2:9)

By contrast, the humble king who was destitute by the world's standards was wealthy in eternal riches. He was willing to share his wealth with all who believed. Christ warned about accumulating riches on earth:

> Do not store up for yourselves treasures on earth, where moths and vermin destroy, and where thieves break in and steal. But store up for yourselves treasures in heaven, where moths and vermin do not destroy, and where thieves do not break in and steal. For where your treasure is, there your heart will be also. (Mt 6:19-21)

A poem attributed to Dr. James Allan Francis speaks to the power of the king, Jesus, who was poor by earthly standards but rich in legacy.

> He was born in an obscure village, the child of a peasant. He grew up in another village, where he worked in a carpenter shop until he was 30. Then, for three years, he was an itinerant preacher.

> He never wrote a book. He never held an office. He never had a family or owned a home. He didn't go to college. He never lived in a big city. He never traveled 200 miles from the place where

he was born. He did none of the things that usually accompany greatness. He had no credentials but himself.

He was only 33 when the tide of public opinion turned against him. His friends ran away. One of them denied him. He was turned over to his enemies and went through the mockery of a trial. He was nailed to a cross between two thieves. While he was dying, his executioners gambled for his garments, the only property he had on earth. When he was dead, he was laid in a borrowed grave, through the pity of a friend.

Twenty centuries have come and gone, and today he is the central figure of the human race. I am well within the mark when I say that all the armies that ever marched, all the navies that ever sailed, all the parliaments that ever sat, all the kings that ever reigned--put together--have not affected the life of man on this earth as much as that one, solitary life. [45]

Earthly standards are often poor indicators of real wealth and power. Some of the most affluent residents of Asia Minor lived in Smyrna, the "jewel of Asia Minor." Living alongside these people were some of the most persecuted and poor Christians of the Anatolian peninsula. However, as in the case of King Herod and Jesus, the ones who had earthly riches had no riches in heaven, and the poorest of the Christians by worldly standards had stored up great treasures in heaven. Jesus assures them that in His eyes, they are the truly "rich" ones.

What are some of the ways that the world's standards deviate from God's ways?

Which are most challenging for you to reconcile?

When is it difficult for you to see people through the eyes of Christ?

Are there times when you find yourself putting more value or importance on those with worldly wealth and power?

I know about the slander of those
who say they are Jews and are not.
Revelation 2:9

THOSE WHO SAY THEY ARE JEWS

The Pharisees were a Jewish religious group and political sect "who prized the study of Jewish laws as it developed through the generations," according to the Shengold Jewish Encyclopedia. From the Ten Commandments, they created 613 additional obligations or duties called Mitzvah.

Jesus criticizes these religious rule lovers in a list of seven woes of the Pharisees:

> "And you experts in the law, woe to you, because you load people down with burdens they can hardly carry, and you yourselves will not lift one finger to help them." (Lk 11:46)

The Mitzvah focused on details. For example, from the Exodus 20:8 commandment to "remember the Sabbath day by keeping it holy," rules were added that stipulated the distance a person could walk, the amount of weight they could carry, and how many knots they could tie on the Sabbath. Man's laws were confused with God's laws.

The idiom that says "the letter of the law versus the spirit of the law" differentiates the exact wording of a law from the underlying purpose and intent of it. This phrase, often used in legal debates, derives from scripture:

> He has made us competent as ministers of a new covenant—not of the letter but of the Spirit; for the letter kills, but the Spirit gives life. (2 Cor 3:6)

Jesus was concerned that the teachers were focused more on obeying set rules than establishing a true relationship with God. The number and specificity of the regulations were overwhelming. By focusing on actions, some of the Jewish leaders forgot that the attitude of the heart is always primary to our Lord. "The Lord does not look at the things people look at. People look at the outward appearance, but the Lord looks at the heart" (I

Sm 16:7). The Lord counsels us to pay attention to our attitudes because He knows that our words and our actions are a by-product of the heart. "Above all else, guard your heart, for everything you do flows from it" (Prv 4:23).

When Jesus was asked the greatest commandment, his answer was succinct and to the heart of the matter:

> "Love the Lord your God with all your heart and with all your soul and with all your mind and with all your strength." The second is this: "Love your neighbor as yourself." There is no commandment greater than these. (Mk 12:30-31)

The Pharisees and teachers of the law encouraged people to follow these laws using the phrase "taking on the yoke of the Torah." A yoke was a wooden farm tool that was placed over the necks of two animals to guide them as they plowed a field. Therefore, the analogy is that the law would be placed upon a person to guide them in the correct way.

While this idea is commendable, Jesus reprimanded the teachers of the law for making this guiding yoke too heavy and complicated for the people to bear:

> Then Jesus said to the crowds and to his disciples: "The teachers of the law and the Pharisees sit in Moses' seat. So you must be careful to do everything they tell you. But do not do what they do, for they do not practice what they preach. They tie up heavy, cumbersome loads and put them on other people's shoulders, but they themselves are not willing to lift a finger to move them." (Mt 23:1-4)

In contrast, Jesus offers an easier and lighter yoke and promises to help bear the burden:

> Come to me, all you who are weary and burdened, and I will give you rest. Take my yoke upon you and learn from me, for I am gentle and humble in heart, and you will find rest for your souls. (Mt 11:28-30)

Due to the ungodly attitude of some of these Jews, the word "Pharisee" garnered a bad reputation. The *Merriam-Webster* Dictionary even made it into an adjective. "Pharisaical" came to be a word describing a person or the actions of a person, "marked by hypocritical censorious self-righteousness." Ouch! Although there were certainly many godly Pharisees, the reputation of the sect was blemished by the actions of those who were not.

Although there were not many, if any, Pharisees in Smyrna, there were pharisaical Jews. These Jewish believers did not accept Jesus as the Messiah. They scorned and hated the Jewish Christians berating them as traitors to the faith and to God. Not only would they blaspheme Christ by denying His deity, but also, they would take revenge on their Jewish brothers and sisters by implicating them to the authorities of the Roman Empire. In the words of the apostle Paul, "No, for not all who are born into the nation of Israel are truly members of God's people!" (Rom 9:6 NLT).

The Roman government recognized the Jewish faith in Smyrna and gave them an exemption to the laws regarding emperor and pagan worship. They were allowed to worship in their synagogues following their prescribed laws and customs. Wealthy, prominent Jewish citizens who had influence over Roman officials would report the Christians to the authorities citing false charges.

Because the synagogue had an exemption for emperor worship, the Jewish parishioners did not have to bow to the idols and altars for Caesar. The Jews would deceive the officials by reporting the names of the Messianic Jews and stating that they were not legitimate Jews. The Romans would seek out these believers and interrogate them asking them to bow to Caesar as a god. When the Christians refused, they were martyred.

Also, the Jews would raise suspicion by misrepresenting the words of Jesus. They quoted Him, out of context, saying, "Take and eat; this is my body" (Mt 26:26). The Jews reported to the Romans that the Christians were cannibals.

The Jews recounted the story of Jesus and his mother and brothers to the Roman officials:

> While Jesus was still talking to the crowd, his mother and brothers stood outside, wanting to speak to him. Someone told him, "Your mother and brothers are standing outside, wanting to speak to you."

He replied to him, "Who is my mother, and who are my brothers?" Pointing to his disciples, he said, "Here are my mother and my brothers. For whoever does the will of my Father in heaven is my brother and sister and mother." (Mt.12:46-50)

The Jews slandered the Christians as people who did not value family, an institution that the Romans held in high regard.

Paul warned of the treachery of these pharisaical Jews:

A person is not a Jew who is one only outwardly, nor is circumcision merely outward and physical. No, a person is a Jew who is one inwardly; and circumcision is circumcision of the heart, by the Spirit, not by the written code. Such a person's praise is not from other people but from God. (Rom 2:28-29)

It is not as though God's word had failed. For not all who are descended from Israel are Israel. (Rom 9:6)

The Jews were pawns in the hand of the enemy. They formed an unholy alliance with the polytheistic Romans to exact revenge on the Christians, many of whom shared the same background and families. These Jews were not acting with the brotherly love God expects from those who believe in Him, which caused Jesus to commiserate with these Christians and assure them that the slander and malevolence waged against them had not gone unnoticed.

The guidelines of the Mitzvah were instituted as standards to bring the Jewish people closer in their relationship with God. Why do you think they got out of hand?

Jesus assures believers then and today that he knows our trials and tribulations. How is this a comfort?

Why do you think the Jews formed an alliance with the pagans against the Christians?

How do you think the Messianic Jews, Jews who believe in Jesus as the Messiah, felt when their fellow Jews were a source of their persecution?

Is it easier for you to follow the letter of the law or the spirit of the law? Why? How does this affect your walk with the Lord?

but are a synagogue of Satan.
Revelation 2:9

SATAN

Billy Sunday, a Philadelphia Phillies outfielder turned evangelist, said this when asked if he believed in Satan: "I know there is a devil for two reasons; first, the Bible declares it; and second, I have done business with him." [46]

Who is this Satan?

The Bible tells us that Satan was initially the best and the brightest of the angelic forces. He was the leader of the Cherubim, the most elite battalion of the angels. This exclusive band is comparable to the Navy SEALs or the Army Green Berets, and Satan was the preeminent one among them:

> You were the seal of perfection, full of wisdom and perfect in beauty.
> You were in Eden, the garden of God; every precious stone adorned you:
> carnelian, chrysolite and emerald, topaz, onyx and jasper, lapis lazuli, turquoise and beryl.
> Your settings and mountings were made of gold;
> on the day you were created they were prepared.
> You were anointed as a guardian cherub, for so I ordained you.
> You were on the holy mount of God; you walked among the fiery stones.
> You were blameless in your ways from the day you were created till wickedness was found in you.
> Through your widespread trade you were filled with violence, and you sinned.
> So I drove you in disgrace from the mount of God, and I expelled you, guardian cherub, from among the fiery stones.
> Your heart became proud on account of your beauty,
> and you corrupted your wisdom because of your splendor.

So I threw you to the earth; I made a spectacle of you
before kings.
(Ez 28:11-18)

Satan had it all. He lived with God in the highest heavens. Then his
heart became hardened and proud. Satan forgot who he was and whose he
was. He acted like a five-star general trying to usurp the power from the
Commander-in-Chief. Pride turned this angel into a devil.

How you have fallen from heaven, morning star, son of
the dawn!
You have been cast down to the earth, you who once laid low
the nations!
You said in your heart, "I will ascend to the heavens;
I will raise my throne above the stars of God;
I will sit enthroned on the mount of assembly, on the utmost
heights of Mount Zaphon.
I will ascend above the tops of the clouds; I will make myself
like the Most High."
But you are brought down to the realm of the dead, to the depths
of the pit. (Is 14:12-15)

He who once existed to glorify and exalt God now only wanted to
promote and elevate himself. He who was a perfect reflection of the light
of the Lord now pretended to be the light. He who bowed to the Master
now desired to be the one to whom homage was paid.

Satan appears in the Garden of Eden as the serpent: "Now the serpent
was more crafty than any of the wild animals the Lord God had made"
(Gn 3:1). In this verse, the word "serpent" is translated from the Hebrew
word for "shining one." This glimmering creation is the serpent who tempts
Adam and Eve to eat from the Tree of the Knowledge of Good and Evil.
This shining angel, who had shone the brightest of all the angels, could have
used his brilliance to show the righteous way to humanity. Now, instead,
he was luring men and women to stray from the light.

Jesus testifies to Satan's fall from heaven: "'I saw Satan fall like light-
ning from heaven'" (Lk 10:18).

Revelation recounts the battle between Satan and his forces and Michael and the angels:

> Then war broke out in heaven. Michael and his angels fought against the dragon, and the dragon and his angels fought back. But he was not strong enough, and they lost their place in heaven. The great dragon was hurled down—that ancient serpent called the devil, or Satan, who leads the whole world astray. He was hurled to the earth, and his angels with him.
> (Rv 12:7-9)

Satan knows that he is a defeated foe. He understands that his time is limited. Therefore, he strikes out with a vengeance:

> But woe to the earth and the sea, because the devil has gone down to you! He is filled with fury, because he knows that his time is short.
> (Rv 12:12)

Another snake acts with a similar desperate ferocity.

The king cobra, a venomous snake, is a delicacy in China. Cobra is an appetizer and specialty soup in the finest restaurants in Asia. In Southern China, a chef was preparing cobra soup when the head of the snake, which he had decapitated twenty minutes earlier, bit him. The snake bite proved fatal.

Sean Bush, a snake expert at the Brody School of Medicine at East Carolina University, confirmed that this was possible. "It's a last-ditch effort to survive, so it's very common. They get real snappy in the throes of death."

Satan, like the cobra, knows his time is limited. Like the cobra, he is snappy in the throes of death. He will do whatever he can to move us away from God. This deceiver is the Satan of whom Christ speaks. He warns the church of this intimidating but defeated foe.

What did you learn about Satan that you did not know?

Why do you think Christ thought it important to inform the church of the identity of their enemy?

Do you think about Satan as a real force in the world?

When you think of conflict in the external world and in your personal world, do you tend to blame it on individuals or the enemy?

What would change in your life if you could focus on Satan as the catalyst instead of a person?

Do not be afraid of what you are about to suffer. I tell you, the devil will put some of you in prison to test you, and you will suffer persecution for ten days.
Revelation 2:10

PERSECUTION

A bumper sticker stated, "Honesty is very valuable. Don't expect if it from cheap people."

Jesus was brutally honest with the church in Smyrna. He did not sugar-coat the message. He did not avoid the topic. He told them that it would get worse before it got better. He warned them: "You will suffer persecution" (Rv 2:10).

Open Doors USA, a nonprofit organization of Christians who come together to support persecuted believers, released the following statistics.

- 245 million Christians experience high levels of persecution
- One in nine Christians worldwide experience high levels of persecution
- On average, eleven Christians are killed every day for their faith [47]

Unfortunately, persecution is still alive and well and is increasing.

Tertullian, a Christian author from the second century AD, asserted that "the blood of the martyrs was the seed of the early church." [48] He correctly noted that persecution did not quench the early church, as was the goal of the oppressors. Instead, persecution and the deaths of Christian leaders seemed to energize the church. Seeds were planted, and church growth accelerated.

The blood of one of the early martyrs, in particular, was a blessing and symbol of hope for those suffering persecution around him. His legendary, brave death exemplified faithfulness under pressure. Polycarp was the bishop of the church of Smyrna. He studied under the tutelage of the apostle John, the very man who penned the letters to the churches.

Polycarp was captured and condemned for being an atheist, one who did not believe in the Roman gods. The Roman guards who captured him granted his request of an hour in prayer. After watching him pray and hearing his passion for the Lord, the guards felt remorse at having arrested him. He was, however, still brought before the proconsul, who gave Polycarp the following reprieve: "Swear, and I will release thee; reproach Christ." [49]

Foxe's Book of Martyrs tells the amazing story of what happened next.

> Polycarp answered, "Eighty and six years have I served (Christ), and He never once wronged me; how then shall I blaspheme my King, Who hath saved Me? I bless Thee for deigning me worthy of this day, and this hour that I may be among Thy martyrs and drink the cup of my Lord Jesus Christ."

> At the stake, to which he was only tied, but not nailed as usual, as he assured them he should stand immovable, the flames, on their kindling the fagots, encircled his body, like an arch, without touching him; and the executioner, on seeing this, was ordered to pierce him with a sword, when so great a quantity of blood flowed out as extinguished the fire. [50]

This blood, which Tertullian deemed the "seed of the early church," was potent enough to extinguish the flames of evil. Polycarp and these early martyrs knew that they were not fighting against the Jews, the crowds of pagans, the guards, or even the Roman Empire. They recognized that they were fighting against the enemy, Satan himself.

The Lord warns us through the pen of Paul: "For our struggle is not against flesh and blood, but against the rulers, against the authorities, against the powers of this dark world and against the spiritual forces of evil in the heavenly realms" (Eph.6:12). We must be vigilant and "not unaware of his schemes" (2 Cor 2:9).

Jesus warns the church of the clear and present danger ahead. He is specific to help them prepare. His initial words are of comfort: "do not be afraid" (Rv 2:10). He informs them of the source of their conflict, "the devil," and of Satan's motivation, "to test you" (Rv 2:10). Jesus even specifies the length of testing, ten days. This time period is not a literal ten days but a Greek idiom meaning "a short time."

Polycarp was an excellent example of holding onto one's faith in times of persecution. However, when the intensity of the struggle increased, the people of Smyrna needed an even better example. They yearned for the flawless hope and the sinless example of Jesus Christ, the first true martyr of the Christian faith.

Jesus knew the pressure. He knew the pain. He knew the difficulty. However, he also knew the final outcome and loved this church enough to be honest with them about the impending persecution.

Tertullian said, "The blood of the martyrs was the seed of the early church." Why do you think this is true?

Why is it helpful to be aware of a trial before it happens?

Jesus warned this church out of his love for them. Have you ever had to tell someone you love something difficult?

Be faithful, even to the point of death,
and I will give you life as your victor's
crown. Whoever has ears,
let them hear what the Spirit says to the churches.
The one who is victorious
will not be hurt at all by the second death.
Revelation 2:10-11

TO THE POINT OF DEATH

As her five-year-old granddaughter was napping in her home, DeDe Phillips put a "Women Who Behave Rarely Make History" sticker on the back of her new truck in the driveway of her home located about 110 miles northeast of Atlanta. When she returned outside to take a picture, she encountered a large bobcat in her driveway.

The bobcat immediately pounced on her. She recalled that her first thought was, "I am not dying today." [51]

Emboldened by adrenaline and her desire to protect her granddaughter, she decided to strangle the animal. "I grabbed it by the shoulders and pushed it back away from me ... and I took it down," she told reporters.

During the struggle, Phillips says she got her hands around the animal's neck and strangled it to death. She did not scream for help until she thought the animal was dead.

"I was scared ... that my granddaughter would come out and I didn't want that to happen," she says. The attack left Phillips with puncture wounds on her hands and some broken fingers, along with cuts and bruises on her body. [52]

DeDe Phillips loved her granddaughter so much that she was willing to die to protect her and keep her safe from the bobcat. She would not scream to summon help to spare her own life in the fear that this would endanger the life of her loved one

Jesus called the Christians in Smyrna to be prepared to go to the point of "death" to receive "life as your victor's crown" (Rv 2:10). The city of Smyrna was associated with the beauty of a crown. Poets compared the city wall that encircled Mount Pagus to a crown. The many torches protruding from the fortification sparkled like jewels.

In the Greek language, there are two words for a crown: *"stephanos"* and *"diadema."* The crown in this passage is *stephanos*. To understand

Jesus's meaning by using *stephanos*, let's first examine the word which he did not use, *diadema*.

Strong's Concordance 1238 states that a *"diadema"* refers to a regal crown, "the kingly ornament for the head."[53] *Diadema* is mentioned three times in Revelation.

The first describes the crown on the head of the dragon of Satan: "Then another sign appeared in heaven: an enormous red dragon with seven heads and ten horns and seven crowns on his heads" (Rv 12:3). The second is the crown on the beast of Satan: "And I saw a beast coming out of the sea. He had ten horns and seven heads, with ten crowns on his horns" (Rv 13:1). The third mention is when Jesus is described with the *diadema* crown: "And on his head were many crowns" (Rv 19:12). This crown represents majesty—the false royalty of Satan and the true imperial divinity of Christ.

The *"stephanos"* crown is associated with faithfulness and obedience. Strong's Concordance 4735 defines it as "a wreath awarded to the victor of the ancient athletic games." [54] Athletes train for long hours and endure physical pain, exhaustion, and the exclusion of other activities to do their best in competition. The same is true of the Christian faith. In the walk of faith, Christians must be willing to endure the struggle for the prize of the *stephanos,* a "victor's crown" (Rv 2:10).

Paul used the imagery of a runner meticulously training and deliberately competing to win the prize of the crown:

> Do you not know that in a race all the runners run, but only one gets the prize? Run in such a way as to get the prize. Everyone who competes in the games goes into strict training. They do it to get a crown that will not last, but we do it to get a crown that will last forever. Therefore I do not run like someone running aimlessly; I do not fight like a boxer beating the air. No, I strike a blow to my body and make it my slave so that after I have preached to others, I myself will not be disqualified for the prize. (I Cor 9:24-27)

Stephanos was also the word given to the floral garland bestowed as a reward for years of devoted service for civil servants. Just as companies today might give a gold watch for thirty years of dedicated employment, ancient cities gave a laurel crown for extended periods of service. Cicero notes that these crowns were often examples of "extravagant praise bestowed on a commonplace person posthumously." [56] The *stephanos* in this context elicits the picture of receiving a reward for long-term loyalty and commitment. This image must have encouraged the Christians who continued to serve the Lord consistently and faithfully as a steadfast daily ritual despite the constant threat of death.

The *stephanos* given to the victorious athlete or the dedicated civil servant is a distinct honor. Its recipient wears it with much pride. However, because it is a wreath made of branches and flowers, the wreath will fade, wilt, and die after several days. Through his words in this verse, "I will give you life as your victor's crown," Jesus assures the believers in Smyrna that He notices their sacrifice (Rv 2:10). They will receive the honor afforded by the laurel wreath with the added benefit of a *stephanos* that will not wilt or wither. Jesus promises them that He will reward their faithfulness to death with eternal life.

What do you think the believers in Smyrna thought when they read this letter?

What type of encouragement could you use right now?

What type of encouragement could you give right now?

What are the things, people, and causes for which you would be willing to die?

What do Christ's words to the suffering church in Smyrna say to you?

What is one takeaway and insight from the letter to the church at Smyrna that resonates with you?

In what way might that insight be calling you into a new way of being and doing?

THE LOYAL CHURCH IN THE EVIL CITY: PERGAMUM

K ing Louis XIV built the Palace of Versailles in the late 1600s to showcase the splendor of the French Crown. The king had been living in the Louvre. Its location in downtown Paris, surrounded by buildings, prohibited the king from enlarging and expanding. The building's footprint was too small to elicit the vision of grandeur he hoped to achieve.

The king searched for options and settled on the site of a small hunting lodge thirteen miles southwest of Paris. The colossal building project commenced.

The land at the site, a swamp, had to be dried out and reclaimed.

In 1678, Louis XIV, the Sun King, turned his attention and money to Versailles and making this hunting lodge into the envy of the regal world. Two hundred lives and the equivalent of $300 million were invested into this 2,300-room palace.[57] This magnificent structure would house unparalleled collections of art and celebrated pieces of sculpture. The name Versailles would become synonymous with opulence.

Centuries earlier, a city was in the infancy of its meticulous design stage. Pergamum was methodically planned with the same intention of creating an illusion of magnificence and lavishness. French archeologist and ancient world historian Maxime Collignon extolled its exquisite architecture and design with these words: King Eumenes II "built up the city, planted a grove in the Nikephorion, and gave votives and libraries and raised the Pergamene urban area to the beauty which she shows to this day." Collignon compared Pergamum's glory to that of Versailles.

Pergamum and Versailles shared many common characteristics. They were both political hot spots. Pergamum was a capital city of Asia Minor, giving it pride and rank exclusive to important seats of government. The city played host to elaborate ceremonies welcoming notable Roman officials and visiting dignitaries from other regions.

The city of Pergamum, similar to Versailles, invested extravagant amounts of money in the arts. As archeologist George M. A. Hanfmann describes, "[Pergamum] created a Greek library, second only to Alexandria, and assembled the first Royal Art Museum brought together for the sake of aesthetic values, that is, for the sake of possessing famous 'classical' art."[58] In the second century BC, purchasing art for the sole purpose of allowing people to enjoy its visual appeal was a revolutionary idea. Although there is little information about Pergamum's art museum, its very existence proved the city's innovative and avant-garde vibe.

Early in their history, the Persians brought their gods to Pergamum, making it a religious city. As Greek influence infiltrated the city, the leaders constructed elaborate temples to the Hellenistic gods. Pergamum boasted temples to Dionysius, the sexually promiscuous god of wine and son of Zeus; Demeter, the goddess of grain; Asclepius, the god of healing; and Caesar Augustus, a Roman Emperor who was worshiped as a god. These buildings, for their time period, rivaled the gorgeous architecture of Versailles and made the city one of the leading architectural sites of Asia Minor.

Pergamum differed from the cities to which the first two letters were sent. Both Ephesus and Smyrna had the advantage of being located on the seacoast and on a river. These cities benefited financially from the trade and commerce these water routes provided. These "highways" transported people, culture, and ideas from the far reaches of the world, enlightening their citizens and exposing them to a wide range of philosophies and lifestyles. Conversely, Pergamum was a mountain town isolated from the prosperity of the trade routes and ease of passage. People who visited Pergamum were deliberately destined there, not passing through on the way to another location.

Come along and see how this backdrop influenced Jesus's words to the church at Pergamum.

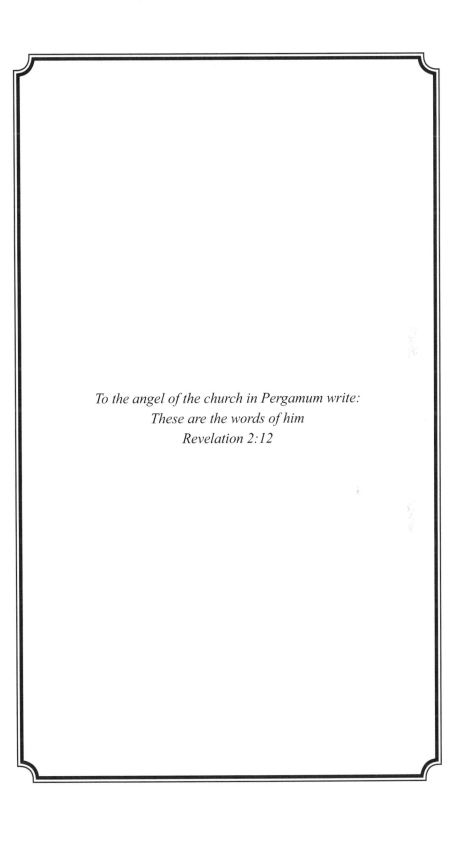

To the angel of the church in Pergamum write:
These are the words of him
Revelation 2:12

WORDS

It is no coincidence that Jesus mentions "words" in his letter to this church. Words were important to the erudite of Pergamum. They were a source of pride and a means of competition. Words, housed in books, were used as a measuring stick of sophistication for this ancient city. In this time period, civilized cities relied on their supersized libraries to testify to their superiority.

Pergamum had a beautiful and prestigious library that stored as many as two hundred thousand manuscripts, an amazing number considering that every volume was written by hand. Eumenes II built this impressive structure. The four rooms inside were lined with shelves. To allow airflow and reduce humidity, the builders ingeniously incorporated an empty space of approximately 20 inches between the shelves and the outer walls. The scrolls were rolled up, marked with a tag, and stored in open-air crates.

This expansive collection of literary works was second only to the collection in Alexandria, Egypt. Cities in this period valued their libraries as an indicator of their region's wealth and sophistication. Therefore, the jealous and zealous Egyptians wanted their library to remain the premier collection in the world.

In an effort to reduce the accessibility and production of new books, the Egyptians limited exports of the writing material, papyrus. This embargo forced the people of Pergamum to manufacture their own writing material from the skins of young animals such as sheep and calves. This new "paper" was called parchment, after the Roman name for the city of Pergamum. Although this new writing material could not be rolled and stored as easily as papyrus, it had the advantage of being useable on both sides, ultimately making it the material of choice for the publication of documents.

Legend has it that Mark Antony gave his new bride, Cleopatra, most of the books from the library at Pergamum as a wedding present. His gift was designed to replace the ones at the library in Alexandria, which had been damaged or destroyed by war.

The words in the books stored in its famous library advanced Pergamum's status in the eyes of the world making it a place of great notoriety and perceived intelligence. However, many of those who were impressed by this scholarly city of words missed the true power of the word.

Genesis tells us that the power of creation was in God's word. The word of the Lord spoke the world into existence. His speech was strong enough to generate life. "And God said, 'Let there be light,' and there was light" (Gn 1:3). The Psalmist reiterates, "By the word of the Lord were the heavens made, their starry host by the breath of his mouth" (Ps 33:6).

The apostle John, the author of the book of Revelation, also wrote the Gospel of John. In it, he refers to Jesus as the "Word" and tells us that Jesus existed before the world was formed.

> In the beginning was the Word, and the Word was with God, and the Word was God. He was with God in the beginning. Through him all things were made; without him nothing was made that has been made. In him was life, and that life was the light of all mankind. (Jn 1:1-4)

In his letter to the church at Colosse, Paul explains that Jesus is the firstborn over all creation.

> (Jesus) is the image of the invisible God, the firstborn over all creation. For by him all things were created: things in heaven and on earth, visible and invisible, whether thrones or powers or rulers or authorities; all things were created by him and for him. (Col 1:15-16)

Scripture tells us that the spoken word of God and the Lord, Jesus Christ, created our world. Through Jesus, the Word, we learn by his example and by His words in scripture.

The majority of the citizens of this proud city missed the significance of the word of the Lord. Their library, overflowing with words, gave them a false sense of worth and value. In their academic arrogance, they missed the real power of the Word, which comes from the Lord.

They mistook the volumes of literature for eternal and lasting truth.

They chose human book knowledge over heavenly wisdom.

They relied on a plethora of fancy-worded philosophies and ignored the living Word.

They did not realize that true wisdom comes from the Lord. "The fear of the Lord is the beginning of wisdom, and knowledge of the Holy One is understanding" (Prv 9:10).

In his letter, Jesus reminds the believers in Pergamum of the importance and prominence of the words that come from him, the true Word.

Today, as in Pergamum centuries ago, people can value other words more than the Word. Many words promise to enrich our lives. The field is crowded and confusing. Friends give advice. Self-help books guide personal advancement. Magazines illustrate the "cool" life. Many words are coming at you. What other words distract you from the true Word?

Outside of the true Word, what words do you rely upon for guidance? What are the positive and negative aspects of these words?

How do you select the source of the words that guide your steps?

How do you find the right words to lead you forward?

The Word of God, as contained in the Bible, gives us guidelines for leading an abundant life. What goals do you need to put in place regarding reading the Bible and memorizing scripture to maximize the Word's influence in your life?

These are the words of him who has the sharp,
double-edged sword.
Revelation 2:12

THE RIGHT OF THE SWORD

Since Pergamum was the capital of Asia, the resident Roman official had the "right of the sword." This edict meant that capital punishment cases, which in most provinces were sent to Rome for trial, were tried locally in Pergamum. The proconsul had the right to decide if an alleged criminal lived or died. This local autonomy put an inordinate amount of power and authority in the hands of the Roman leaders governing this city.[59]

This power was unique to this region. The local leaders of other provinces did not possess the ability to condemn a prisoner to death. They had to refer the case to higher Roman authorities. A familiar example can be found in the trial of Jesus in the Roman province of Palestine. The ruling Jewish Sanhedrin and High Priests did not have the jurisdiction to condemn Jesus. Therefore, they conspired to send him to Pontius Pilate, the Roman official with this authority, to sentence Jesus to death.

The power of the sword was of particular significance to the Christians as Pergamum had a temple for Caesar Augustus. If they refused to profess that "Caesar is Lord," they could be hastily tried and convicted of treason and atheism and killed on the spot without the due process of an appeal to a Roman court.

Jesus assures these persecuted believers that He is the one with the true power of the sword. The double-edged sword of the Lord represents the power of the Word of God both in the scripture and in the deity of Christ. In the first chapter of Revelation, John describes Jesus: "and out of his mouth came a sharp double-edged sword" (Rv 1:16). Jesus reiterates this twice in this letter: "These are the words of him who has the sharp, double edge sword" (Rv 2:12), and "I will soon come to you and will fight against them with the sword of my mouth (Rv 2:16).

The believers with knowledge of the Hebrew scripture could have drawn further comfort as they clung to the words of Isaiah as he prophesizes the future redeemer, the servant of the Lord, coming with a sword in His mouth:

> Listen to me, you islands; hear this, you distant nations;
> Before I was born the Lord called me;
> from my birth he has made mention of my name.
> He made my mouth like a sharpened sword,
> In the shadow of his hand he hid me;
> He made me into a polished arrow and concealed me in
> his quiver.
> (Is 49:1-2)

The imagery of Jesus as a judge would also be a reassurance for these faithful followers who were condemned without a fair trial:

> He will not judge by what he sees with his eyes,
>   or decide by what he hears with his ears;
> but with righteousness he will judge the needy,
>   with justice he will give decisions for the poor of the earth.
> He will strike the earth with the rod of his mouth;
>   with the breath of his lips he will slay the wicked.
> Righteousness will be his belt
>   and faithfulness the sash around his waist.
> (Is 11:3-5)

What comfort these martyrs from Pergamum must have felt when Jesus assured them that He, not a Roman official, was the real judge. They saw their family members and friends executed by a brutal Roman magistrate. No justice was given to them. These believers were helpless and hopeless in the mock courts that convicted and condemned them. The trials in this city were particularly expedient and biased. The persecuted believers clung to the hope that Jesus is a righteous judge and that He will avenge the evil deeds committed against them.

The apostle Paul also speaks of a sword much more powerful than the double-edged sword they feared. In his letter to the Ephesians, he describes the armor of God:

Therefore, put on the full armor of God, so that when the day of evil comes, you may be able to stand your ground, and after you have done everything, to stand. Stand firm then, with the belt of truth buckled around your waist, with the breastplate of righteousness in place, and with your feet fitted with the readiness that comes from the gospel of peace. In addition to all this, take up the shield of faith, with which you can extinguish all the flaming arrows of the evil one. Take the helmet of salvation and the sword of the Spirit, which is the word of God. (Eph 6:14-17)

Note that the belt, the breastplate, the shoes, the shield, and the helmet are all defensive pieces of equipment. These are important fortifications against the attacks of the enemy. The only offensive component of the armor is the sword which is the word of God. The word is so powerful that no other weapon is needed.

When Jesus fought in head-to-head battles with Satan in the wilderness, He won all three conflicts by quoting scripture. Jesus conquered the enemy with the sword of the word of God, saying, "It is written" (Mt 4:6, 7, 10). We will look at this in more depth in the next section.

The book of Hebrews in the Bible compares the power of the Word of God to a sword:

For the word of God is alive and active. Sharper than any double-edged sword, it penetrates even to dividing soul and spirit, joints and marrow; it judges the thoughts and attitudes of the heart. (Heb 4:12)

These believers woke up every morning with the harsh realization that today could be the day that an official with the "right of the sword" condemned them or one of their loved ones to a gruesome death. When the sentence came, they were allowed no defense. They had no legal rights and no protection.

By reminding this church of His double-edged sword, Jesus gives them hope and strength to endure and persevere knowing that the true "right of the sword" belongs ultimately to the Lord.

——

What situations, habits, or people make you feel hopeless and helpless?

How could remembering the power of the double-edged sword of Jesus help you?

How can you sharpen your "sword," the knowledge of the Bible?

How can you take comfort in knowing that Jesus is the final judge?

I know where you live—
where Satan has his throne.
Revelation 2:13

WHERE SATAN HAS HIS THRONE

Carl Humann, a German engineer, was appalled and saddened by what he discovered. The priceless ancient ruins of Pergamum's beautiful past were being plundered and pillaged by looters. The locals were collecting pieces of marble from the magnificent Altar of Zeus and using them for building materials. In the mid to late 1860s, Humann was preparing for the construction of roads in Anatolia when he visited the once-thriving metropolis. By 1878, he garnered support and money from Germany and permission from the Ottoman government to excavate the marble ruins and ship them to Berlin, creating the Pergamon Museum.[60]

Acquiring this magnificent altar, which was world-renowned as one of the finest examples of Hellenistic sculpture, elevated the world's view of Germany's sophistication. A great deal of nationalistic pride centered around this monument. Even today on the museum website, they boast of their accomplishment:

> The extraordinary achievements of German archaeology during the years of the German Empire resulted in huge swathes of objects being brought to Berlin so that the museums soon began to rival much older comparable collections in Paris and London.[61]

One of the many visitors to the museum was Albert Speer, Adolf Hitler's chief architect and later the Reich Minister of Armaments and War Production for Nazi Germany. Inspired by the grand Altar of Zeus, Speer designed an immense parade ground and grandstand to showcase the strength, might, and power of the Third Reich and to spotlight its leader, Chancellor Adolf Hitler.

The grounds were used for the Nuremberg rallies displaying the might of the regime through a series of parades and processions of Nazi party faithful.

Many of the ceremonies were held at night with hundreds of columns of lights extending into the black night sky, creating an aura of excitement and mystery. Speer placed a magnificent podium in the location where the sacrificial brass altar of Zeus stood in the original Pergamum temple. In the ancient world, brass and bronze represented power and judgment, adding to the importance of this particular spot. This large, brass, bowl-like structure was where animals, human babies, and adults were burned as a sacrifice to please and appease Zeus.

Speer orchestrated these spectacles with precise choreography. Thousands of Germans attended and were spellbound and awestruck by the auspicious venue. Speer later said that he was trying to unify the people with the setting.

> It was not my aim that the (single spectator) should feel anything. I only wanted to impose the grandeur of the building upon the people who are in it. If people who may have different minds are pressed together in such surroundings, they all get unified to one mind. That was the aim of the stadium.

In this same piece, Speer commented about the featured speaker at these events, Adolf Hitler, "One seldom recognizes the devil when he is putting his hand on your shoulder." [62]

At one of these rallies, Hitler announced the Nuremberg Laws which took away Jewish people's rights, citizenship, and property.

> Bitter complaints have come in from countless places citing the provocative behavior of Jews. We have no choice but to contain the problem through legislative measures. If this attempt fails, it will be necessary to transfer (the problem) to the National Socialist Party for a final solution by law.[63]

This final solution he alluded to in his speech became known as the Holocaust—a word whose Greek meaning is a "wholly burnt animal sacrifice."

The original Altar of Zeus had precipitated the death of innocents in the first century AD. Some of these women, men, and children of Pergamum died because they were Christians. The recreation of this altar in Nuremberg

---

centuries later foretold the deaths of innocents who would die because they were Jewish.

Jesus labels Pergamum as the city "where Satan has his throne" (Rv. 2:13). Scholars are not certain of the specific place to which Jesus is referring. The Altar of Zeus is just one of the contenders for the title of Satan's throne. This pagan stronghold housed several different sites contributing to this designation of evil and worshipping different gods. These deities all had beautiful temples, unique worship rites, and exclusive rewards. Ray Vander Laan explains, "Each of the cults in Pergamum was a counterfeit, a clever copy of the blessings that God alone provides. Each god took credit or honor away from the true God and attributed his blessing to something else."[64]

The Altar of Zeus could have been the throne to which Jesus alluded. Here the pagans paid homage to the counterfeit "king of kings" and "lord of lords." Unlike the real King of kings, Zeus is not portrayed as omnipotent or morally good. Many stories involving Zeus show him cheating on his wife, consorting with gods or mortals for his selfish gain, and seeking pleasure for himself. However, Zeus was perceived as a source of supremacy, and pagans came to honor and worship him in an attempt to gain power and prestige, making this a possible throne of Satan.

Another option for the throne of Satan was the Temple of Asclepius. Worshipers came here seeking healing. One of the treatments involved patients spending the night on the floor of the darkened temple in a drug-induced sleep. Nonpoisonous snakes would crawl over the sick, supposedly bringing healing by their touch. For this reason, Asclepius was known as the snake god. Satan is shown as the serpent in the Garden of Eden, leading many scholars to conclude that this temple of a snake god could have been the throne of Satan.

The city offered many other options for the throne of Satan designation. The Temple of Dionysius, the god of wine and revelry, was there for the pleasure-seekers. Dionysius was the mythological son of the king of the gods, Zeus, and a mortal woman, Semele. Zeus's wife arranged Semele's death in a jealous rage. In the last moments of her life, Zeus secretly took their son, Dionysius, from her dying body and sent him to the valley of Nysa to be raised by nymphs. As an adult, he traveled to the underworld to resurrect his mother from the dead. He took her to Mount Olympus, where she would be able to have eternal life. Worshipers of Dionysius drank excesses of wine and committed sexually immoral acts to pay homage to this illicit god. The level of revelry incited by this worship reached such high levels that it was banned in portions of the Roman Empire. This sensual lure for fun and fantasy was difficult for pagans, and possibly some of the early believers, to resist. Again, this god mimicked the truth of Christ being the son of a god and having the ability to raise a person from the dead to eternal life, making this another possible location for the throne of Satan.

The goddess of grain, Demeter, promised food and prosperity for her worshipers. Demeter, the sister of Zeus, was a deity of great importance to the working-class people who were concerned about feeding their family. A worshiper would come to her temple in search of a good harvest and bountiful crops. One of the religious rites associated with her worship involved the blood of a bull. The animal was killed on a grate covering a pit. Worshipers gathered below to let the blood drip on them. The followers sacrificing the animal were supposedly saved by the washing of the blood of the beast. Again, this lie could be confused with the truth of the blood of Christ, which truly saves. This shrine that imitated the truth could have been the locale to which Jesus was referring.

The Temple of Athena solicited those who sought wisdom and solutions. She was heralded as the source of all wisdom, from personal love requests to national battle plans. Again, this temple could have been perceived as the location of Satan's throne as it imitated the true wisdom found in Proverbs: "The fear of the Lord is the beginning of wisdom, and knowledge of the Holy One is understanding" (Prv 9:10).

If a person was looking for political favors and an inside track to power, emperor worship was alive and well in the city's Temple of Trajan. This royal temple could have been the throne of Satan.

Many scholars have debated the exact location of the throne of Satan. The site is not as important as the message. The vital lesson from this letter is that there are many counterfeit options that will pull our allegiance away from God. The enemy's strategy is to take advantage of human needs and wants, promising to satisfy these with his fake options. The French mathematician and theologian, Blaise Pascal, said, "There is a God-shaped vacuum in the heart of each man which cannot be satisfied by any created thing but only by God the Creator, made known through Jesus Christ." [65] Satan's deception is that this vacuum can be filled with the things of this world. He misleads with lies that hold a shade of truth. This tactic has been around since the beginning of time in the Garden of Eden. Don't fall for the lies of the enemy. He may try to establish his throne in your territory.

Hear the good news. God is in charge. The "one who is in you is greater than the one who is in the world" (1 Jn 4:4). You don't have to settle for the false gods and the fake promises. The prince of lies will never overcome the Lord of truth. The throne of Satan will be knocked down by the King of kings.

Satan is alive and well today. He still offers counterfeit solutions and cheap substitutes. What lies is the enemy feeding you?

What is that haunting thought in the back of your mind that holds you back?

What is that thought that unsettles you just when you are starting to find peace?

What is that attitude that creeps in to steal your joy?

What deeply buried thoughts keep you from being the person God wants you to be and from living the life that God wants you to live?

How are you going to knock down the throne of Satan in your world?

Yet you remain true to my name.
You did not renounce your faith in me,
not even in the days of Antipas, my faithful
witness, who was put to death in your city
Revelation 2:13

ANTIPAS, THE FAITHFUL WITNESS

You hear your name. You take the witness stand. The clerk administers the oath. You hear the words, "the whole truth and nothing but the truth, so help me God."

Your mind wanders to the day of the accident. The sunny and mild weather tempted you to select a table outside with a clear view of the street. As you sat nibbling on the bread, you mindlessly stared at the cars making their way through the downtown maze. Your peaceful thoughts were interrupted by a harsh squeal of tires and the crunch of metal on metal. From your café vantage, you had a front-row view of the accident. By the time the police arrived, the drivers were in an angry exchange. One of the motorists pointed to you as a witness.

So, here you are—a witness. What should have been a simple insurance claim has turned into a complicated case. When the attorney called you to testify on behalf of her client, you declined. You felt as if you did not know enough to be a witness. After all, you don't know the intricacies of the law, the people involved, or the details or situations surrounding the incident. The attorney assured you that you possess all the knowledge required to be a witness. A witness is simply one who has personal knowledge of something. She explained that you do not have to know the cars or their features. You do not have to know the drivers or their history. You don't need to be an expert on traffic laws. All you need to know is what you observed. She reassured you that your role is to convey no more than your personal experience and knowledge.

This definition of a courtroom witness applies to witnessing for Christ as well. Many are hesitant to share their faith because they feel inadequate. Excuses for holding back are varied:

- My Bible memory bank could fit in a thimble.
- My past is so hot it would curl your hair.

- My life is the furthest thing from the perfect example of Christ.
- I don't want people to think that I think that I am God's gift to holiness.

God calls us to be His witnesses: "You were chosen to tell about the excellent qualities of God, who called you out of darkness into his marvelous light" (I Pt 2:9). He does not ask you to wait until you are smart enough, well-behaved enough, or succinct enough. He wants you to share your personal knowledge of how your walk with Christ has changed your life. He wants you to witness.

Interestingly, the Greek word for "martyr" is "*martus,*" which means to witness. We often think of a martyr as one who suffers or dies for his or her faith. Suffering and sacrifice often accompany a life of serving Christ. However, the original meaning is simply a witness, one who shares personal knowledge.

For the citizens of Pergamum living in the city where Satan has his throne, witnessing for Christ was synonymous with the modern connotation of a persecuted martyr. To live a life for Jesus in that city invited financial hardship, exclusion from friends and family, and possible torture and death.

Scholars do not know the identity of the person, Antipas, whom Jesus references in His letter. Antipas may have been the first resident of Pergamum to die for his faith. One tradition holds that he was roasted in a brazen bull-shaped altar in a pagan purification ceremony. He may have been brought to the city to be killed in this "throne of Satan" as an example for other Christians.

Although we do not know that particular details of his life and death, we do know that Jesus thought so highly of Antipas that he gave him the title "faithful witness" (Rv 2:13). These two words are the exact ones that Jesus used to describe himself: "and from Jesus Christ, who is the faithful witness" (Rev 1:5). The recurrence of these words shows the high regard Christ had for Antipas.

Jesus offers these believers encouragement. He assures them that he knows their trials in this Satanic city and commends those who are willing to be witnesses and martyrs.

There are costs to anything worth pursuing. What price do you pay for living a Christian life?

What are the costs of witnessing for Christ?

When you think of your sacrifice, what is most difficult for you to give up?

Christ was a witness and martyr for our sakes. What did Christ give up? Why did He do it?

As you pray about and ponder this passage, did the Holy Spirit give you insights you can use for yourself and share with others?

Where Satan lives
Revelation 2:13

WHERE SATAN LIVES

Sheepishly, a young wife brought home a new dress. Her exasperated husband reminded her of their vow to save money and put their spending on hold. "We promised each other to stop buying and start saving."

She explained, "As I was walking by my favorite store, I saw this dress in the window and didn't think there was any harm in trying it on. I loved the dress, but then I remembered our pledge to save money. I called out, 'Satan, get behind me.' To which he replied, 'Whoa, it looks good from back here too.'"

This simplistic anecdote references a profound truth often overlooked by the believer. There is an unseen power at work in the world. Satan is alive and well. He is a real force. To have a balanced view, we should not excessively fear or focus on the enemy. However, we should also be aware of his presence.

Sun Tzu, a military leader and strategist born in China in the mid-fifth century BC, wrote a book on battle tactics and philosophies that is still used to train our armed forces and intelligence agencies today. He issues this warning in his book, *The Art of War*:

> If you know the enemy and know yourself, you need not fear
> the result of a hundred battles. If you know yourself but not the
> enemy, for every victory gained you will also suffer a defeat.
> If you know neither the enemy nor yourself, you will succumb
> in every battle.[66]

This advice is true for our battle with Satan. We must know and understand him as the enemy if we are to overcome him. We must also know ourselves and where we are most vulnerable to his attack.

Jesus reveals in this letter that Satan has his throne on the earth. The enemy is dwelling among us. In the book of Job, Satan tells the Lord that he has been "roaming through the earth and going back and forth in it" (Jb 1:7). Peter warns us that "your enemy the devil prowls around like a roaring lion looking for someone to devour" (I Pt 5:8). John cautions us that "the whole world is under the control of the evil one" (1 Jn 5:19).

When we are in a crisis, our natural tendency is to blame the people around the conflict. Paul warns us in Ephesians that we must realize our true enemy is Satan. The struggle is against him, not people.

> For our struggle is not against flesh and blood, but against the rulers, against the authorities, against the powers of this dark world and against the spiritual forces of evil in the heavenly realms. (Eph 6:12)

It is difficult to grasp the power or presence of the enemy because he does not often mount a full-scale frontal attack. He is much too clever for obvious tactics. Instead, he uses subtle nuances to deceive the believer. He misleads us with mere shades away from the truth. The differences are so minute that it becomes difficult to separate the truth from his lies.

Let's take a look at the enemy's deceptive tactics in the first temptation recorded in the Bible. The enemy, in the form of a serpent, visited Eve in the Garden of Eden. He meticulously picked the best time to lure his prey at her weakest point. He caught Eve when she was alone. The crafty serpent did not make any rash statements belittling God or his directions. Instead, he asked a simple leading question:

> Now the serpent was more crafty than any of the wild animals the Lord God had made. He said to the woman, "Did God really say, 'You must not eat from any tree in the garden'?"
> The woman said to the serpent, "We may eat fruit from the trees in the garden, but God did say, 'You must not eat fruit from the tree that is in the middle of the garden, and you must not touch it, or you will die.'" (Gn 3:1-3)

Eve recalled God's command and quoted it to the enemy. However, she was not exactly correct. The Lord did not say anything about touching it. Here were the exact instructions from the Lord. With such a formidable foe as the devil, it is wise to know precisely what the Lord says:

And the Lord God commanded the man, "You are free to eat from any tree in the garden; but you must not eat from the tree of the knowledge of good and evil, for when you eat from it you will certainly die." (Gn 2:16-17)

The enemy now twisted the truth into a lie to entice the woman to disobey the commandment of the Lord. The enemy was successful, and Eve and Adam succumbed to the temptation:

"You will not certainly die," the serpent said to the woman. "For God knows that when you eat from it your eyes will be opened, and you will be like God, knowing good and evil." When the woman saw that the fruit of the tree was good for food and pleasing to the eye, and also desirable for gaining wisdom, she took some and ate it. She also gave some to her husband, who was with her, and he ate it. (Gn 3:4-6)

Confronted with his disobedience, Adam played the blame game and pointed to Eve as the culprit. He seemed to insinuate that God may be at fault since He is the one who created Eve to be with him. Adam never accused Satan of manipulating the situation, nor did Adam take responsibility for his actions:

The man said, "The woman you put here with me—she gave me some fruit from the tree, and I ate it." (Gn 3:12)

Now let's look at another scene of temptation in the Bible. Matthew told of Jesus's temptation in the wilderness. First, notice that Satan repeated his strategy of attacking a person at his weakest. Jesus had been without food for forty days. He was hungry, thirsty, and exhausted:

Then Jesus was led by the Spirit into the wilderness to be tempted by the devil. After fasting forty days and forty nights, he was hungry. The tempter came to him and said, "If you are the Son of God, tell these stones to become bread." Jesus answered, "It is written: 'Man shall not live on bread alone, but on every word that comes from the mouth of God.'"

Then the devil took him to the holy city and had him stand on the highest point of the temple. "If you are the Son of God," he said, "throw yourself down. For it is written:
'He will command his angels concerning you,
and they will lift you up in their hands,
so that you will not strike your foot against a stone.'"
Jesus answered him, "It is also written: 'Do not put the Lord your God to the test.'"
Again, the devil took him to a very high mountain and showed him all the kingdoms of the world and their splendor. "All this I will give you," he said, "if you will bow down and worship me." Jesus said to him, "Away from me, Satan! For it is written: 'Worship the Lord your God, and serve him only.'" Then the devil left him, and angels came and attended him. (Mt 4:1-11)

Unlike Adam and Eve, Jesus was fully aware that the temptation was coming from Satan. He addressed him directly. Unlike Eve, Jesus knew scripture well enough to realize that the enemy was twisting words and lying. Jesus confronted this master of lies and battled him with the power of the Lord from the word.

In the letter to the believers in Pergamum, Jesus reminds them that Satan lives and reigns in their city. Jesus reveals that although the face of the persecutor is a Roman soldier, a slanderous Jew, or a spiteful neighbor, Satan himself is behind the evil deeds.

How do you think this knowledge changed the perspective of the early believers in Pergamum?

Paul reminds us in Ephesians that we are fighting against the "powers of the dark world," not "flesh and blood." When you have conflict in your life, do you attribute it to a person, a habit, or a situation, or do you attribute it to Satan?

How would you act differently if you approached temptation as a battle against Satan?

How well do you know yourself? What are Satan's best ploys against you?

When are you most vulnerable?

Armed with this knowledge, how could you better protect yourself from the enemy?

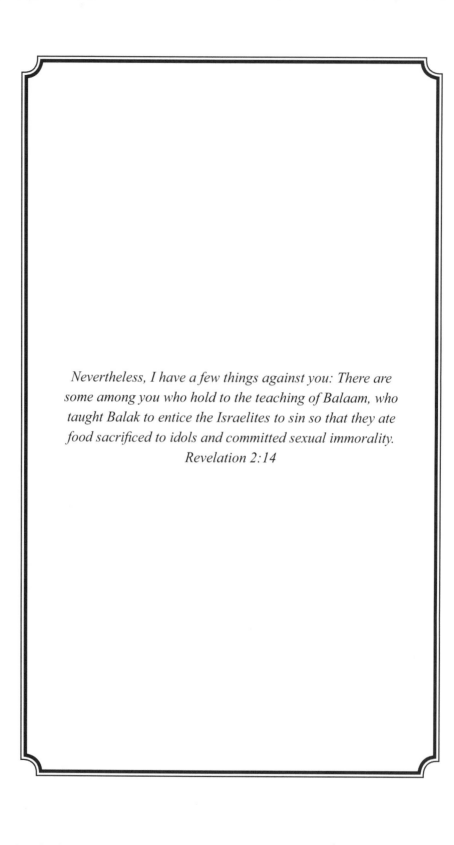

Nevertheless, I have a few things against you: There are some among you who hold to the teaching of Balaam, who taught Balak to entice the Israelites to sin so that they ate food sacrificed to idols and committed sexual immorality.
Revelation 2:14

BALAAM

The Israelites had been freed from slavery in Egypt and were approaching the promised land in Canaan. The occupying nations fought them to defend their territories. The Lord blessed the Hebrew people with great victories on the battlefield. The book of Numbers reports that the Jewish people's amazing conquests were not overlooked by King Balak of Moab or by his people.

> Now Balak son of Zippor saw all that Israel had done to the Amorites, and Moab was terrified because there were so many people. Indeed, Moab was filled with dread because of the Israelites. (Nm 22:2-3)

King Balak devised a plan. He called on Balaam.

Balaam was a prophet for profit. He would bless anyone he was paid to bless and curse those he was paid to curse. The king sent messengers with gold to try to persuade the prophet to come back with them to Moab. God appeared to Balaam instructing him not to go to Moab. Balaam sent the messengers back to the king with a "no."

King Balak sent another envoy with more influence and more gold. This time, God told Balaam he could go to Moab. However, he was only to say what God told him.

> Balaam got up in the morning, saddled his donkey and went with the Moabite officials. But God was very angry when he went, and the angel of the LORD stood in the road to oppose him. Balaam was riding on his donkey, and his two servants were with him. When the donkey saw the angel of the LORD standing in the road with a drawn sword in his hand, it turned off the road into a field. Balaam beat it to get it back on the road.
> Then the angel of the LORD stood in a narrow path through the vineyards, with walls on both sides. When the donkey saw the

angel of the LORD, it pressed close to the wall, crushing Balaam's foot against it. So he beat the donkey again.

Then the angel of the LORD moved on ahead and stood in a narrow place where there was no room to turn, either to the right or to the left. When the donkey saw the angel of the LORD, it lay down under Balaam, and he was angry and beat it with his staff. Then the LORD opened the donkey's mouth, and it said to Balaam, "What have I done to you to make you beat me these three times?"

Balaam answered the donkey, "You have made a fool of me! If only I had a sword in my hand, I would kill you right now."

The donkey said to Balaam, "Am I not your own donkey, which you have always ridden, to this day? Have I been in the habit of doing this to you?"

"No," he said.

Then the LORD opened Balaam's eyes, and he saw the angel of the LORD standing in the road with his sword drawn. So he bowed low and fell facedown. The angel of the LORD asked him, "Why have you beaten your donkey these three times? I have come here to oppose you because your path is a reckless one before me. The donkey saw me and turned away from me these three times. If it had not turned away, I would certainly have killed you by now, but I would have spared it."

Balaam said to the angel of the LORD, "I have sinned. I did not realize you were standing in the road to oppose me. Now if you are displeased, I will go back."

The angel of the LORD said to Balaam, "Go with the men, but speak only what I tell you." So Balaam went with Balak's officials. (Nm 22:21-35)

Balaam approached the king and warned him that he could "speak only what God puts in my mouth." Three times, the king took Balaam out to curse the Israelites. Three times, Balaam blessed the Hebrew people. King Balak was furious.

Balaam, letting his greed overtake him, knew that he would be well compensated if he helped King Balak, so he left the king with this advice.

Balaam encouraged King Balak to let the Israelite men spend time with the women of Midian and Moab so that they would forget the one true God and worship Baal to please the women. Then, the blessing of the Lord would depart from the Hebrew people.

Balaam's advice proved to be correct.

> While Israel was staying in Shittim, the men began to indulge in sexual immorality with Moabite women, who invited them to the sacrifices to their gods. The people ate the sacrificial meal and bowed down before these gods. So Israel yoked themselves to the Baal of Peor. And the Lord's anger burned against them. (Nm 25:1-3)

To the Hebrew mind, Balaam represents compromising values and indulging in sin. Jesus warns the church about the danger of getting involved in immoral practices. Getting involved in practices that are not pleasing to God, even ones that seem insignificant and harmless, can pull us away from the ways of the Lord. As Paul wrote twice in the letter to the church at Corinth, "'I have the right to do anything,' you say--but not everything is beneficial. 'I have the right to do anything' but not everything is constructive" (I Cor. 6:12; 10:23). Jesus exhorts them to stay pure in their faith and not to let the Balaams of the world lure them away from the Lord.

In what ways do you feel you are compromising your faith?

What freedoms could you justify pursuing while knowing *that they are not beneficial to your walk with the Lord?*

Do you have a person, a friend group, a habit, or other influence that is similar to Balaam, something that tempts you to go in a direction away from God?

How can you break free of this bond?

Likewise, you also have those who hold
to the teaching of the Nicolaitans.
Repent therefore!
Otherwise, I will soon come to you and will fight
against them with the sword of my mouth.
Revelation 2:15

THE TEACHING OF THE NICOLAITANS

Robert Leroy Parker was a good boy and a kind man. His sisters, his neighbors, and his mother all agreed.

He was born in Beaver, Utah, in 1866, the first of thirteen children. He was raised in a strict Mormon home by parents who had immigrated from England ten years earlier. According to his sister Lulu Parker Betenson, Bob, as she called him, was kind and compassionate. One night, Bob broke into a closed store and took a pair of jeans. He left the proprietor a note promising to return and pay for the item. The store owner pressed charges and took Bob to court. Bob was acquitted. However, this incident marked the beginning of a long stream of conflicts with the law.

Bob fell in with the wrong crowd of people and ended up being influenced by a cattle rustler named Mike Cassidy. Mike led Bob astray and became his mentor in crime. Not wanting to embarrass his mother, Bob took on Mike's name and was forever known as Butch Cassidy.

The Bible is very clear about the importance of the moral quality of a person's friends and associates. "Do not be misled: 'Bad company corrupts good character'" (I Cor 15:33). One of my teachers used to warn that if you want to see what you will be like in five years, look at the company you keep.

Jesus exhorts the church members to isolate themselves from those who prescribe to the teaching of the Nicolaitans. He commands them to repent for the sins that seem to have been precipitated by the influence of this group. He compares this to the story of King Balak. Just as Balaam led the children of Israel into sin, the Nicolaitans led the church members in Pergamum into sin. The name Balaam is made up of roots in Hebrew with the same meaning as the roots of Nicolas in Greek. In essence, the names Balaam and Nicolas are the same. Jesus warns them not to let the influence of the Nicolaitans be as detrimental to their church as Balaam's influence was on the Hebrew people.[67]

Bible scholars have several theories on the meaning of the Nicolaitans.

As we mentioned previously, one theory derives from the roots of the words. *"Nikao"* means to conquer, and *"laos"* means the people.[68] The word "laity" is derived from *"laos."* Thus, the Nicolaitans could have been a priestly group who supported the premise that ministers and pastors should rule over a church's laypeople, inserting a hierarchy between followers and Jesus. God does not require a professional religious official to establish and maintain your relationship with God. This Nicolaitan philosophy directly contradicts Jesus's teaching.

> Jesus answered, "I am the way and the truth and the life. No one comes to the Father except through me. If you really know me, you will know my Father as well. From now on, you do know him and have seen him." (Jn 14:6-7)

Another theory suggests that the Nicolaitans followed the deacon Nicolaus referenced in the book of Acts. "This proposal pleased the whole group. They chose Stephen, a man full of faith and of the Holy Spirit; also, Philip, Procorus, Nicanor, Timon, Parmenas, and Nicolas from Antioch, a convert to Judaism" (Acts 6:5). These followers encouraged others to eat meat which had been sacrificed to the idols. Partaking of this food often involved participating in the pagan temple rituals, associating with the priests of these temples, and worshipping the polytheistic gods. The Nicolaitans also convinced the believers to compromise their values to engage in sexual behavior, which was against scriptural guidelines.[69]

William Barclay summarizes the concern this way:

> Those teachers who encouraged the Christians of Pergamos to commit fornication were urging them to conform to the accepted standards of the world and to stop being different. The early church was in constant danger of being tainted by and relapsing into the standards of the world.[70]

Jesus is concerned for the believers. He does not want the Nicolaitans to lead the church into sin as Balaam led the men of Israel astray by introducing them to the pagan Midianite women centuries earlier. He threatens that He will "come and fight against them with the sword" of His mouth (Rv 2:16). Notice that he is not coming to attack the believers but to defend them. Out of His great love, He vows to fight against those who propagate the teachings of this cult, not the believers who are being deceived.

Jesus has a passion for punishing those who lead others astray. He issued this warning.

> "If anyone causes one of these little ones—those who believe in me—to stumble, it would be better for them to have a large millstone hung around their neck and to be drowned in the depths of the sea." (Mt 8:6)

In this passage, the term "little ones" refers to any easily swayed believers. Jesus will rush to their protection and avenge the deeds precipitated by a negative influence.

Would Bob Parker, aka Butch Cassidy, have made his mother proud and kept his given name if he had not fallen under the bad influence of the cattle rustlers? No one knows. We do, however, know that Jesus is urgently calling the believers in Pergamum to rid their church of the Nicolaitans and their bad influence on the congregation.

How about you? Are there any influences in your life that lead you away from the Lord?

How can you escape these influences?

Are there ways in which you are a bad influence on others?

How passionately does Jesus react to people who persuade others away from the path of Christ?

Whoever has ears,
let them hear what the Spirit says to the churches.
To the one who is victorious,
I will give some of the hidden manna.
Revelation 2:17

"WHAT IS IT?"

The Lord had made the impossible happen—repeatedly. Ten miraculous plagues had humbled the great and mighty Egyptians. The proud Pharaoh had at long last lifted the terrible burden of harsh slavery off the backs of God's chosen people, the Hebrew nation. Not only did the Egyptians let them go, but they also gave them parting gifts.

> The Israelites did as Moses instructed and asked the Egyptians for articles of silver and gold and for clothing. The Lord had made the Egyptians favorably disposed toward the people, and they gave them what they asked for; so they plundered the Egyptians. (Ex 12:35-36)

This band of travelers could have numbered in the millions. When the pharaoh realized the impact of this exodus, he changed his mind and decided to recall his workforce, forcibly. He sent chariots and horses to pursue them and bring them back to their bondage. God protected his people by parting the Red Sea.

> But the Israelites went through the sea on dry ground, with a wall of water on their right and on their left. That day the Lord saved Israel from the hands of the Egyptians, and Israel saw the Egyptians lying dead on the shore. (Ex 14:29-30)

These amazing miracles should have convinced the Israelites of God's power and might. They should have been confident in His love and grace. However, after only a short time in the desert, they were already grumbling and doubting God's provision. They complained that they were hungry and thirsty.

The Hebrew word for grumbling used in Exodus 16:2 and 9 is an onomatopoeia, a word that sounds like its definition, such as murmur, babble, and mumble. The people were quick to forget the grace and undeserved gifts of the Lord.

Dr. Rob Blackburn sums it up this way: "After a short stay in the desert, they had already formed the 'Back to Egypt' committee."

> In the desert the whole community grumbled against Moses and Aaron. The Israelites said to them, "If only we had died by the Lord's hand in Egypt! There we sat around pots of meat and ate all the food we wanted, but you have brought us out into this desert to starve this entire assembly to death." (Ex 16:2-3)

The nostalgia they reportedly remembered about Egypt was not close to the reality of their living conditions there. The Egyptians "made their lives bitter with harsh labor in brick and mortar and with all kinds of work in the fields; in all their harsh labor the Egyptians worked them ruthlessly" (Ex 1:14).

The Lord granted them another miracle. Every evening, the camp swarmed with quail for them to eat, and in the morning, thin flakes appeared on the ground for their breakfast. The people saw this and said, "What is it?" (Ex 16:13). From that day forward, the edible wafers were called "manna," which means "what is it?" By God's grace, the children of Israel were fed. To feed the sojourners, the Lord covered the ground every morning with a sweet cake.

> The people of Israel called the bread manna. It was white like coriander seed and tasted like wafers made with honey. Moses said, "This is what the Lord has commanded: 'Take an omer of manna and keep it for the generations to come, so they can see the bread I gave you to eat in the wilderness when I brought you out of Egypt.'"
>
> So Moses said to Aaron, "Take a jar and put an omer of manna in it. Then place it before the Lord to be kept for the generations to come."
> As the Lord commanded Moses, Aaron put the manna with the tablets of the covenant law, so that it might be preserved. (Ex 16:31-34)

Later, God commanded them to build the Ark of the Covenant. "This ark contained the gold jar of manna, Aaron's staff that had budded, and the stone tablets of the covenant'" (Heb 9:4). Jewish tradition says that the prophet, Jeremiah, hid the manna when the temple in Jerusalem was destroyed. He will return to bring it back when the Messiah appears.

Moses explained the deeper meaning and significance of manna:

> He humbled you, causing you to hunger and then feeding you with manna, which neither you nor your ancestors had known, to teach you that man does not live on bread alone but on every word that comes from the mouth of the Lord. Your clothes did not wear out and your feet did not swell during these forty years. Know then in your heart that as a man disciplines his son, so the Lord your God disciplines you. (Dt 8:3-6)

In the desert, the Children of Israel were forced to rely on God for their sustenance. Moses challenged them to obey the Lord and rely on His grace in situations in which there is a choice.

"Jesus declared, 'I am the bread of life. Whoever comes to me will never go hungry'" (Jn 6:35). Jesus is telling the believers in Pergamum that He is the hidden manna. His love and grace are raining down on them like the manna rained down from heaven on the Israelites. He encourages them to be strong and rely on the hidden manna.

What is it? The true bread of life is Jesus Christ.

In what areas of your life is it tough to rely on God?

How can you put more trust in Him in these areas?

Do you feel yourself grumbling amidst great blessings like the Israelites?

How do you acknowledge the blessings and miracles of the Lord every day?

I will also give that person a white stone
with a new name written on it,
known only to the one who receives it.
Revelation 2:17

THE TEMPLE OF ASKLEPIOS

Mark Twain humorously warned, "The public is sensitive to little things, and they wouldn't have full confidence in a college that didn't know how to spell 'John.'" [71]

Despite the spelling conundrum, Johns Hopkins University is one of the most prestigious and respected public health universities and medical centers in the country. The facility was named for the philanthropist who gave the money to fund this first research university in the United States. Johns Hopkins, the founder, was named for his great-grandmother, Margaret Johns. People from across the country come to this hospital for healing.

The city of Pergamum housed the premier medical center of its day. Just as with Johns Hopkins, people from around the ancient world traveled to the Temple of Asklepios in search of good health. To this day, the medical profession gleans words and symbols from this snake god, also known by his Roman name of Asclepius. A surgeon's knife, a scalpel, derives its name from the god's name. The Rod of Asclepius, a stick with a snake wrapped around it, represents the medical profession today.

To avoid tarnishing the name of Asklepios, priests interviewed potential patients and turned away those who were too sick to save. A patient's death during treatment would hurt the reputation of the god. Therefore, gravely ill people (no pun intended) and pregnant women were denied access to the temple.

Those patients who were well enough to be admitted would walk into the depths of the temple. Voices piped in through holes in the walls comforted them with reassuring words designed to convince them that they would get well soon. Patients would soak in hot baths and mineral waters. They would receive spa-like treatments for medicinal purposes.

At night, however, the treatment became less recreational and more gripping. The patients would lie on the floor of the darkened temple in a drug-induced sleep. Nonpoisonous snakes would crawl over them, allegedly bringing healing by their touch. This shock treatment was purportedly the ultimate measure for those in search of good health.

If a patient were to die while in the temple, the priests would discreetly take the corpse out the back exit. The people who appeared to have recovered were discharged with great fanfare. A white stone with the patient's name recorded on it was displayed to show the theoretical omnipotence of the snake god, Asklepios.

Jesus uses this analogy of the white stones of Asklepios to exhort and encourage the church. He assures them that He can provide the believers true healing and recovery from those who hold to the teaching of Balaam and the Nicolaitans, and from the persecution in this city with the throne of Satan. If they rely on His strength to repent and persevere, He will reward them with the white stone. A new name will be written on the stone to signify the new person they will each become in Christ:

> Therefore, if anyone is in Christ, the new creation has come: The old has gone, the new is here! All this is from God, who reconciled us to himself through Christ and gave us the ministry of reconciliation: that God was reconciling the world to himself in Christ, not counting people's sins against them. And he has committed to us the message of reconciliation. (2 Cor 5:17)

The diseases in Pergamum were not the types of ailments that could be treated at the Temple of Asklepios or even at a first-rate facility such as Johns (note the *s*) Hopkins. Only the great physician Jesus Christ could restore these believers. He encourages their repentance and obedience with the reward of the white stone.

Why do you think people would submit themselves to the dark and dubious practices of having snakes crawl on them?

These believers were plagued with people in the church leading them astray with false doctrine. They were also beleaguered with people outside the church persecuting them. What is overwhelming you or inundating you?

What would you ask the Great Physician to examine in your life?

What is one takeaway and insight from the letter to the church at Pergamum that resonates with you?

In what way might that insight be calling you into a new way of being and doing?

THE PERSEVERING CHURCH IN THE ORDINARY CITY: THYATIRA

There was nothing extraordinary about this man. He was not too short or too tall. His lineage was not regal, and his family was not influential. He was a timid and humble man who described himself in this manner: "My clan is the weakest in Manasseh, and I am the least in my family" (Jgs 6:15).

He was not abnormally strong, nor was he particularly brave or courageous. On this day, he was hiding in the low-lying area of his winepress. The harvested wheat was ready for threshing and winnowing. Threshing grain involves crushing it to separate the edible components from the husk and straw. Winnowing removes the useless chaff from the grain. This process typically takes place on a threshing floor deliberately located on a high hill where the grain stalk can be crushed and held up to the open-air so that the breeze can assist in removing the debris. The edible grain falls to the threshing floor, and the unusable portions are taken away by the wind. Without the open air to assist him, the winnowing process had been difficult.

Our man, Gideon, took his wheat crop down to this inconspicuous area in an attempt to hide the grain from the Midianite raiding parties.

> Whenever the Israelites planted their crops, the Midianites, Amalekites and other eastern peoples invaded the country. They camped on the land and ruined the crops all the way to Gaza

and did not spare a living thing for Israel, neither sheep nor cattle nor donkeys. They came up with their livestock and their tents like swarms of locusts. It was impossible to count them or their camels; they invaded the land to ravage it. Midian so impoverished the Israelites that they cried out to the Lord for help. (Jgs 6:3-6)

The angel of the Lord answered their call by visiting our man. Gideon must have looked around to find the heroic champion who was given this greeting: "The Lord is with you, mighty warrior" (Jgs 6:12). The words "mighty warrior" do not seem to elicit the image of Gideon. After all, he was a man cowering in his winepress with grain and chaff dangling from his hair, struggling to eke out a meager existence on salvaged wheat. It took Gideon a few days and a couple of fleece tests to finally realize that the Lord was going to use him, an ordinary guy, to save his people, the Israelites.

Isn't that just like God? He uses the ordinary to accomplish the extraordinary.

Brothers and sisters, think of what you were when you were called. Not many of you were wise by human standards; not many were influential; not many were of noble birth. But God chose the foolish things of the world to shame the wise; God chose the weak things of the world to shame the strong. God chose the lowly things of this world and the despised things— and the things that are not—to nullify the things that are, so that no one may boast before him. (1 Cor 1:26-29)

God often takes people whom the world deems commonplace and accomplishes His great and glorious will through these regular folks.

Thyatira was an ordinary city. The first three cities whose churches received letters had exceptional traits and reputations. Ephesus was a religious center housing one of the famous Wonders of the World, the Temple of Artemis. Smyrna claimed to be the "Glory of Asia," the "First in Beauty," and the "Crown of Asia." Pergamum was the opulent capital city of Asia Minor. Thyatira was without superlative. Historian Colin Hemer compares Thyatira to the other six cities that were sent letters: "Thyatira was the least known, least important, and least remarkable of the cities."[72] Yet the Lord sent his longest and most detailed letter to this seemingly insignificant church in this inconsequential city.

Thyatira was situated thirty miles outside of Pergamum and acted as a sentinel town for the capital city. When an enemy approached the capital, they were forced to fight through the town of Thyatira first. This skirmish delayed the adversary long enough for Pergamum to fortify and prepare for the battle. Thus, Thyatira was destroyed and rebuilt numerous times and was in constant danger of attack. This small and insignificant town was merely a step on the way to a larger prize.

Thyatira's biggest asset was its most profitable industry: dye. Colored cloth was highly valued in the ancient world as a symbol of status and wealth. Thyatira specialized in a purple dye, which was extracted from the murex, a tiny shellfish, or from the root of a plant which thrived in that region.

One of the most recognizable citizens of the city and the first convert in Asia Minor was Lydia, a seller of purple:

> One of those listening was a woman from the city of Thyatira named Lydia, a dealer in purple cloth. She was a worshiper of God. The Lord opened her heart to respond to Paul's message. When she and the members of her household were baptized, she invited us to her home. "If you consider me a believer in the Lord," she said, "come and stay at my house." And she persuaded us. (Acts 16:14-15)

Let's venture to this ordinary town to hear the extraordinary word from our Lord.

To the angel of the church in Thyatira write:
These are the words of the Son of God, whose
eyes are like blazing fire and whose feet are like
burnished bronze. I know your deeds, your love
and faith, your service and perseverance, and that
you are now doing more than you did at first.
Revelation 2:18-19

OMNISCIENT JUDGEMENT

Margalit Fox begins her fascinating book with this account:

> It was one of the most notorious murders of its age. Galvanizing
> early twentieth-century Britain and before long the world, it
> involved a patrician victim, stolen diamonds, a transatlantic
> manhunt, and a cunning maidservant who knew far more than
> she could be persuaded to tell.[73]

In 1908, Miss Marion Gilchrist, an older woman, was robbed and
murdered in her luxurious apartment in Glasgow, Scotland. Oscar Slater,
a German Jew who had recently arrived in the country, had been trying
to pawn a diamond brooch similar to one stolen from Miss Gilchrist.
Witnesses said that they thought they saw him fleeing the apartment that
night. Slater was charged and tried. After less than an hour of deliberation,
a jury convicted this innocent man of murder. He ended up serving his life
sentence hewing granite in miserable conditions in a raw northern prison
nicknamed "Scotland's gulag."

In desperation, Slater managed to relay a secret message from prison
to a doctor asking for his help. The physician believed his story enough to
investigate the facts. Further investigation of the brooch revealed that Slater
had the piece before Miss Gilchrist's death. In the end, the witnesses divulged
their uncertainty of the murderer's identity. The court transcripts showed
signs of racial and religious prejudice from the judge and the prosecution.
Enough evidence was uncovered to release Oscar Slater after nineteen
years in prison. Much of the credit for his release goes to this physician,
Sir Arthur Conan Doyle, the author of the Sherlock Holmes mysteries.

Although our legal systems are generally reliable, they are not perfect.
Many innocent people are convicted of crimes they did not commit. A judge
and jury do not always know or seek to find the sum of the truth.

In His letter to the church at Thyatira, Jesus identifies himself as the "Son of God...whose feet are like burnished bronze" (Rv 2:18). As He does in all the letters, Christ is referencing the beginning of the Revelation where he identifies himself as the "Son of Man" (Rv 1:13) whose "feet were like bronze glowing in a furnace" (Rv 1:15). His reference to himself as the Son of God and as the Son of Man point to the fact that Jesus was fully a man during his time on earth and is for all eternity fully God.

The allusion to bronze represents strength and judgment. When worshipers entered the Tabernacle, the first room was an area of sacrifice to cleanse themselves from their sins. All these implements were made from bronze.

> Make all its utensils of bronze—its pots to remove the ashes, and its shovels, sprinkling bowls, meat forks and firepans. Make a grating for it, a bronze network, and make a bronze ring at each of the four corners of the network. Put it under the ledge of the altar so that it is halfway up the altar. Make poles of acacia wood for the altar and overlay them with bronze. (Ex 27:3-6)

The believers knew that bronze represented the judgment of the Lord and subsequent washing away of the sins which had been pointed out by Jesus and acknowledged by the sinner. Animal sacrifice was the first method of atonement. Christ replaced this method of sacrifice by offering himself as the sacrifice. We are atoned by His blood. The words "at one" appear in the word *atone*. Jesus' blood makes us at one with God. Jesus erased our sins by giving up His life on the cross for us. Without the presence of sin, we are adjudicated as "not guilty." By presenting himself with feet like burnished bronze, he is alluding to Himself as not only our judge but also our savior.

Christ compares His eyes to a "blazing fire" (Rv 2:18). He assures us that his eyes see all and can burn through to the truth within the heart and soul.

You have probably heard of a Gillette razor blade, but do you know what Gillette means?

Gillette was the term for the early unit of measurement for a laser. A Gillette was equivalent to the energy required to burn through one Gillette-brand razor blade. In 1957, the word "laser" was coined as the acronym for "light amplification by stimulated emission of radiation." Lasers work by focusing the broad range of colors into white light to create a super-concentrated beam of one color with one wavelength.

Today lasers are used in a wide range of applications including scanning purchases, transmitting data on a fiber-optic cable, correcting vision by LASIK surgery, making precise cuts in manufacturing and a myriad of other tasks. The moon even has a laser measurement device on its surface to accurately calculate the distance between it and the Earth. The largest laser in the world is the size of three football fields. An article from *Discover Magazine* explained this laser's capability to focus its energy: "The megalaser can deliver the same amount of energy released by a couple of pounds of TNT to a target the size of a pea."[74]

Jesus advises the believers in Thyatira that His eyes are blazing fires with the power of a megalaser. They can burn and cut through to see the true heart of the believer. They can measure motivations. His eyes have the power to scan and read our souls. As our Judge, he knows all. He is omniscient.

The word omniscient comes from two Latin words. The first is *"omni,"* meaning all. Examples of words using this prefix are "omnivorous" (those who eat all foods) and "omnipotent" (all-powerful). The second word is the Latin word *"scire,"* meaning knowledge. Derivatives from this root are "science" and "conscience."

Jesus stated, "I know," in commendation for the church's actions (Rv 2:19). When He says, "I know," He knows. This fact was both comforting and unsettling to the church. First, He commended them for the good that He knew they had been doing. Then He chastened them for some conflicts within the church. His laser vision generated a warning and a reassurance.

Just as He "knew" the positives and the negatives of the church at Thyatira, Jesus clearly sees our activities and our shortcomings. With full knowledge of us, he stills loves us unconditionally. His love for us is not dependent upon our actions. In relationships with other people, our love for them can fluctuate based on their activities and attitudes toward us. This variance is not true for Jesus. He loves us with a deep and abiding love. There is no great deed we can do to make the Lord love us more. There is no horrible sin we can commit that would make Him love us less. Although this level of love is difficult for us to comprehend, it is comforting to know that there is nothing that "will be able to separate us from the love of God that is in Christ Jesus our Lord" (Rom 8:39).

A human judge will sometimes hand down an unjust verdict or will convict a person out of personal prejudice. In His omnipotence, with his eyes like blazing fire and his feet like burnished bronze, our judge is always good and right. He knows us, and He loves us.

The church at Thyatira had some internal struggles. How could Christ's complete knowledge of this unnerve the believers? How could it be comforting?

Christ's eyes, like blazing fire, can see your heart and motivation. Is this comforting for you? Is it intimidating? What elicits your specific reaction?

Jesus loves us so much that even though he recognizes our faults, he can still see through to the good in us. Do you feel that love and acceptance in His omniscience?

Nevertheless, I have this against you:
You tolerate that woman Jezebel,
who calls herself a prophet.
By her teaching she misleads my servants into sexual
immorality and the eating of food sacrificed to idols.
I have given her time to repent of her immorality,
but she is unwilling.
So I will cast her on a bed of suffering,
and I will make those who commit adultery with her
suffer intensely, unless they repent of her ways.
I will strike her children dead.
Then all the churches will know that I am
he who searches hearts and minds,
and I will repay each of you according to your deeds.
Revelation 2:20-23

JEZEBEL

King Ahab ruled the Northern Kingdom of Israel beginning in about 874 BC. Instead of relying on the power of the Lord, Ahab felt the need to form an alliance with a pagan king from Phoenicia, the coastal area northeast of Israel. He, therefore, married the Phoenician princess from the city of Sidon, Jezebel.

> In the thirty-eighth year of Asa king of Judah, Ahab son of Omri became king of Israel, and he reigned in Samaria over Israel twenty-two years. Ahab son of Omri did more evil in the eyes of the Lord than any of those before him. He not only considered it trivial to commit the sins of Jeroboam son of Nebat, but he also married Jezebel daughter of Ethbaal king of the Sidonians, and began to serve Baal and worship him. He set up an altar for Baal in the temple of Baal that he built in Samaria. Ahab also made an Asherah pole and did more to arouse the anger of the Lord, the God of Israel, than did all the kings of Israel before him. (1Kgs 16:29-33)

Tragically, a pagan queen now ruled over God's chosen people. She had tremendous influence over her husband and over the people of Israel. Jezebel worshiped the false gods of Baal and Asherah. They were fertility gods. Their religious rites were sexual in nature and often involved temple prostitutes. Shrewdly, Queen Jezebel did not ban the worship of God. Instead, she set up Baal worship alongside the worship of the one true God, making it appear that it was acceptable to serve both. She housed and fed four hundred and fifty prophets of Baal and four hundred prophets of Asherah at the expense of the chosen people of Israel. By her official actions, the people felt justified in compromising their faith. The people soon forgot that only God is God. When the prophet Elijah confronted the supposed Hebrew believers in Israel, they were silent in their devotion to God.

> Elijah went before the people and said, "How long will you waver between two opinions? If the LORD is God, follow him; but if Baal is God, follow him." But the people said nothing. (1Kgs18:20-21)

To heat up the people's lukewarm dedication to the Lord, Elijah proposed a contest between the false gods of Baal and Asherah and the one true God.

> Then Elijah said to them, "I am the only one of the LORD's prophets left, but Baal has four hundred and fifty prophets. Get two bulls for us. Let Baal's prophets choose one for themselves, and let them cut it into pieces and put it on the wood but not set fire to it. I will prepare the other bull and put it on the wood but not set fire to it. Then you call on the name of your god, and I will call on the name of the LORD. The god who answers by fire—he is God." Then all the people said, "What you say is good." (1 Kgs 18:22-24)

It took a miraculous pyrotechnics show of power and force to bring the people of Israel back to the Lord.

> Then the fire of the Lord fell and burned up the sacrifice, the wood, the stones and the soil, and also licked up the water in the trench.
> When all the people saw this, they fell prostrate and cried, "The Lord—he is God! The Lord—he is God!" (1 Kings 18:38-39)

Jezebel did not launch a full attack on God. Instead, she led the believers astray by degrees. The attack on the Lord came from within the country, not from an outside force.

Pastor and theologian, Adrian Rogers, frames this subtle deception with this question:

> Which is more dangerous, a clock that is five minutes wrong or a clock five hours wrong? You would be prone to say a clock that is five hours wrong, but you are wrong. A clock five minutes

wrong is more dangerous than one that is five hours wrong. If you look at a clock that is five hours wrong, you know that is wrong. But if you look at a clock that is five minutes wrong, you are liable to miss a train, a plane, or bus or an important appointment.[75]

Jesus warns the church at Thyatira that a prophetess comparable to Queen Jezebel of Israel was infiltrating the church and leading the believers astray. Rogers says, "Perhaps they thought they were broadening their minds. But they were merely stretching their consciences."[76]

Like the Jezebel of old, this woman was in a position of power within the organization and attacked the church from the inside. This type of attack is different from the assaults on the first three churches. All the letters before this attest to attacks from the outside. Thyatira, however, had a different type of battle—one from the inside.

Another similarity between Queen Jezebel of old and the prophetess in Thyatira is that her misleading teachings were construed as close to the truth. They were five minutes wrong, not five hours wrong. Queen Jezebel did not disallow the worship of the living God. Such decisive action could have started a rebellion of the people. Instead, she set up another option of worship. The prophetess, whom Jesus calls Jezebel, operated similarly. She did not attack the basic precepts of the faith. She merely accepted sexually promiscuous activities and practices associated with the pagan gods. Often these subtleties are harder to discern and combat than those philosophies that are blatantly and openly against the Word of God.

Jesus warns the church in Thyatira, and us today, to dissociate from Jezebel.

An inside force within the church led the believers within it astray. Do you see these forces at work in your church or other organizations?

What is the best way to defend against these internal battles?

Do you feel a Jezebel force in your life?

How would you confront this?

Have you seen this subtle moving away from God in other people's lives?

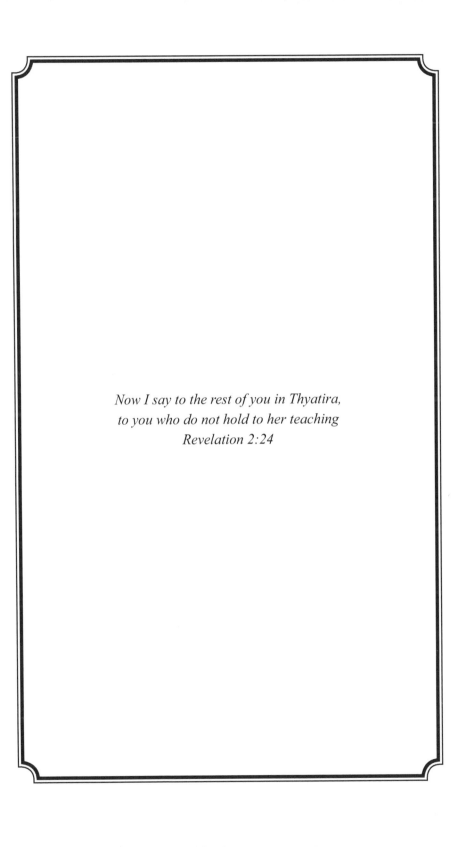

Now I say to the rest of you in Thyatira,
to you who do not hold to her teaching
Revelation 2:24

THE TEACHER

Jesus emphasizes the importance of teachers and their influence in His letter to the congregation at Thyatira. He warns how the doctrines of Jezebel are misleading the congregation and pulling them away from the Lord. Bill Bratt tells the story of a different kind of leader. This one, a teacher, used her influence to change a life positively.

Jean Thompson stood in front of her fifth-grade class on the very first day of school in the fall and told the children a lie. Like most teachers, she looked at her pupils and said that she loved them all the same, that she would treat them all alike. And that was impossible because there in front of her, slumped in his seat on the third row, was a little boy named Teddy Stoddard.

Mrs. Thompson had watched Teddy the year before and noticed he didn't play well with the other children, that his clothes were unkempt and that he constantly needed a bath. And Teddy was unpleasant.

At the school where Mrs. Thompson taught, she was required to review each child's records, and she put Teddy's off until last. When she opened his file, she was in for a surprise. His first-grade teacher wrote, "Teddy is a bright, inquisitive child with a ready laugh. He does his work neatly and has good manners. He is a joy to be around."

His second-grade teacher wrote, "Teddy is an excellent student well-liked by his classmates, but he is troubled because his mother has a terminal illness and life at home must be a struggle."

His third-grade teacher wrote, "Teddy continues to work hard, but his mother's death has been hard on him. He tries to do his best, but his father doesn't show much interest, and his home life will soon affect him if some steps aren't taken."

Teddy's fourth-grade teacher wrote, "Teddy is withdrawn and doesn't show much interest in school. He doesn't have many friends and sometimes sleeps in class. He is tardy and could become a problem."

Before Christmas break, her children brought her presents, all in beautiful ribbon and bright paper, except for Teddy's, which was clumsily wrapped in the heavy, brown paper of a scissored grocery bag. Mrs. Thompson took pains to open it in the middle of the other presents. Some of the children started to laugh when she found a rhinestone bracelet with some of the stones missing and a bottle that was one-quarter full of cologne. She stifled the children's laughter when she exclaimed how pretty the bracelet was, putting it on, and dabbing some of the perfume behind the other wrist.

Teddy Stoddard stayed behind just long enough to say, "Mrs. Thompson, today you smelled just like my mom used to."

After the children left, she cried for at least an hour. On that very day, she quit teaching reading and writing. Instead, she began to teach children. Jean Thompson paid particular attention to one they all called "Teddy." As she worked with him, his mind seemed to come alive. The more she encouraged him, the faster he responded. On days there would be an important test, Mrs. Thompson would remember that cologne. By the end of the year he had become one of the smartest children in the class. He had also become the "pet" of the teacher who had once vowed to love all of her children exactly the same.

A year later she found a note under her door, from Teddy, telling her that of all the teachers he'd had in elementary school, she was his favorite. Six years went by before she got another note from Teddy. He then wrote that he had finished high school, third in his class, and she was still his favorite teacher of all time. Four years after that, she got another letter, saying that while things had been tough at times, he'd stayed in school, had stuck with it, and would graduate from college with the highest of honors. He assured Mrs. Thompson she was still his favorite teacher.

Then four more years passed and yet another letter came. This time he explained that after he got his bachelor's degree, he decided to go a little further. The letter explained that she was still his favorite teacher, but that now his name was a little longer. The letter was signed, Theodore F. Stoddard, MD.

The story doesn't end there. You see, there was yet another letter that spring. Teddy said he'd met this girl and was to be married. He explained that his father had died a couple of years ago, and he was wondering if Mrs. Thompson might agree to sit in the pew usually reserved for the mother of the groom. And on that special day, Jean Thompson wore that bracelet, the one with the rhinestones missing. And on that special day, Jean Thompson smelled the way Teddy remembered his mother smelling on their last Christmas together. They hugged each other, and Dr. Stoddard whispered in Mrs. Thompson's ear, "Thank you, Mrs. Thompson, for believing in me. Thank you so much for making me feel important and showing me that I could make a difference."

Mrs. Thompson, with tears in her eyes, whispered back. She said, "Teddy, you have it all wrong. You were the one who taught me that I could make a difference. I didn't know how to teach until I met you.[77]

Scripture is clear on the importance of teaching and taking the role seriously. James, the brother of Jesus, says in his letter that a teacher bears a grave burden. Students will be motivated and influenced by the words and actions of one holding authority. Therefore, teachers are held to a higher standard.

Not many of you should become teachers, my fellow believers, because you know that we who teach will be judged more strictly. We all stumble in many ways. Anyone who is never at fault in what they say is perfect, able to keep their whole body in check. (Jas 3:1-2)

Parents are one of the primary authorities and influences on a child's development. My mom used to say that "the apple doesn't fall far from the tree." She meant that regardless of their intent or desire to be similar to their parents, many children turn out to be surprisingly similar. As I have seen our friends' children grow up and start their own families, I have found this to be true.

In the same manner, the student can become like the teacher. Jesus reiterates this fact saying, "The student is not above the teacher, but everyone who is fully trained will be like their teacher" (Lk 6:40).

Jesus knew that a strong leader, like this Jezebel in Thyatira's congregation, had the power and persuasion to lead the parishioners down the wrong path. He reminds them that teachers like Mrs. Thompson have the power to lift others to a higher level. However, they also have the power to negatively impact others like the Jezebel in their congregation. He commends those who realized that as followers of Christ, they must evaluate the teaching of the leader against the teaching of the Word.

We all have those in authority above us. How do you evaluate the validity of their teaching?

What can you do when you feel that a teacher's guidance is not godly?

Think about a situation in which you had a Jezebel as a leader. How did you react in this situation?

Think about a situation in which you had a godly leader. What were you able to learn from this person?

Whom do you teach? Family members? Employees? Friends?

How strongly do you focus on the impact you are having on them?

Are you giving your best influence?

How could you improve?

Now I say to the rest of you in Thyatira,
to you who do not hold to her teaching
and have not learned Satan's so-called deep secrets,
'"I will not impose any other burden on you,
except to hold on to what you have until I come."
Revelation 2:24

SATAN'S SO-CALLED DEEP KEPT SECRETS

Russell Freedman described the images that photographer, Lewis Hine, captured in the early 1900s in the United States.

> Manuel is five years old but big for his age. When the whistle blows at three o'clock in the morning, he pulls on his clothes and hurries over to the shrimp and oyster cannery where he spends the day pulling shells off iced shrimp. He has been working as a shrimp picker since he was four.

> Thousands of young boys descend into the dark and dangerous coal mines every day, or work above ground in the stifling dust of the coal breakers, picking slate from coal with torn and bleeding fingers. Small girls tend noisy machines in the spinning rooms of cotton mills, where the humid, lent-filled air makes breathing difficult. They are kept awake by having cold water thrown in their faces. [78]

Lewis Hine had been a teacher. He was horrified by the working conditions of children who should have been at school or play. Russell Freedman included these images in his book, *Kids at Work: Lewis Hine and His Crusade Against Child Labor*. Hine reasoned that if people could see what these children endured, there would be a public outcry for reform. He hoped to persuade philanthropic groups and workers' organizations to pressure government officials to enact legislation and policies to improve working conditions in the short term and eliminate child labor in the long run. [79]

In the years before World War I, children occupied many of the lowest paying, most dangerous, and least healthy jobs. Individuals like Lewis Hine helped bring the issue to the attention of the American public. Organized labor unions took this a step further. Many of the organizations worked to eliminate child labor. The first convention of the American Federation of Labor (AFL) in 1881 passed "a resolution calling on states to ban children under 14 from all gainful employment."[80] Labor unions were created to protect their workers and promote the interests of the community as a whole.

In the ancient world, the trade guild was the forerunner of the labor union. Thyatira was a city with a large number of trade guilds disproportionate to its small population. Inscriptions unearthed from archeological digs show more trade guilds existed in this town than in much larger cities. Thyatira's most powerful artisans were the potters, coppersmiths, and dyers.

Every artisan was required to belong to a guild to participate in the trade. The guilds would negotiate contracts for large and small projects and allocate the work to its members. Christians did not belong to the trade guilds because of their pagan and illicit practices. Before a guild meeting, a sacrifice would be offered to a false god. The guild would gather socially and hold sexually promiscuous parties serving meats which had been sacrificed to idols. Because of their loyalty to the Lord, Christians did not participate in these trade guilds. Therefore, the Christian was unable to practice his or her trade and make a living.

In some cities, the Christian's life was threatened because of his or her faith. In Thyatira, the Christian's livelihood was threatened.

The "Jezebel" came into the church at Thyatira with a compromise. She suggested tolerating the sin and embracing the wicked ways of this heathen world.

If the members of the church followed her ways, they could justify joining the trade guilds for the purpose of economic survival. Her teaching permitted the Christians to belong to the trade guilds even though they involved practices that compromised the values of the believers. Jezebel encouraged them to go along and get along so that they could feed their families.

Other early teachers encouraged Christians to participate in immoral debauchery to test and strengthen their faith. They suggested experimenting with evil and ungodly things, "Satan's so-called dark secrets" (Rv 2:24). William Barclay summarizes it this way: "In effect, they were teaching that a man must sow his wild oats, before he could really appreciate what virtue was. Such teaching was to encourage men to know the deep things of Satan and not the deep things of God."[81]

Jude, the brother of Jesus, warns about these godless men in his letter:

> Dear friends, although I was very eager to write to you about
> the salvation we share, I felt compelled to write and urge you
> to contend for the faith that was once for all entrusted to God's
> holy people. For certain individuals whose condemnation was
> written about long ago have secretly slipped in among you.
> They are ungodly people, who pervert the grace of our God
> into a license for immorality and deny Jesus Christ our only
> Sovereign and Lord. (Jd 1:2-4)

Jesus commends those who did not succumb to the temptations of
Jezebel, the trade guilds, or Satan, and encourages them to "hold on to what
you have until I come" (Rv 2:24). He praises them for not compromising.

*Joining the trade guild and participating in their prescribed pagan practices
could be a parent's only way to provide food for their family. How might
some people justify this?*

What arguments could you give them to hold on and not compromise?

What do you think were "Satan's deep so-called secrets" in that time period?

What do you think they are today?

In what areas do you see your church compromising?

Are there areas in your life where you deviate from your faith to fit into society?

What are ways you can "hold on" and stay true to the Lord?

To the one who is victorious
and does my will to the end,
I will give authority over the nations—
that one "will rule them with an iron scepter
and will dash them to pieces like pottery"—
just as I have received authority from my Father.
I will also give that one the morning star.
Whoever has ears,
let them hear what the Spirit says to
the churches.
Revelation 2:27-29

AUTHORITY AND RULE

"The best blood of England flows in my veins; on my father's side I am a Northumberland, on my mother's I am related to Kings, but this avails me not."[82]

These bitter words came from a brilliant and wealthy man. He was denied entrance into Parliament. He was denied the right to hold a public office. He was denied the academic accolades bestowed on those less gifted and less deserving than he. He was denied the rights of his father's title as the Duke of Northumberland. He was even denied entrance into the church.

These doors were closed to him through no fault of his own. He was denied these rights because of his birth. James Macie was the illegitimate child of the British Duke of Northumberland and Elizabeth Hungerford Keate Macie, a descendant of King Henry VII.

Knowing that the stigma of illegitimacy would be passed on to any children he had, Macie never married. Instead, he devoted himself to excelling in his research in the fields of chemistry and mineralogy.

Macie was frustrated by his situation in life. Society held him back. The systems pushed him down. Regardless of how diligently he worked, he was destined to be marginalized and forgotten. He feared that the Northumberland family's powerful and influential name would be remembered and chronicled, but that his name would fade into obscurity.

The believers at Thyatira must have dealt with many of these same frustrations. They worked hard, yet they were held back by the society of their time. The powerful trade guilds denied them entrance unless they bowed to the pagan gods. Without this membership, they were unable to sell their goods. The trade guilds were not the only authority holding them back. The mighty Roman Empire could, at any time, take their lives as traitors for not worshiping the emperor. This little church felt frustration that control belonged to the potent pagans, who used it to its fullest extent to suppress the Christians.

Jesus assures them that things are not as they seem. The seemingly weak will overcome the outwardly strong. The persecuted Christians are the true dominant victors, and by their obedience to Him, they will prevail:

> To the one who is victorious and does my will to the end, I will give authority over the nations-that one 'will rule them with an iron scepter and will dash them to pieces like pottery'—just as I have received authority from my Father. (Rv 2:27)

In the end, the Kingdom of God will reign. Jesus quotes portions of this powerful psalm in which the Lord assures the psalmist that He is the sovereign Lord and those who follow Him inherit the right and privilege of His might:

> Why do the nations conspire and the peoples plot in vain?
> The kings of the earth rise up and the rulers band together
> against the Lord and against his anointed, saying,
> "Let us break their chains and throw off their shackles."
> The One enthroned in heaven laughs: the Lord scoffs at them.
> He rebukes them in his anger and terrifies them in his wrath, saying,
> "I have installed my king on Zion, my holy mountain."
> I will proclaim the Lord's decree: He said to me,
> "You are my son; today I have become your father.
> Ask me, and I will make the nations your inheritance,
> the ends of the earth your possession.
> You will break them with a rod of iron;
> you will dash them to pieces like pottery."
> (Ps 2:1-9)

Perhaps Jesus used the imagery of pottery because of the large number of artisans in the city. They could easily imagine the damage done by a mighty hand swinging a sturdy rod, easily and completely shattering pieces of pottery. Jesus engages this imagery to compare it with the strength that the believers in the kingdom of heaven will have over the things of this

---

world. He gives a peek into the future where the victorious believers will, at last, be rewarded.

The faithful believers were "victorious" because they remained true to Christ and did not follow the teaching and example of Jezebel. Jesus promised these loyal few power and authority over the nations. This dominance must have been unimaginable to these Christians who had been marginalized.

Christ confirmed yet another gift. This honor is unsurpassed by any privilege or riches of the powerful heathens in Thyatira. Jesus promises these believers that they will receive the Morning Star Himself:

> "'I, Jesus, have sent my angel to give you this testimony for the churches. I am the Root and the Offspring of David, and the bright Morning Star.'" (Rv 22:16)

James Macie, just like the Christians at Thyatira, was treated unfairly by the society in which he lived. However, after his death, he did realize his dream to overcome those who purposefully and prejudicially defamed his reputation and robbed him of the honors and privileges he had earned. He was able to have his name, at last, respected and revered.

Although Macie had never visited the United States, he donated his estate to the colonies recently freed from the British Empire that had snubbed him. He put several stipulations on his contribution. The gift was to be earmarked for research conducted in his name. He changed his name from his mother's maiden name, Macie, to Smithson, the name of his father. His will stipulated that the money was to be allocated in this manner:

> "to found at Washington, under the name Smithsonian Institution, an establishment for the increase and diffusion of knowledge among men."[83]

Today the Smithsonian Institute consists of "nineteen world-class museums, galleries, gardens, and a zoo."[84] The Smithsonian Institute's name is recognized throughout the world. In contrast, the Northumberland name and fame has faded into the annals of the past.

Similarly, the glory of the Roman Empire has faded. The powerful trade guilds of Thyatira have been forgotten. However, the glory of the Lord continues and will crescendo with the second coming of Christ.

> Therefore God exalted him to the highest place
>> and gave him the name that is above every name,
> that at the name of Jesus every knee should bow,
>> in heaven and on earth and under the earth,
> and every tongue acknowledge that Jesus Christ is Lord,
>> to the glory of God the Father.
> (Ph 2:9-11)

Thanks be to God!

Have you ever felt marginalized by a system or society?

What did you do to counter this?

The promise of receiving the Morning Star was a blessing for the faithful believers in Thyatira. They will look forward to that day. However, the followers of the Jezebel in that church have good reason to fear the day. How would each of these groups respond to the coming of Christ?

How would you respond?

What is one thing you can do today to prepare yourself for the coming of Christ?

What is one takeaway and insight from the letter to the church at Thyatira that resonates with you?

In what way might that insight be calling you into a new way of being and doing?

THE DEAD CHURCH IN THE
GOLDEN CITY: SARDIS

O nce upon a time, there was a self-indulgent ruler named King Midas. He spent his days eating excesses of rich foods, drinking too much fine wine, and indulging in foolish antics to entertain and please himself. The self-centered king burdened and oppressed his subjects to maintain his flamboyant and gaudy lifestyle. The only other person this egotistical monarch cared for was his only child, his daughter.

One day King Midas saw a satyr lying in his garden. These wild creatures were part man and part beast, with the body of a man but ears and a tail similar to a horse. They were servant companions of the god Dionysus engaging in the debauchery which that god represented—wine, women, and song. This particular satyr was passed out recovering from a night of revelry. The king, realizing that this was an opportunity to be noticed and perhaps rewarded by Dionysus, took the satyr into the palace to care for him. Dionysus rewarded Midas by granting him one wish.

Although the greedy king was surrounded by abundance and wealth, he lamented that all of this was not enough. He asked Dionysus to grant him the wish that all he touched might turn to gold. The god granted the king's wish.

Immediately, Midas started touching all the items in his palace. His stone goblets became gold. The plates from which he ate turned into gold. The statues in his garden transformed into the shining metal. He touched walls, chairs, flowers, and trees, changing them into valuable objects. He exhausted himself running from place to place to snatch objects for their conversion.

To revive himself, he reached for a cup to drink some water. However, when the water touched his lips, it turned to gold. He reached for some grapes but could not eat them as they were now precious metal.

Fatigued and hungry, he lay on his bed. Midas cried out as he reclined on the pillows which had been soft but now turned to hard, cold gold. Hearing his cry, his beloved daughter ran to see what had happened to her father. To the king's horror, as his daughter grabbed his hand, she was also turned to gold.

Midas realized the folly of his ways and begged Dionysus to bring his daughter back to life. The god granted his release from his wish and commanded him to bathe in the Pactolus River. As the king bathed, the objects in his home, which he had touched, returned to their former states. At last, his precious daughter regained her life.

To this day, pieces of gold are found in the riverbed. The story claims that these treasures are the remnants of gold washed off from the repentant king's folly.

Although the story of King Midas is a myth, the alluvial gold in the river is real. Some of the richest sources of gold and silver in the ancient world were located in Sardis, making it a prime location for the capital of Lydia's empire. The Pactolus River and other stream beds flowing on the north side of Mount Tmolus are still filled with nuggets of these precious metals.

One man who benefitted from the deposits in the Pactolus River was the Lydian ruler in Sardis from 560-547 BC, King Croesus. His wealth funded the construction for the Temple of Artemis at Ephesus. His father minted the first coins. Money from his court supported the writer Aesop, from whom we got the famous "Aesop Fables." King Croesus's wealth caused him to overestimate his strength and underestimate that of his enemies. The abundance of resources made the king and his subjects soft and unprepared in many different ways, especially in the area of national security. King Croesus challenged Cyrus the Great. The Persian army surprised the king, infiltrated the city, and defeated the Lydians.

Even under Persian rule, wealth came easily to the people of Sardis. Several factors led to this affluence. Sardis was strategically located at a crossroads connecting the interior of Asia Minor and the Aegean coast, making it a valuable trade route. Raw materials and goods from the eastern Mesopotamian lands of Assyria, Babylon, and Persia came through this city and were exchanged for manufactured products from the Mediterranean kingdoms. The citizens in Sardis profited by taxing goods as they flowed through and by housing and feeding the merchants along their route.

Yet another advantage of Sardis's location was its rich supply of natural resources. The fertile agricultural land of the plain, the timber and mineral resources of the mountains, and the fresh, flowing water from the streams, springs, and lakes made this area prosperous.

To add to its impressive resume as a city, Sardis was built on two mountains. The rulers of the city built their fortress and important build-ings on the peak of the higher mountain. This height was a significant advantage in defending the city. Enemies had to scale the heights to reach the high ground and capture it. To add to the defenses, the Pactolus River circled the mountain, forming a moat that further fortified this seemingly impregnable citadel. These assets gave the area's military leaders a false sense of security.

The blessings of wealth, prosperity, and good location caused the city and its residents to be spoiled and overconfident. The townspeople garnered a reputation for being soft and superficial. The city had a reputation for shallow luxury living and lax moral values.

The church at Sardis had been a strong influence for Christ in a city known for ostentatious excess and ease. The church members had "a repu-tation for being alive" (Rv 3:1). At one time, they had been instrumental in bringing the authentic truth to this artificial city. However, they lost their fervor. Their zeal for the Lord died.

As we look at the letter to the church at Sardis and how the Lord's words relate to its history, keep in mind the area's many assets. Let's journey there and see how this easy affluence and success affected the church and the Lord's comments.

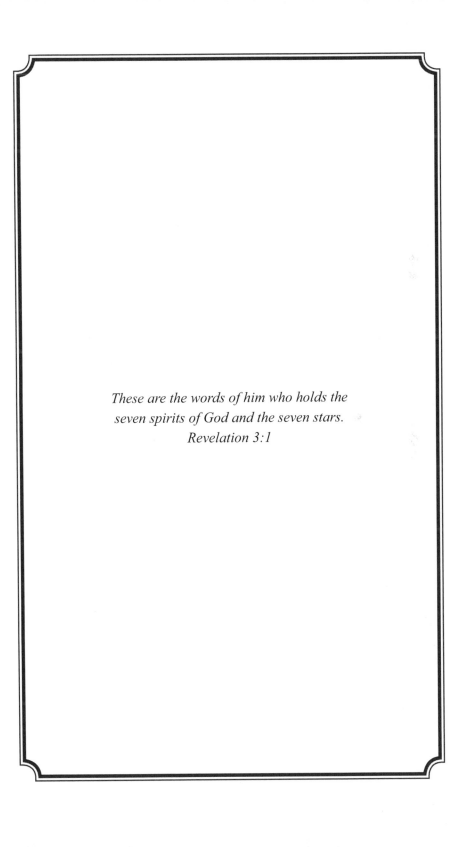

These are the words of him who holds the
seven spirits of God and the seven stars.
Revelation 3:1

HOLDS THE SEVEN SPIRITS AND THE SEVEN STARS

The years following World War II were filled with fear and apprehension as the world entered the Cold War period. The Western world was apprehensive about the Soviet Union and its nuclear arms. Suspicion and distrust ruled this era.

In a first-grade classroom, a teacher instructed his innocent and carefree six- and seven-year-olds in a duck-and-cover drill. This safety precaution was designed to protect against the dangers and side effects of a Soviet nuclear attack. He told the children to crawl under their desks face down and to cover their heads and necks with an article of clothing or a book, explaining that the explosion's impact would likely shatter windows and walls, sending dangerous debris across the room. Propaganda circulated with slogans casting doubt about the Communist bloc countries, our own country, and our neighbors.

These Cold War years were a time of paranoia and suspicion. Many believed these days signaled the end of the world. People felt helpless amid the threat of a danger over which they had no control. Then in the late 1950s, a thirteen-year-old boy came out with a hit that calmed fears and inspired hope. Ace Collins explains it this way in his book, *Music for the Heart*:

> In the midst of all this hopelessness, a child's voice reassured the world that God was still in charge. Laurie London, a young British boy, stepped into the recording studio and cut an American song that was likely a century and a half old. When released, millions seized "He's Got the Whole World in His Hands" as if it were life preserver thrown to a drowning shipwreck victim. Audiences the world over simply couldn't get enough of the affirmation that God was out there and caring about them.[85]

This apprehensive generation in the 1950s and 1960s needed the assurance that a higher authority was in charge. This slave anthem, sung by a child's sweet voice, reminded this post-war world to put its faith and trust in God.

Jesus knew that the church in Sardis would benefit from this promise as well. In His letter, he introduces himself as the omnipotent one "who holds the seven spirits of God and the seven stars" (Rv 3:1). He interprets this for us: "The mystery of the seven stars that you saw in my right hand and of the seven golden lampstands is this: The seven stars are the angels of the seven churches, and the seven lampstands are the seven churches" (Rv 1:20). The number seven represents completion, indicating that Jesus is powerful enough to hold all the ministers and churches throughout the ages in His hands.

These are important words for a church in a city like Sardis. The city misplaced its security in its own riches. Ease of wealth made this city soft and overconfident. The leaders' arrogance caused them to make decisions detrimental to the safety of the citizens, as we will see in future sections. The result was insecurity and uncertainty. Christ knew that the church members in this city needed the assurance of an almighty Lord and Savior who is able to hold the spirits and stars in His hands.

Isaiah prophesied that Jesus will be filled with "the seven spirits of God" (Rv. 3:1). He refers to Jesus's lineage as a descendant of Jesse, the father of King David, calling him a "Branch." He then lists the seven as the Spirit of the Lord, wisdom, understanding, counsel, power, knowledge, and the fear of the Lord.

> A shoot will come up from the stump of Jesse;
> from his roots a Branch will bear fruit.
> The Spirit of the Lord will rest on him—
> the Spirit of wisdom and of understanding,
> the Spirit of counsel and of might,
> the Spirit of the knowledge and fear of the Lord—
> and he will delight in the fear of the Lord.
> (Is 11:1-2)

Jesus is the embodiment of these Spirits. Matthew describes the Spirit descending on Jesus after he was baptized:

At that moment heaven was opened, and he saw the Spirit of God descending like a dove and lighting on him. And a voice from heaven said, "This is my Son, whom I love: with him I am well pleased." (Mt 3:16-17)

When we put our faith in the Lord, the Holy Spirit enters us as well. "Do you not know that your bodies are temples of the Holy Spirit, who is in you, whom you have received from God?" (I Cor 6:19). With the Spirit indwelling, we can produce the fruit of the Spirit. "But the fruit of the Spirit is love, joy, peace, forbearance, kindness, goodness, faithfulness, gentleness and self-control" (Gal 5:22-23). Jesus demonstrates for us a life lived immersed in the Spirit. Although we are only able to engage a small portion of the power of the Spirit, we can follow the example of Christ and taste the fruit of the Spirit.

Jesus uses the full extent of the power. He assures the church of Sardis that nothing will escape His omniscient eye. His omnipotent hands are holding them. With this power of the Spirit, Jesus assures the church that He truly has the whole world in His hands.

What assurance do you think the church at Sardis gained by knowing Jesus's power?

What assurance do you gain by knowing Jesus's power?

How does Jesus show us how to live a Spirit-filled life?

How can you live a more fruitful life?

What fruit of the Spirit challenges you?

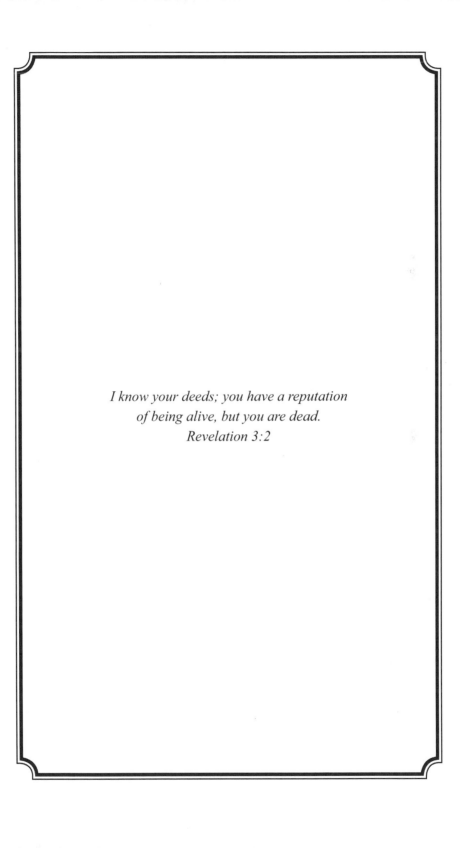

I know your deeds; you have a reputation
of being alive, but you are dead.
Revelation 3:2

DEAD OR ALIVE

The human body is constantly rejuvenating itself. To keep us alive, the body has to actively engage in the process of creating new cells to replace the old ones. As Margaret Thompson Reese writes,

> The life span of each type of tissue depends upon the work load endured by its cells. Cells lining the acid filled stomach last only about five days. The outer layer of skin is recycled about every two weeks. An adult human liver replaces itself about once every year to year and a half. The entire human skeleton is thought to be replaced every ten years or so in adults. [86]

The body is not designed to be dormant. It is created to cyclically revitalize and refresh itself. The body must always be creating and restoring. One of the ways a medical examiner determines the time of death is by studying cells.

The same is true in a church. A church cannot live off its past accolades and former works. Easy and fast success tends to create a soft and shallow organization. The organization must continue to grow and move forward. The church in Sardis had quickly developed a stellar reputation as a vivacious congregation accomplishing great works. This publicity became a detriment, as they became overly confident and arrogant and forgot the source of their gifts and their need for the Lord.

Adrian Rogers describes the church at Sardis in *Tapestry, Promises, and Prophecy*:

> The tragedy was this church wasn't alive at all. The organism had become an organization, and the movement had become a monument, and they were dead. When a person dies, the spirit departs. And that's exactly what had happened to this church.

The life of any church is the Holy Spirit of God. And when the Spirit leaves, the life is gone.[87]

Jesus uses the word "dead" to describe the church. Perhaps this reference would conjure thoughts of the Necropolis in the minds of the Sardis reader. Necropolis translates from Greek as the city *"polis"* of the dead *"necro."* This huge cemetery, located in Sardis, could have been the largest in the world at that time, rivaling the pyramids of Egypt. The mound served as the burial place for a dignitary and was approximately 1100 feet in circumference and over 225 feet high. Graves of other persons were located around it, earning it the name "cemetery of 1000 hills." The people of Sardis were very proud of the Necropolis and liked to look back at its glory and the former glory of its inhabitants.

Jesus sees this church as an organization that is as dead as the bodies in the Necropolis. He warns them to stop focusing on their vibrant past and to start living for the future.

Easy and fast success tends to create a shallow and soft individual or church. Jesus told a parable about seeds sown in soil. The seeds grew and prospered to differing degrees based on where they landed:

> "Listen! A farmer went out to sow his seed. As he was scattering the seed, some fell along the path, and the birds came and ate it up. Some fell on rocky places, where it did not have much soil. It sprang up quickly, because the soil was shallow. But when the sun came up, the plants were scorched, and they withered because they had no root. Other seed fell among thorns, which grew up and choked the plants, so that they did not bear grain. Still other seed fell on good soil. It came up, grew and produced a crop, some multiplying thirty, some sixty, some a hundred times." (Mk 4:3-8)

The believers in Sardis were comparable to the soil in rocky places where the plants grew quickly but withered because they had not developed a sturdy root structure.

The human body relies on the continuous growth and rejuvenation of cells for survival. Jesus exhorts the church to come alive with new growth.

Why do you think the citizens in Sardis revered the Necropolis?

How is it sometimes easier to look back than to look forward?

How does getting things easily lead to soft and superficial people?

Jesus exhorts the Sardis church to return to its former glory out of love. Do you feel that call on your heart?

Is there an organization or individual you see as being dead in their faith? How can you help them and pray for them?

Is there an area of your walk in which you feel "dead?"

Wake up!
Strengthen what remains and is about to die,
for I have found your deeds unfinished
in the sight of my God.
Revelation 3:2

WAKE UP!

These words were written on November 8, 1833, by a man who survived, without so much as a scratch, the first recorded train wreck in US history:

> Blessed, ever blessed be the name of God, that I am alive and have escaped unhurt from the most dreadful catastrophe that ever my eyes beheld! The scene of sufferance was excruciating. Men, women, and a child scattered along the road, bleeding, mangled, moaning, writhing in torture, and dying, as a trial of feeling to which I had never before been called; and when the thought came over me that a few yards more of pressure on the car in which I was would have laid me a prostrate corpse-like him who was before my eyes or a cripple for life; and, more insupportable still, what if my wife and grandchild had been in the car behind me![88]

This man had retired from one job and was now three years into his new career. He was traveling to work on the Camden and Amboy Railroad.

The train had been traveling at the top rate of the day-twenty miles per hour. Near Hightstown, New Jersey, an axle broke, causing the second car to derail and overturn. All twenty-four passengers in that coach were injured. Two passengers died, making them the first railroad fatalities in America.

This fortunate passenger, unscathed by the train wreck, was horrified by the scene. He realized the importance of the rail in the growth and commerce of our country. He further grasped that we, as a country, needed to "wake up" and put into place a deliberate plan for reform and design. The American public needed a logically organized transportation system to succeed as an industry and keep our country moving.

This passenger, former President and then-Congressman John Quincy Adams, did just that. Anton Chaitkin praises the congressman for the work he did to undergird this fledgling transportation system:

> He launched an infrastructure building spree that revolutionized the transportation network of the country. He did not wait upon public opinion, he led it: "The great object of civil government is the improvement of the condition of those who are parties to the social compact, and no government ... can accomplish [its] lawful ends but as it improves the conditions of those over whom it is established." [89]

President Adams took charge of the project by commissioning the Army Engineers at West Point to survey the land for the purpose of determining the best routes. He was proactive in planning and designing the infrastructure for our country's railway system, giving it a vibrant base upon which to build.

The president understood the importance of, in the words of our Lord, "waking up" and deliberately "strengthening" that which is in place.

President John Quincy Adams was not the only famous man riding the rails on the Camden and Amboy on the fateful day of the crash. Unlike the president, this gentleman did not avoid injury from the wreck. This passenger, in his late thirties, received cracked ribs and a punctured lung. He was heard vowing to never again ride the rails.

As it turned out, he did not honor that vow. He did, in fact, ride the rails again and was one of the most influential pioneers in the railroad industry. During this time period, railroads were a losing investment. States invested capital in the rail. However, they were underutilized by travelers. The cost of the capital was high, and the number of passengers was low. With high expenses and low revenue, the rails were slow to show a positive return on investment. Thus, states lost large sums of money, making railway building unpopular and politically dangerous. In an attempt to encourage private investment in the rail, states granted benefits to companies, such as monopoly rights and limited liability. Railroads also began to dominate trading on the New York Stock Exchange, making them an increasingly attractive investment.

This particular passenger was a keen observer of all these factors. Although his expertise in business was centered around steamboats, he began to take over the rail routes that connected to his shipping routes. The rail was required to take the products he transported by steamboat into the heart of the country. Using the knowledge he acquired from running his steamboat business, he found more efficient ways to run the rails.

In the late 1830s, the traveler, known to some as the Commodore and more formally to others as Cornelius Vanderbilt, orchestrated a brilliant takeover of the New York, Providence, and Boston Railroad known as the Stonington Line. The Commodore realized that he could control transportation in and out of Long Island Sound if he could control the Stonington. T. J. Stiles describes it this way in *The First Tycoon*:

> So (the Commodore) took a steamer to Stonington, boarded a train, and rode up the line to Providence. "There's nothing like it," he told the line's chief engineer three years later. "The first time I ever traveled over the Stonington, I made up my mind." It was the fastest route to Boston, potentially the key to the entire battle for the Sound.[90]

The Commodore took control of the line by lowering fares on other railways offering the same service. The Stonington lost passengers, revenue, and profit, which drove its stock price down. The Commodore was then able to buy the stock at a discount, obtaining a controlling interest. He became president of the company in 1847. It was the first of the many railroads he took over.

The Commodore deliberately endeavored to "wake up" and see the "strengths" around him. The New York & Harlem was a railroad with high debt and low value on Wall Street. Mr. Vanderbilt, however, realized that this line had an asset that no other line could claim. All the other lines connected the rail with the shipping docks to move freight. The Harlem was the only rail to enter the city of New York and go straight into Manhattan, making it the city's first and only passenger-friendly rail.

Both President John Quincy Adams and Cornelius Vanderbilt "woke up" and were aware of the climate surrounding them. They both, in their different spheres of influence, realized the importance of the infrastructure they were developing and took decisive action to strengthen the railway system. Their plans were calculating and deliberate.

Jesus called the church in Sardis to "wake up." Evidently, at one time, the church had a strong presence and influence on the pagan culture around it. However, Jesus told the believers that they had gone to sleep and lost their fervor for spreading the Good News. Unlike many of the seven churches, this church was being attacked from within its walls, not from without. He challenged them to aggressively assess the situation around them and to take the appropriate action to strengthen what remains, just as our two rail passengers did.

Why is it that organizations are unaware of the negative activity happening within?

The church at Sardis had more attacks from within than from without. What are the advantages and disadvantages of the problem coming from inside the organization?

In what ways could your church "wake up" and "strengthen what remains" for your congregation?

What are the areas you need to monitor in your life that could be heading in the wrong direction?

How do Christ's directives motivate you?

Remember, therefore,
what you have received and heard;
hold it fast.
Revelation 3:3

THE SALT OF THE EARTH

Consider this biographical passage:

> She's lived for over a century. And she doesn't look a day over 8-years-old. A true barometer of our culture, (she) has seen a lot in her time – from motion pictures and the miracle of flight – to the first moon landing and music videos. She's seen fashion fads come and go and come back around. And she's heard everything from rock-and-roll to rap. She's even into social media.
>
> She's also done a lot in her time. She's flavored our food for generations, softened our water, melted ice, and snow, improved industrial processes, made pharmaceuticals more effective, and so much more. All this from one little girl.[91]

"She" is the Morton Salt Girl. She carries her umbrella in one hand to shield her from the pouring rain. On the other hand, she holds a cylindrical box, its open spout pouring salt behind her and proving the patented words to be true: "When It Rains It Pours®."

A problem with table salt in the early 1900s was that it would clump in damp weather, rendering it unusable. The Morton Salt Girl, premiering in 1914, promoted the fact that her company's salt would pour freely in rainy and damp weather due to its patented pouring container and the addition of magnesium carbonate to the salt compound.

Salt has been a treasured commodity throughout the ages and has a myriad of important uses. At the time in which the letters in Revelation were written, supply was low, and demand was high, making salt an economic standard for a high price.

At that time, Roman soldiers received a ration of this rare commodity as part of their wages. They would trade their salt for other products. The etymology of the word, *"soldier,"* breaks down *"sal,"* meaning salt and *"dare"* meaning to give. A soldier was one who gave salt. The word *"salary"* is derived from the Latin *"salarium"* itself deriving from *"sal"* or salt.[92]

Since salt was a scarce luxury, it was considered a standard of measurement. A common saying is that someone is "worth his salt," meaning that the individual is competent and reaching his potential.

Agreements in Bible times were consummated with salt. To ingest salt with someone was a sign that the two parties were sealing the deal: "Don't you know that the Lord, the God of Israel, has given the kingship of Israel to David and his descendants forever by a covenant of salt?" (2 Chr 13:5). The covenant of salt symbolizes a timeless agreement of permanent obligation. This covenant is passed from one generation to the next. "It is an everlasting covenant of salt before the LORD for both you and your offspring" (Nm 18:19).

Salt was added to the offerings presented to God, making this sacrifice even more valuable and special. The book of Leviticus instructs the priests, members of the tribe of Levi, on methods of conducting worship. The scripture articulates this specific instruction: "Season all your grain offerings with salt. Do not leave the salt of the covenant of your God out of your grain offerings: add salt to all your offerings" (Lv 2:13). In Hebrew culture, when a statement is repeated three times, as in the passage above, the writer is emphasizing the importance of this statement. In our culture, this would be similar to typing something in boldface and all capital letters.

Adding the costly salt to the offering was a visible sign that the believer was willing to sacrifice that which was precious to them. This act of worship signified trust in God's provision.

In Matthew 5:13, Jesus exhorts believers, "You are the salt of the earth." In His letter to the church at Sardis, He reminds them of this responsibility. "Remember, therefore, what you have received and heard; hold it fast" (Rv 3:3). They, like all believers, had received the gift of the Holy Spirit when they accepted Christ as their Lord and Savior. They had heard the call. Now they needed to continue to hold it fast.

Christ challenges them to examine if they are, in the words of the saying, "worth their salt." Let's look at a couple of salt's attributes and evaluate how Christ might compare these to the ministry of the church at Sardis.

One of the greatest values of salt in the ancient world was as a preservative and an antiseptic. Salt reduces the water activity in substances. Without the greater amount of water, microbial growth and chemical reactions are slowed. By reducing the substance and the space in which bacteria can grow, food lasts longer. Before refrigeration, this was a tremendous benefit. The same principle applies to treating wounds with saltwater. The salt reduces the amount of potentially bacteria-laden liquids, giving the wound a better chance of healing. In both cases, the arena for the damage has been reduced, making the substances more stable.

Another benefit of salt was as a catalyst. People in this time used salt as a fire accelerant. Salt mixed with animal manure produced fuel for their cooking ovens. The salt acted as a chemical agent to increase the temperature of the fire.

The church at Sardis had, at one time, acted as an antiseptic bringing the cleansing power of Christ to a world saturated with the filth of false gods. Its message of the truth had slowed the growth of false teaching just as salt slows the proliferation of bacteria. The church had been enough of a catalyst for change that it had earned a "reputation of being alive" (Rv 3:1). It had been the salt the world needed. But something caused its members to forget what they knew and to lose their vitality.

In his book *The Early Church,* Ray Vander Laan attributes this decline to the compromise of their beliefs. He describes one of the most striking buildings in Sardis, the combination of Greek gymnasium and Roman bathhouse.[93] The Greek gymnasium was built to glorify man. Athletes exercised and competed in the nude, again emphasizing the beauty and perfection of the human body. The gymnasium promoted a narcissistic and self-centered lifestyle with the love of man superseding the love of God.

The Roman bathhouse connected to the gymnasium was a place where men and women came together to relax and socialize in hot, warm, and cold baths. Gatherings often included illicit activities.

Surprisingly, archaeologists have uncovered a large synagogue built in the corner of this ungodly complex. Vander Laan poses this question about the Jews in Sardis:

> Did the Jews of Sardis place their synagogue in the gymnasium
> in order to influence the culture, or had they so adopted the pagan

lifestyle that they saw no discrepancy between worshipping God and participating in gymnasium activities?[94]

Vander Laan reports that archeologists have discovered objects with Christian symbols, such as the cross and the sign of the fish, alongside pagan markings. He again poses a question that was relevant to the church at Sardis and remains relevant to us today:

> Salt doesn't do its job or fulfill its purpose until it is mixed in with what it is supposed to flavor. But salt that becomes diluted by what it is supposed to flavor can't do its job either. If Christians are to be the salt of the earth, how involved with the secular world and secular people must we be in order to be "salt" and communicate the message of Jesus?[95]

Jesus cautions us about the dangers of compromise:

> "You are the salt of the earth. But if the salt loses its saltiness, how can it be made salty again? It is no longer good for anything, except to be thrown out and trampled underfoot." (Mt 5:13)

Paul gives a similar warning in his letter to the church at Corinth: "Do not be deceived: 'Bad company ruins good morals.' Wake up from your drunken stupor as is right and do not go on sinning" (1 Cor 15:33).

Thomas Watson, a Puritan preacher and author, summed it up well:

> All the danger is when the world gets into the heart. The water is useful for the sailing of the ship; all the danger is when the water gets into the ship; so the fear is when the world gets into the heart.[96]

Traders in Asia Minor would take the valuable salt and mix it with sand to make it go further. However, when they put too much sand in the mixture, it neutralized the salt. The members of the church at Sardis had compromised their faith to the point that they lost their efficacy. They no longer looked different to the world.

This combination represents a delicate balance. If a church never reaches out to the unsaved, it doesn't have the opportunity for impact. However, if a church becomes so involved in the world that it begins to adapt to sinful ways, then it compromises its influence. Using our salt analogy, the salt has to get out of the shaker to make a difference. At the same time, once out of the shaker, it must continue to maintain its unique chemical structure.

John described this in his first epistle:

> Do not love the world or anything in the world. If anyone loves the world, love for the Father is not in them. For everything in the world-the lust of the flesh, the lust of the eyes, and the pride of life comes not from the Father but from the world. The world and its desires pass away, but whoever does the will of God lives forever. (1 Jn 2:15-17)

The challenge for the believers in Sardis as well as for us today is to be in the world but not of the world. Jesus calls us to be the salt of the earth.

Why do you think the Jewish believers built a synagogue in the Greek gymnasium and Roman bath?

How do you think they justified this?

What are ways that we compromise our faith?

How do we justify our compromise?

Why is this dangerous for the church?

What are the dangers to us if we compromise?

How can this impact our witness?

But if you do not wake up,
I will come like a thief,
and you will not know
at what time I will come to you.
Revelation 3:3

LIKE A THIEF

This is the tale of two cities.

More correctly, it is the tale of one city twice.

Remember the old adage, "Fool me once, shame on you. Fool me twice, shame on me?" Sardis was defeated by the same maneuver not once, but twice.

The first time was during the reign of King Croesus. He ruled over the kingdom of Lydia from 560-546 BC. Croesus was wealthy, self-reliant, and successful. His kingdom consisted of fertile land for farming and timber, freshwater streams, and heavy mineral deposits. He had the safety of an impregnable citadel.

Perhaps it was this sense of security that led King Croesus to believe that he could conquer Cyrus the Great and defeat the mighty ruler of the Persian Empire. Unfortunately for King Croesus, Cyrus's superior forces captured and surrounded the citadel of Sardis in 546 BC, sequestering the troops in their fortress on Mount Tmolus on the acropolis of Sardis. The two armies were in a standoff. The soldiers of Sardis secured the citadel and stopped any attempts to infiltrate their fortress. Night after night, the Persian soldiers watched and waited. As the days slipped slowly by, Cyrus's soldiers vigilantly tried to compose a plan to invade Sardis.

Then, one fateful night, it happened. Greek historian and master story-teller Herodotus tells it this way:

> This is how the Persians captured Croesus and Sardis. When the fourteenth day of the siege arrived, Cyrus sent around his horsemen and proclaimed to his army that he would give a reward to the first man to scale the wall. After this, the army tried to scale the walls but failed. Then, when all the rest had given up, a Mardian named Hyroeades attempted to climb up at the part of the acropolis where no guard had been posted, since

it was so steep and apparently impenetrable there that no one
had ever feared that the acropolis could be taken from there....
It so happened that the day before, Hyroeades the Mardian had
seen one of the Lydians climb down at this part of the acropolis
and recover a helmet that had tumbled from above. Hyroeades
watched him carefully and committed to memory what he saw.
Then the next day, he ascended the height at the same place
with other Persians following behind. In this way, when many
had made that climb, the acropolis of Sardis was taken and the
whole city fell and was sacked. [97]

Cyrus the Great conquered King Croesus's impenetrable fortress not
because of superior manpower, superior training, or superior equipment. He
conquered Lydia because they fell asleep and did not keep a vigilant watch.

Here is the crazy twist to the story: Approximately 350 years later, the
same scene occurred. An enemy army, this time the Greek army of King
Antiochus of the Seleucid Empire, surrounded the Sardis soldiers in the
citadel atop Mount Tmolus. Again, Sardis occupied the high ground and
waited. The Greeks camped around the base, unable to mount an attack on
this seemingly impenetrable fortress. As before, the soldiers of the sieging
army were waiting and watching, trying to find a way to infiltrate this
stronghold. History repeated itself, and an astute soldier realized that part
of the wall was not being guarded. He saw the soldiers from Sardis throw
garbage off the top of the wall. Scavenger birds flocked to enjoy this feast
and remained sitting on the wall. The Greek soldier realized that if there
had been guards on that section of the wall, the birds would have flown
away, which indicated that portion of the wall was unguarded. That night,
the Greek army invaded through this vulnerable entrance and captured the
sleeping city of Sardis.

Sardis was overly confident in their security, which caused them to be
careless. Christ warns the church at Sardis to wake up and be prepared.

In the early 1930s, US Admiral Harry Yarnell, concerned about the
safety of our naval forces in Hawaii, led a military exercise using two aircraft
carriers, the Lexington and the Saratoga. The admiral positioned these ships
on an unpatrolled northeastern route to prevent them from being detected
by American troops. On February 7, 1932, from this desolate position near

the Aleutian Islands, he was able to launch 152 fighter planes without being spotted, simulating a full-scale attack first on the airfields and then the ships on Pearl Harbor's Battleship Row. The surprise attack rendered the US Army and Navy defenseless and unable to commence a counter-attack. The Navy war-game umpire ruled the attack successful, proving that the admiral's fears were merited.

The naval hierarchy, however, ignored the report. No changes were made to the naval base. Security was not tightened. Pearl Harbor stayed the same. Several news agencies reported the exercise, including several Japanese writers. The Japanese did not ignore the exercise. They studied the plan with interest.

In the fall of 1941, four Japanese Imperial Navy officers came to Honolulu disguised as stewards. They tested the ability to arrive from the northeast without being detected by US reconnaissance. The officers bought maps, scoped out the area, and even took pictures from tourist plane rides over Pearl Harbor.

Early Sunday morning, December 7, 1941, while most of the island slept, the Japanese replayed Admiral Yarnell's exercise nine years and ten months later. However, this time, the stakes were real. The losses were tragic. The United States lost 3400 men, eight battleships, and 188 aircraft. The US Navy had ignored the reports. While they were asleep, not keeping watch, an enemy attacked.

Jesus refers to His second coming in a similar way:

> But about that day or hour no one knows, not even the angels in heaven, nor the Son, but only the Father. As it was in the days of Noah, so it will be at the coming of the Son of Man. For in the days before the flood, people were eating and drinking, marrying and giving in marriage, up to the day Noah entered the ark; and they knew nothing about what would happen until the flood came and took them all away. That is how it will be at the coming of the Son of Man. Two men will be in the field; one will be taken and the other left. Two women will be grinding with a hand mill; one will be taken and the other left.
>
> Therefore, keep watch, because you do not know on what day your Lord will come. But understand this: If the owner of the

house had known at what time of night the thief was coming, he would have kept watch and would not have let his house be broken into. (Mt 24:36-43)

In this passage, Jesus warns all His followers to be ready for His second coming. He uses the example of Noah. In 120 years, Noah did not convert one person to the ways of God. When the rains came, it was too late. Only Noah and his family were spared.

Christ cautions us to be ready at all times. The homeowner in the story would have been diligently prepared if he knew the night of the robbery. He would have made sure that all the windows and doors were locked, and he would have been on guard. However, he does not know, so he has to be continuously fortified.

Similarly, believers need to get their lives right with the Lord and keep them that way. They should not delay asking for forgiveness from the Lord or forgiveness from a friend. They should live a life today that is pleasing to God and be prepared to meet Him with a clean heart.

In His letter to the parishioners in Sardis, Jesus compares the judgment that will fall on the city of Sardis His second coming. He does not want them to be unprepared like the historical warriors of their city who failed to keep a diligent watch.

How does Christ ask the church at Sardis to prepare themselves?

How does Christ ask us as believers to prepare ourselves?

What emotions do you feel when you hear about the second coming of Christ?

What do you need to do to prepare yourself for the second coming?

Yet you have a few people in Sardis
who have not soiled their clothes.
Revelation 3:4

SOILED CLOTHES

The stoat is a furry brown animal, similar in size to a squirrel, and lives in the colder climates of North America, Europe, and Asia. The stoat was a prevalent resident in the area of the seven churches. As temperatures drop, the stoat's fur turns white. In the coldest of the winter months when snow is on the ground, the stoat's coat will be a pristine white, camouflaging it and protecting it from its predators. The only dark remaining on its body is an ink-black section on the tip of its tail. The change of the color of its coat comes with a name change. The stoat becomes an ermine.

Royalty wore the coat of this beautiful animal for years as a symbol of purity and strength. In the 1300s in England, King Edward III banned anyone who was not a part of the royal family from wearing ermine.[98] The fur became an expensive and prized commodity.

The ermine itself appreciates the beauty and unspoiled look of its fur and will, therefore, go to extremes to keep it clean. Hunters and trappers took advantage of this characteristic to capture this valuable creature by smearing the door of its home with grease or mud while the ermine was out of its burrow. The hunters would then loose the dogs to find and pursue the ermine. When the ermine reached the safety of its home, it would realize that the entrance was filthy. If the ermine went inside, the dirt would soil its coat. The ermine would stay outside and fight the dogs instead of escaping to the protection of its home to keep the purity of its coat intact. The ermine would rather die than soil its fur.[99]

Jesus commended the members of the church at Sardis who had not soiled their clothes. Just as the ermine forfeited its safety to keep its white fur clean, a "few people" of the early church in Sardis surrendered their lifestyles to keep themselves holy and spotless.

They had to sacrifice the easy path of conforming to popular beliefs and remember and obey the teaching of Christ. Often this requires isolating yourself from other people and connecting with the Lord. The psalmist expressed this separation with this lovely poetry.

> Blessed is the one
>> who does not walk in step with the wicked
> or stand in the way that sinners take
>> or sit in the company of mockers,
> but whose delight is in the law of the Lord,
>> and who meditates on his law day and night.
> That person is like a tree planted by streams of water,
>> which yields its fruit in season
> and whose leaf does not wither—
>> whatever they do prospers. (Ps 1:1-3)

To remain pure, these few had to dissociate themselves from the pagans in their city and even from some of the church members. Dwight L. Moody summarizes it: "If I walk with the world, I can't walk with God."[100]

These ermine-like Christians in this pagan culture would often distance themselves from friends and family who were participating in inappropriate activities. They refused to compromise their beliefs to fit in with those around them. Practices that were considered socially acceptable contrasted with the teaching of Jesus. The people in Sardis and perhaps even some in the church might have looked down upon them as close-minded and old-fashioned. However, just as the ermine chose to die with a pristine coat, these few Christians chose to live a life set apart for the Lord with an unsoiled heart and conscience. Jesus commends them for their steadfast faith and obedience.

Today, we face similar challenges. Jesus still calls us to forfeit business deals, activities, and even time with certain people who soil our relationship with our Lord.

Have you seen a time when a church has "soiled its coat" in an effort to fit into society?

What happens when believers compromise their faith?

———

What types of temptations do you face that could soil your relationship with God?

In what ways do you see yourself protecting your purity like the ermine?

In what areas could you be more protective?

They will walk with me.
Revelation 3:4

WALKING WITH THE LORD

C. Austin Miles was a brilliant pharmacist with prestigious degrees from the Philadelphia College of Pharmacy and the University of Pennsylvania. However, it is not his career as a pharmacist that distinguishes him. He is most often recognized for his work coming out of an event that happened on the day chronicled below:

> One day in April 1912, I was seated in the darkroom where I kept my photographic equipment, and also my organ. I drew my Bible toward me, and it opened at my favorite book and chapter, John chapter twenty. I don't know if this was by chance or by the work of the Holy Spirit. I will let you the reader decide. That story of Jesus and Mary in John 20 had lost none of its power and charm.
>
> It was though I was in a trance, as I read it that day, I seemed to be part of the scene. I became a silent witness to that dramatic moment in Mary's life when she knelt before her Lord and cried, "Rabboni." I rested my hands on the open Bible, as I stared at the light blue wall. As the light faded, I seemed to be standing at the entrance of a garden, looking down a gently winding path, shaded by olive branches. A woman in white, with head, bowed, hand clasping her throat, as if to choke back her sobs, walked slowly into the shadows. It was Mary. As she came unto the tomb, upon which she placed her hand, she bent over to look in and ran away.
>
> John, in a flowing robe, appeared looking at the tomb. Then came Peter, who entered the tomb, followed slowly by John. As they departed, Mary reappeared leaning her head upon her arm at the tomb, she wept. Turning herself, she saw Jesus standing

there, so did I. I knew it was He. She knelt before Him, with arms outstretched, and looking into His face cried, "Rabboni."

I awakened in sunlight, gripping my Bible with my muscles tense, and nerves vibrating, under the inspiration of the Holy Spirit. I wrote as quickly as the words could be formed the lyrics exactly as it is sung today. That same evening, I wrote the tune. It is sung today as it was written in 1912.[101]

The popular hymn, *"In the Garden,"* was written this night by this inspired and talented songwriter. Perhaps the hymn's popularity derives from the comfort believers feel when walking with our Lord. Throughout the Bible, believers cherished these walks with the Lord.

Austin Miles described the experience in this way:

I come to the garden alone,
While the dew is still on the roses;
And the voice I hear, falling on my ear,
The Son of God discloses.

Refrain:
And He walks with me, and He talks with me,
And He tells me I am His own,
And the joy we share as we tarry there,
None other has ever known.

2 He speaks, and the sound of His voice
Is so sweet the birds hush their singing;
And the melody that He gave to me
Within my heart is ringing. [Refrain]

3 I'd stay in the garden with Him
Tho' the night around me be falling;
But He bids me go; thro' the voice of woe,
His voice to me is calling. [Refrain][102]

The disciples had the opportunity to walk with Jesus in person. As they journeyed from town to town, He would make their time meaningful. Instead of a mindless walk, the expedition became a lecture hall for knowledge and wisdom. The Shema, which the Jewish believer recited twice a day, encouraged this mobile classroom.

> Hear, O Israel: The Lord our God, the Lord is one. Love the Lord your God with all your heart and with all your soul and with all your strength. These commandments that I give you today are to be on your hearts. Impress them on your children. Talk about them when you sit at home and when you walk along the road, when you lie down and when you get up. (Dt 6:4-6)

On the disciples' walk along the road, Jesus would use commonplace items to convey exceptional doctrines. His parables involved lilies, mustard seeds, grapevines, and many other ordinary objects that he used to exemplify extraordinary truths.

As He walked with them, He taught them.

After the resurrection, Cleopas and his friend plodded on the road from Jerusalem to Emmaus. Their shoulders sagged, and their heads drooped with disappointment and discouragement. They had hoped that Jesus would change their world. They had dared to believe that He could restore the nation of God's people to its former glory. They were disillusioned and disheartened. The man they expected to transform the world had been humiliated, tortured, and crucified.

To add to their frustration, a stranger had joined them on their seven-mile journey. This man seemed to be totally unaware of the horrid events of the weekend. They must have wondered how this stranger could have been so naïve. The men gave their abbreviated synopsis of the tragic chain of events. The new arrival asked a couple of questions and then talked about the Scriptures that prophesized the suffering of the Messiah. It wasn't until this stranger, who was the resurrected Christ, prayed with them at dinner that they realized they were traveling in the presence of the Messiah of whom they spoke. Although they did not recognize His identity, they sensed the magnitude of the presence accompanying them on their walk. "Were not our hearts burning within us while he talked with us on the road and opened the Scriptures to us?" (Mt 24:32).

As He walked with them, He inspired them.

Mary Magdalene tossed and turned all night. Jesus had rescued her from seven demons and transformed her life. Now she feared she would never see Him again. Unable to bear the pain and grief anymore, she jumped up and ventured out into the dark of the early morning. She did not even stop to think that she would be unable to access the inside of the tomb due to the large rock covering the opening. The bleak haze in her mind resembled the predawn emerging of the day.

To her horror, when she arrived at the tomb, the stone was removed, and Jesus's body was gone! In a panic, she ran back to alert the disciples. Peter and John hurried back with her to find the empty tomb, and the burial cloth neatly folded. The men returned to their homes, but Mary Magdalene, overcome with grief, remained weeping at the tomb.

A man, whom she presumed to be the gardener, asked her why she was crying. She did not recognize Him until He called her by her name. Just as sheep can distinguish their shepherd's voice, Mary recognized Jesus's voice and realized that she was with the Lord.

As He walked with her, He comforted her.

Walking with the Lord is always an active endeavor. We don't "sit" or "stop" with Lord. We move forward with Him. Sometimes it is to teach us. Sometimes it is to inspire us. Sometimes it is to comfort us. In the words of Henry Ford, "Those who walk with God always reach their destination."[103]

Jesus promised the few faithful at the church in Sardis that He would walk with them. He vowed to accompany them to their appropriate destination and give them the wisdom, inspiration, or comfort they needed for the journey. His offer is the same for us today.

What do you think the disciples thought of the stories as they journeyed with Jesus?

Why do you think Jesus joined the men on the road to Emmaus?

Why do you think that Jesus waited until the disciples left to reveal himself to Mary Magdalene?

Do you deliberately take time to walk quietly with the Lord?

Where and when do you meet Him?

How could you reschedule your life to spend more time in deliberate step with Jesus?

The one who is victorious will, like them,
be dressed in white, for they are worthy.
I will never blot out the name of that person
from the book of life,
but will acknowledge that name
before my Father and his angels.
Whoever has ears,
let them hear what the Spirit says to the churches."
Revelation 3:5-6

DRESSED IN WHITE

According to the Executive Strategy Director for Tide laundry detergent, Veb Anand:

> There's a 40 percent chance that whatever you're wearing has been washed in the last week and a 38 percent chance that the detergent it sloshed around in was Tide. The brand has over 4 million fans on Facebook. Many families have used Tide for generations. Tide is so firmly rooted that it's been difficult for any competitor to displace.[104]

The rise of Tide (no pun intended) is very interesting. In the early 1940s clothes were washed by hand with soap that did not dissolve in hard water. Dick Byerly, a chemist with Proctor & Gamble, found the winning compound after fourteen years of research. The product he developed was able to lift stains out of clothing.

The president of Proctor & Gamble compared the cleaning power of this new product to the fresh, clean sand on the beach after the tide rolls out. Thus, the new soap was named Tide. As *Adweek* Senior Editor Robert Klara writes:

> Tide was billed as a wash day miracle but the real miracle was the marketing. Home washing machines were just coming onto the market, and P&G arranged to drop a sample box of Tide into them-a practice that continued well into the 1970s. Many housewives who tried Tide never tried anything else, which goes a long way to explaining the brand's continued dominance. "It's been passed from mother to daughter-and to sons," said P&G fabric care spokesperson Anne Candido. "People think, 'My mom used it, so I can use it.'"

But there's another reason Tide still rules the detergent shelf-that fragrance. As Brand Union's Anand explains, the smell of fresh laundry is an immensely comforting thing. "Tide is like coffee," he said. "It's the smell of home, and that's quite valuable." Indeed, it is. Today, Americans spend $2.8 billion yearly-more than they do on Halloween candy, more than on weight-loss products-on Tide.[105]

The popular detergent back in the day of the Letters in Revelation was a plant called hyssop. Similar to our modern laundry detergent, it has a chemical compound that works well with water to remove stains. As a bonus, it also has an aromatic, minty scent. Just as the article points out that the fragrance of Tide elicits a pleasant and comforting feeling of home, the minty smell of hyssop most likely evoked the same emotions in those launderers in the ancient world.

King David was the powerful ruler during the Kingdom of Israel's glory years. David committed adultery and then perpetrated several sins to try to hide his indiscretion. When he turned to the Lord for forgiveness, he compared the cleaning power of hyssop to the inner cleansing of repentance. He asked God to wash away his iniquity with His forgiveness.

> Cleanse me with hyssop, and I will be clean;
>> wash me, and I will be whiter than snow.
> Let me hear joy and gladness;
>> let the bones you have crushed rejoice.
> Hide your face from my sins
>> and blot out all my iniquity.
>
> Create in me a pure heart, O God,
>> and renew a steadfast spirit within me.
> Do not cast me from your presence
>> or take your Holy Spirit from me.
> (Ps 51:7-11)

The city of Sardis was known for its red wool. Today, this deep hue is referred to as Turkish Red. Because of the expense of dyeing the wool, this fabric and the clothes made from it carried a certain prestige. Jesus modified the trend to replace the fashionable and desirable color of the city from red to white.

However, the Bible shows us that we are not able to whiten our garments by our own strength. The power of the Lord does this for us. God promises to make us as white as wool despite our red stains of sin:

"Come now, let us settle the matter,"
    says the Lord.
"Though your sins are like scarlet,
    they shall be as white as snow;
though they are red as crimson,
    they shall be like wool.
(Is 1:18-19)

In ancient cultures, even in pagan worship, parishioners were expected to clean themselves and their clothes before coming before the altars. The color white represented this purity and cleanliness.

Jesus gives the few faithful in Sardis a two-pronged agreement. He will not blot out their names, and He will acknowledge them before His Father and the angels. Being a gracious host, He will make sure that they have clothes appropriate for the occasion. They will be donned in white just as He, the Victor, is in white. What a glorious time that will be! I can almost smell the aroma of fresh laundry.

God offers us the same promise of blotting out our sins and cleansing us. Do you believe His promise?

What do you need to bring to the Lord for washing?

Do you find it hard to acknowledge Him in certain situations? What are those and why?

What is one takeaway and insight from the letter to the church at Sardis that resonates with you?

In what way might that insight be calling you into a new way of being and doing?

THE FAITHFUL CHURCH IN THE IMMORAL CITY: PHILADELPHIA

"I love your outfit," a stranger compliments.

"I would love to go to Hawaii," a young girl dreams.

"I love you and want to marry you," a man proposes.

The ancient Greeks would struggle with our word "love." The Greek language has at least six words describing the shades and degrees of this diverse sentiment. A Hellenistic speaker needs variations on the emotion and intent behind the verb to choose the word appropriate for a given situation.

"Philadelphia" derives its root from one of the Greek words referring to love. Phileo is characterized as brotherly love. In his book *How Should We Live? Great Ideas from the Past for Everyday Life*, Roman Krznaric explains the characteristics of this type of love. Krznaric proposes that Phileo love is the most valued form of love by the Greeks:

> [Phileo] was the most profound friendship that developed between comrades who had fought side by side on the battlefield. These brothers-in-arms had seen one another suffer and often risked their lives to save their companions from being impaled by a Persian spear. They considered themselves as equals, and would not only share their personal worries but also display extreme loyalty, helping one another in times of need without expecting anything in return.[106]

Philadelphia was a city perched on a high terrace in the Lydian region. The remains of the city have had little excavation or archeological research and lay beneath the modern city of Alasehir. This city has a small population because it is located on a seismic hazard zone and was near the epicenter of an earthquake in 1969. Volcanic cliffs surrounded Philadelphia. Due to the earthquakes and volcanos, Philadelphia was a city that was continually built and rebuilt. Residents were familiar with fleeing from their homes to escape to open-air fields for a greater likelihood of safety during an earthquake or volcanic eruption. [107]

The volcanic ash in this region created fertile soil that was exceedingly good for growing vines. This area produced a bountiful and quality harvest of grapes. Philadelphia became known for its wine. Because of this designation, Philadelphia had Dionysius, the god of the vine, as its patron saint. Edith Hamilton, one of the premier experts on mythology, describes Dionysus's popularity and influence on the culture of the city in this way:

> Under his influence, courage was quickened and fear banished, at any rate for the moment. He uplifted his worshippers; he made them feel that they could do what they had thought they could not. All this happy freedom and confidence passed away, of course, as they either grew sober or got drunk, but while it lasted it was like being possessed by a power great than themselves. So people felt about Dionysus as about no other god. He was not only outside of them he was within them, too. They could be transformed by him into being like him. They could themselves become divine.

> The god of wine could be kind and beneficent. He could also be cruel and drive men on to frightful deeds. Often, he made them mad. The Maenads, or the Bacchantes, as they were also called, were women frenzied with wine. They rushed through woods and over mountains uttering sharp cries waving pine-cone-tipped wands, swept away in a fierce ecstasy. Nothing could stop them. They would tear to pieces the wild creatures they met and devour the bloody shred of flesh.[108]

This gateway city was located at the culmination of three countries, Phrygia, Mysia, and Lydia, and the border from Europe to Asia. As such, Philadelphia served as a missionary city to spread Hellenism to the east. The Hellenists charged them with disseminating the pagan religions, the literature, the language, and the lifestyle of the Greeks to the less sophisticated barbarians to the east.

The church in Philadelphia existed in the midst of this volatile situation. These parishioners had to endeavor to live a pure life amid a rowdy culture. They had to be on guard for natural disasters, moral temptations, and unwarranted persecution.

With all these factors working against them, this small congregation did not have the big name and reputation of the larger churches, such as the one in Sardis. However, this church was large in the eyes of the Lord. Philadelphia and Smyrna are the only two churches for which Jesus has no words of condemnation. He only has praise and encouragement for this faithful group of obedient believers. Just as succulent grapes grew out of the ashes, this resilient church flourished out of the heathenistic culture surrounding it.

Come along and see how this faithful church survived and thrived in this immoral city.

To the angel of the church in Philadelphia write:
These are the words of him who is holy and true,
who holds the key of David.
What he opens no one can shut,
and what he shuts no one can open.
Revelation 3:7

OPEN AND SHUT

The second book of Kings in the Bible tells us that Hezekiah ascended to the throne of the Kingdom of Judah at the age of twenty-five. He ruled for twenty-nine years.

> Hezekiah trusted in the Lord, the God of Israel. There was no one like him among all the kings of Judah, either before him or after him. He held fast to the Lord and did not stop following him; he kept the commands the Lord had given Moses. (2 Kgs 18:5-6)

King Hezekiah relied heavily on his two top advisors: Eliakim, the palace administrator, and Shebna, the secretary. On several occasions documented in the Bible, these two leaders in the palace were emissaries who met with dignitaries on the king's behalf. One of Shebna's privileges and responsibilities was to be the steward who possessed the keys to the palace that King David had built years before. With these keys, Shebna had access to all the palace's many rooms, including the storerooms containing gold and other precious commodities. As the holder of the keys, Shebna was one of the most important and influential men in the kingdom.

Evidentially, Shebna started to think of himself more highly than he should. As some would say, he started believing his own press releases.

Shebna started stealing money and possessions away from the king. He also carved the stone out of a cave for a burial tomb to memorialize himself after his death. This luxury was reserved for royalty.

Hezekiah sent Eliakim and Shebna to Isaiah to relay information between the king and Isaiah. The Lord revealed Shebna's indiscretions and embezzlements to Isaiah, and Isaiah exposed his deeds to the king:

> This is what the Lord, the Lord Almighty, says:
> "Go, say to this steward,

to Shebna the palace administrator:
What are you doing here and who gave you permission
    to cut out a grave for yourself here,
hewing your grave on the height
    and chiseling your resting place in the rock?

Beware, the Lord is about to take firm hold of you
    and hurl you away, you mighty man.
He will roll you up tightly like a ball
    and throw you into a large country.
There you will die
    and there the chariots you were so proud of
    will become a disgrace to your master's house.
I will depose you from your office,
    and you will be ousted from your position."

In that day I will summon my servant, Eliakim son of Hilkiah.
I will clothe him with your robe and fasten your sash around
him and hand your authority over to him. He will be a father to
those who live in Jerusalem and to the people of Judah. I will
place on his shoulder the key to the house of David; what he
opens no one can shut, and what he shuts no one can open.
(Is 22:15-22)

Shebna was stripped of his power and prestige. The Lord gave the honor
to Eliakim, the dutiful servant who is loyal and obedient. Eliakim proved
himself to be humble and reliable.

Jesus introduces Himself to the church in Philadelphia as "him who is
holy and true, who holds the key of David. What he opens no one can shut,
and what he shuts no one can open" (Rv 3:7). Jesus alludes to these verses
to assure the readers that He is the authority with the ultimate power over
access and closure.

Jesus declares that He is the Eliakim. He is the "holy and true" one
who has proven Himself reliable and trustworthy. He has overthrown the
deceiver, the enemy, Shebna. Jesus is in charge. Jesus asserts that this authority belongs to Him.

The parishioners in Philadelphia must have felt bullied. They endured natural disasters such as earthquakes and volcanos. They weathered persecution from the Jews and ridicule from the pagans. In his introduction, Jesus comforts them with the truth that He has this ultimate power and loves them enough to use it on their behalf.

Have you seen an organization or group that seems to always be under attack?

Was there a redeemer for this group?

When have you felt bullied by people or situations?

What is your response to this?

How do you take on overwhelming situations?

Jesus offers His power and authority to the members of the church in Philadelphia and to believers today who will obey and call on His name. How can you put your trust in Him in the challenges of your life?

I know your deeds.
Revelation 3:8

YOUR DEEDS

Jesus assures the congregation at the church in Philadelphia that he knows their deeds. He first commends them that they have "kept my word and not denied my name" (Rv 3:8). By this, He praises their obedience and firm faith. His next acclamation is that they have endured patiently.

Under the inspiration of the Holy Spirit, Paul says that we are saved by grace and downplays our works: "For it is by grace you have been saved, through faith-and this is not from yourselves, it is the gift of God-not by works, so that no one can boast" (Eph 2:8-9). Paul is rightfully reminding us that our deeds do not save us.

James, the half-brother of Jesus, looks at this from a different vantage. He exhorts us to work to show our faith. He urges us to do good deeds as a visible sign of our commitment to the Lord.

> What good is it, my brothers and sisters, if someone claims to have faith but has no deeds? Can such faith save them? Suppose a brother or a sister is without clothes and daily food. If one of you says to them, "Go in peace; keep warm and well fed," but does nothing about their physical needs, what good is it? In the same way, faith by itself, if it is not accompanied by action, is dead.
> But someone will say, "You have faith; I have deeds."
> Show me your faith without deeds, and I will show you my faith by my deeds. You believe that there is one God. Good! Even the demons believe that-and shudder.
> You foolish person, do you want evidence that faith without deeds is useless? Was not our father Abraham considered righteous for what he did when he offered his son Isaac on the altar? You see that his faith and his actions were working together, and his faith was made complete by what he did. And

the scripture was fulfilled that says, "Abraham believed God, and it was credited to him as righteousness," and he was called God's friend. You see that a person is considered righteous by what they do and not by faith alone.

In the same way, was not even Rahab the prostitute considered righteous for what she did when she gave lodging to the spies and sent them off in a different direction? As the body without the spirit is dead, so faith without deeds is dead. (Jas 2:14-26)

James is making the case that real faith is not invisible. Faith is seen by its works. One pastor used the analogy that you know a house has a fire in the fireplace by the smoke coming out of the chimney.

James uses the examples of Abraham and Rahab in his letter to these Hebrew people. The Jewish reader recognized that these two people are opposites. Abraham is revered as the father of their faith. He was a man who was held in the highest regard. Rahab was a prostitute. She was a woman and a gentile earning her low marks on the Hebrew scales. However, both are credited with righteousness by their works. By using these two polar examples, James is proving to his Jewish audience that every person, regardless of his or her station in life, is justified by faith.

This question is often asked: Is Paul right or is James right? The answer is that they are both correct. Paul is giving the root of our salvation, and James is showing us that we should do good deeds because of our salvation.

Martin Luther summed it up this way. "We are saved by faith alone, but the faith that saves is never alone."[109]

The church in Philadelphia was small and weak. It had not had tremendous success recruiting new converts from this city, dubbed "Little Athens" and designated as a monument to Hellenism and pagan worship. The church in Philadelphia did not make headlines like the church in Sardis.

However, Jesus lovingly reassures them that He knows the truth. He knows their deeds and has nothing but praise for this little church.

Do you focus more on your faith or on your deeds?

What is the best way to balance the two?

———

Which area could you strengthen?

Would the Lord be complimentary of the deeds of your church?

How about your personal deeds?

Ask the Lord to help you see if there are areas in which you could do more for Christ?

See, I have placed before you an open door
that no one can shut.
Revelation 3:8

AN OPEN DOOR THAT NO ONE CAN SHUT

On the morning of August 13, 1961, the citizens of Berlin were horrified to wake up to a barbed-wire wall separating Soviet-occupied East Berlin from the free city of West Berlin. Thousands of East Germans had been commuting to the West to work and play. But on the night of August 12, a barricade was secretly, swiftly, and stealthily erected, imprisoning everyone on the East side, regardless of their residence. Those there that night were forced to remain there. Parents were isolated from their children. Loved ones were unable to reunite. Business associates were divided. Though they often lived only several hundred yards apart, in reality, these people were worlds away from each other. This separation lasted for twenty-eight long years.[110]

The East Germans defended the building of the wall as a necessary protective measure to keep Western spies out. The truth was that the Communist East Germans needed to stop the outpouring of lives fleeing from the East to the West, as the numbers had escalated to over three million defectors.

One of the many families forever impacted was that of Anna Kaminsky. She is a child of the wall. Her father is Swedish, and her mother is from East Berlin. The Communist German Democratic Republic (GDR) would not approve their marriage nor allow her father into East Berlin.

On August 12, 1961, Anna's mother was allowed to go to Sweden. Leaving Anna's brother, a toddler, in East Berlin with his grandparents, her mother departed. An ABC News interview tells her story:

> Then on Aug. 13, overnight, the Berlin Wall went up. Kaminsky's grandparents and her brother, as with so many thousands of German families, were suddenly stranded on opposite sides of an impossible barrier.

The East German government would not allow Kaminsky's brother – a toddler – to leave the country to join his parents. They would also not allow his mother to come and collect him.

She could return, but she would have to stay. And, if she didn't return, the government had threatened to send her son to an orphanage. Either way, her Swedish fiancé had no chance of entering East Germany. A writer with a political agenda opposing that of the East German government, he had been branded an enemy of the state. They never married.

Months later, in 1962, Kaminsky's mother made a heartrending decision: She took the one-way trip back to East Germany, to her son. By then, she was pregnant with Anna.

Anna Kaminsky would never meet her father. He died in the early 1980s before the wall came down.[111]

Anna is one of the thousands of people whose lives were inexorably changed on the night the wall went up. The closure of the passage isolated families and shut down hopes and dreams. The Berlin Wall demonstrates the frustration and pain of opportunity and freedom lost.

In her book *The Collapse: The Accidental Opening of the Berlin Wall*, Mary Elise Sarotte tells the fascinating convergence of events that led to the collapse of the wall. The GDR was starting to make mistakes. At the same time, peaceful protesters were organizing and finding ways to resist and outsmart the Stasi, the GDR's secret police and intelligence agency.

In a press conference on November 9, 1989, Günter Schabowski, an official of the Politburo, read a poorly written announcement in a live broadcast which stated that East Germans would get new travel freedoms. The press release did not disclose the myriad of fine-print rules surrounding the new edict or the visas that would be required for passage.

Schabowski later cavalierly explained that he did not proofread the announcement prior to giving it, saying, "I can speak German, and I can read a text out loud without mistakes so no preparation was necessary."[112]

The protesters heard the announcement and came out in droves. Tens of thousands of people descended on the border checkpoints, telling the border guards about Schabowski's broadcast.

One border guard, Harald Jäger, saw the press conference on television. By seven that evening, several people had gathered to cross out of the East to freedom in the West. Jäger called his commanding officer, who told him to send the people home. However, by 8:30 p.m., the crowd had increased to hundreds of people. When the crowds refused to disperse, General Heinz Feilder approved a plan to allow the East Germans to leave. However, the border patrols were to stamp their passports to invalidate them, negating the citizens' ability to return.

Sarotte describes the evening:

> Among the first people let out had been young parents. The parents had only wanted to take a quick look in the immediate area just to the west of Bornholmer and then rejoin their young children, who were at home in bed and asleep. They had returned quickly to the western entry of the checkpoint and had happily presented their IDs, saying in merry tones, "Here we are again! We are coming back!" And in response, they heard that they could not go home. No one had told them that the stamps on their ID photos in their outstretched hands represented their permanent expulsion from East Germany.
> Jäger told the young parents that he could make an exception for them. Hearing that, other East Germans standing near the western outpost who also wanted to return asked to be allowed back in as well.[113]

Jäger repeatedly called his commanding officers for counsel. They berated him for his inability to handle the situation, calling him a coward and offering no meaningful advice. As the crowds swelled to tens of thousands of people chanting, "Open the gate," Jäger began to fear for the lives of his men and doubt the importance of limiting the freedom of those at the wall.

At 11:30 p.m., Jäger gave the orders to open the gate.

Sarotte details the emotional conclusion to the night. One of the guards at the gate later recounted:

> "Why have a been standing here for the last twenty years?" Jäger was on the verge of tears. To prevent his men from seeing their acting commander cry, he ducked into a near control

building. There he found one of his subordinates, already hunched over and weeping. The East Germans who passed through the gate also shed tears, but theirs were of joy, not confusion or sorrow. [114]

Jäger said years later, "I didn't open the wall. The people who stood here, they did it. Their will was so great, there was no other alternative but to open the border."[115]

This unusual chain of events had peaceably opened the wall that had separated lives, loves, and families for twenty-eight years.

These stories about the Berlin Wall illustrate the bleakness, despair, and isolation of closure. Conversely, they exemplify the hopefulness, optimism, and promise of openness.

Jesus promises the hope of an open door. He brought this good news to a church which could have easily lost heart. He assures them that with His power, He will keep the doors of opportunity open to the church. Through His strength, they could have an open door that no one could shut. They could, for once, have hope that no one could crush.

As Paul said in his letter to the Corinthians, we become our most powerful as we rely on Christ. In our weakness, His power prevails:

> "My grace is sufficient for you, for my power is made perfect in weakness." Therefore I will boast all the more gladly about my weaknesses, so that Christ's power may rest on me. That is why, for Christ's sake, I delight in weaknesses, in insults, in hardships, in persecutions, in difficulties. For when I am weak, then I am strong. (2 Cor 12:9-10)

The only way this small and weak congregation could literally and figuratively keep their doors open was through the One who is strong enough to keep the outside forces from shutting them. Through the power of Christ, they were able to live, to serve, and to evangelize as Christians in their perilous setting.

Many external forces threatened to shut the doors of their church and their faith. They lived in a precarious zone of earthquakes and volcanos that cost them their homes and stability. They constantly had to build and rebuild their city. This unpredictable environment created physical insecurity.

This faithful congregation also experienced spiritual challenges. Philadelphia was dubbed the "Gateway to the East" and was established to spread Greek polytheism, philosophy, and culture. The city contained such a large number of temples to pagan gods that it earned the nickname "Little Athens." The church was an oasis for God in a cesspool of pagan sin and revelry.

Persecution threatened to close them down. This vulnerable congregation lived in fear of torture and death. Throughout the ages, whenever an individual or organization furthers the kingdom of God, this entity comes under attack. They were making a difference for the Lord and, thus, were under assault from the enemy.

Even with all these factors hindering them, Jesus used this gateway, this "open door," as an evangelistic tool for the Gospel. This little church believed the words of the prophet Isaiah. They knew that the world's view of their strength and ability to influence the unstable environment surrounding them was different than God's view. They trusted that when they persisted in doing their good deeds, keeping His word, and not denying His name, the Lord would keep open the doors for their effectiveness for His glory.

> "As the heavens are higher than the earth,
> so are my ways higher than your ways and my thoughts than
> your thoughts.
> As the rain and the snow
> come down from heaven,
> and do not return to it
> without watering the earth
> and making it bud and flourish, so that it yields seed for the
> sower and bread for the eater,
> so is my word that goes out from my mouth:
> It will not return to me empty,
> but will accomplish what I desire and achieve the purpose for
> which I sent it." (Is 55:9-11)

Historical accounts record that the believers in the churches in Smyrna and Philadelphia suffered under harsh persecution. In contrast, the information on the churches in Sardis, Thyatira, and Laodicea shows a less severe level of harassment. Why do you think this disparity occurred?

What caused Jesus to come to the aid of this church?

Philadelphia faced physical and spiritual challenges. In what areas does your church or organization face the most difficult trials?

What are the most challenging areas in your life? What makes you feel overwhelmed or ineffectual?

How can you turn these challenges over to God and rely on Him to keep the doors open for you?

I know that you have little strength,
yet you have kept my word and
have not denied my name.
Revelation 3:8

LITTLE STRENGTH

Medical missionary Dr. William Leslie of Ontario, Canada, went to a remote area of the Democratic Republic of the Congo in 1912. This mission field was an unlikely place for the Gospel to take root. The belligerent indigenous tribes often fought against each other. Some tribes were cannibals.

The country was under the harsh rule of King Leopold of Belgium. His occupying soldiers cruelly mistreated and abused the black Africans. "I greatly regret that it is all too true and that the representatives of King Leopold have been guilty of many of the atrocities charged against them," said Dr. Leslie. "With my own eyes, I have witnessed many of the most horrible examples of cruelty practiced upon the poor natives in that country."

For seventeen years, Dr. Leslie provided medical assistance and spiritual feeding in this brutal environment. He returned home discouraged, believing that only the medical part of his mission had been accomplished. He did not think that he had done anything to spread the love of Christ. In 2010, years after his death, a team led by Eric Ramsey with Tom Cox World Ministries visited Vanga, where Dr. Leslie had been based. Here is what they discovered:

"The team found a network of reproducing churches hidden like glittering diamonds in the dense jungle, where Dr. Leslie was stationed." [116]

Based on his previous research, Ramsey thought the Yansi might have some exposure to the name of Jesus, but no real understanding of who He is. They were unprepared for their remarkable find.

> When we got in there, we found a network of reproducing churches throughout the jungle. Each village had its own gospel choir. They wrote their own songs and would have sing-offs from village to village. [117]

Ramsey and his team visited eight villages in the area, and each of them had a church. He noted that in one village, the tribe had built a stone church that could seat one thousand people. That church was built in the 1980s, but with this building filling up and people walking long distances to attend services, the leadership decided to start churches in other villages. Ramsey said Dr. Leslie's goal "was to spread Christianity. He felt he never really made a big impact, but the legacy he left is huge."[118]

Dr. Leslie persevered and planted seeds in a soil and culture that seemed unlikely to reap a harvest. Perhaps the workers at the church in Philadelphia felt the same way. They were poor people in a city that prided itself on pagan and hedonistic practices. Despite opposition and persecution, the believers in Philadelphia remained true to the word of God and kept the faith in honoring Christ's name.

They probably did not expect a bountiful harvest to come from their obedience and loyalty. However, the harvest was plentiful. Just as the exceptional grapes in this region grew from soil containing scorched ashes, great faithfulness came from this congregation planted in adversity.

In God's garden, the rules are different. Paul explains it this way:

> I planted the seed, Apollos watered it, but God made it grow. So neither he who plants nor he who waters is anything, but only God, who makes things grow. The man who plants and the man who waters have one purpose, and each will be rewarded according to his own labor. (1 Cor 3:6-8)

Dr. Leslie's story is similar to that of the church at Philadelphia. Despite the odds in the Congo, Dr. Leslie made an impact for Christ. Similarly, despite the odds in Philadelphia, the church made an impact for Christ. Luke says that "all the Jews and Greeks who lived in the province of Asia heard the word of the Lord" (Acts 19:10).

God blessed their work in the garden and made it grow.

Have you been part of an organization in which you felt the work was not making a difference?

Have you been surprised by an unexpected harvest from work you have done?

What aspect of your life makes you feel that you have little strength?

How can you incorporate the Lord in your work?

I will make those who are of the synagogue of Satan,
who claim to be Jews though they are not,
but are liars—
I will make them come and fall down at your feet
and acknowledge that I have loved you.
Revelation 3:9

THE ATTACK OF SATAN

The Shelby Kennedy Foundation released this story in their Bible study of 1 Peter:

> The dry breeze stung Nadia's face as she looked out over the grassy plain at the herd of gazelles grazing. It was mid-summer in Africa, and newly born calves were romping together on the savannah grass. Silently she studied their every move, careful not to make a sound, not wanting to startle them, the slightest noise threatened to send the entire herd running away at over 50 miles per hour! Her girlfriends, Laila, Shaina, and Maya, could see the same view, but from different vantage points.
>
> Shaina and Maya were crouched nearest to each other and silently studied the herd of gazelles. They noticed that the youngest gazelles clung close to their mothers and the mothers, similarly, clung close to the greater herd. The mothers knew that their young were easy targets for predators and were careful to provide them the protection of the herd. Maya quietly commented that the behavior of the older gazelles was not much different than that of the young. Though they had lost the physical power of their younger counterparts, these older gazelles were wise. They had spent many years on the plains of Africa and knew that due to their weakening bodies, they too could be easily taken out by their carnivorous neighbors. Even the stronger most powerful gazelles clung close to the herd.
>
> Laila, Nadia's best friend, was focused on an adolescent gazelle that had wandered away from the herd. She noted that the young gazelle, though fully grown physically, had not achieved the same girth as the other males in the herd. He was thin and

sinewy- his muscular strength clearly defined. Though his body had reached full maturity, he was still a child. He had found a particularly sweet bush to graze on and had left the safety of the herd in order to do so. Silently, Laila caught Shaina's gaze and directed it to the young gazelle near the bush.

Nadia and her friends continued to study the gazelles calmly, quietly, until the sun began to set. Then, as dusk fell, in a seemingly choreographed movement, Shaina, Laila, and Maya charged on to the plain. With skill and accuracy, the lionesses attacked the adolescent gazelle. Because of his tremendous speed, they couldn't capture him- in fact, they didn't even try. Instead, the three lionesses herded him straight to where Nadia patiently waited- straight into the arms of the one who would destroy him. With a powerful pounce, Nadia bounded out of hiding and clenched the young gazelle's rump in her powerful jaws and flung him to the ground. In a singular movement, she had brought down a stunning animal that was significantly faster than she. Nadia and her friends had taken advantage of the pride of the young gazelle. He had believed, wrongly, that since he had reached his full height, he was able to leave the safety of the herd, that his strength would protect him.

The lion is one of God's most revered creations. Both beautiful and deadly, it has long been a symbol of strength and power. The lion does not succeed in a hunt because of superior speed but as a result of tactics and planning. She knows the time at which her prey will be the most vulnerable-she does not attack in broad daylight, but at dusk, when she will be more difficult to spot and can better blend into the scenery. The lion's success lies in her ability to catch her prey off-guard, to attack when they are vulnerable and unprepared to flee. [119]

This story is a sobering reminder of the tactics of our enemy, Satan. Just as the lioness attacked the gazelle at dusk when he was away from the herd, Satan plans his assault for the time and place when we are at our weakest.

The lionesses played off the gazelle's pride and used his speed to lure him into their trap. Satan uses these same tactics.

Peter warns us about the enemy prowling around:

> Be alert and of sober mind. Your enemy the devil prowls around like a roaring lion looking for someone to devour. Resist him, standing firm in the faith, because you know that the family of believers throughout the world is undergoing the same kind of sufferings. (1 Pt 5:8-9)

Satan admits that he is roaming around looking for someone to trick, to deceive, to manipulate. In Job, the Lord talks to him: "The Lord said to Satan, 'Where have you come from?' Satan answered the Lord, 'From roaming throughout the earth, going back and forth on it'" (Job 1:7).

For Eve, Satan took the form of a snake instead of a lion. Ever since he misled Eve in the garden of Eden, he has continued to stick his fangs into people. His knows us well and plays off of our weaknesses, striking at vulnerable times such as when we are tired, lonely, or proud. He concocts a plan tailored specifically to attack us at the optimum time and place for his benefit. His bite comes in many different shapes and sizes.

Let's examine some examples in the Bible.

- Was it his bite that roused Herod the Great to kill the babies in Bethlehem?
- Was it his acrimonious attack that persuaded the high official in the Persian Empire, Haman, to suggest the decree that would kill Esther and destroy the Jewish people?
- Was it his poisonous strike that coaxed Judas to betray our Lord?
- Was it his venomous assault that persuaded the Jews in Philadelphia to harass the Christians?

Although the enemy is a defeated foe, he is a formidable opponent. His goal is to thwart God's plan of salvation and to prevent people from spending eternity with God in heaven. The enemy is actively working against us in ways we may not realize.

The Roman Empire often sent a community of Jewish families to colonize a city. This fact may explain the influential number of Jews in Philadelphia. The government allowed the Jews to worship as they pleased. Satan used this group of Jews to impede the efforts of the church. The Jewish synagogue leaders reported the Christians as infidels and traitors to the Roman authorities, citing the fact that the Christians refused to worship Caesar as God. They turned them in as atheists, exposing that they refused to worship the pagan gods. This duplicity led to persecution by the Roman authorities.

Jesus called these treacherous Jews "a synagogue of Satan" because their actions carried out the evil plan of the enemy. They were playing into the devil's hand. Jesus was chiding the source of the plan, Satan.

Similarly, when Jesus first predicted his death, Peter rebuked Him. Jesus responded by revealing the source of evil, Satan:

> From that time on Jesus began to explain to his disciples that
> he must go to Jerusalem and suffer many things at the hands
> of the elders, the chief priests and the teachers of the law, and
> that he must be killed and on the third day be raised to life.
> Peter took him aside and began to rebuke him. "Never, Lord!"
> he said. "This shall never happen to you!"
> Jesus turned and said to Peter, "Get behind me, Satan! You are
> a stumbling block to me; you do not have in mind the concerns
> of God, but merely human concerns." (Mt 16:21-23)

Satan still uses people to accomplish his devilish ends. The good news is that we can take this advice from James, brother of Jesus: "Resist the devil and he will flee from you" (Jas 4:7).

We need to pray for help and guidance to defeat this old foe. One preacher illustrated it this way: When Satan comes knocking at your door, send Jesus to answer it.

Jesus assures the church at Philadelphia, just as He declares to us, that our victory is sure in the Lord. Satan and his followers are defeated by Christ and will have to "come and fall down at your feet and acknowledge that I have loved you" (Rv 3:9).

What tactics could the enemy use to entice the Jews to harass the Christians? Jealousy? Anger? What other strategies?

What is your perception of Satan?

Do you feel there are times when the enemy is taking advantage of you?

How do you, in the words of James, "resist the devil?"

Since you have kept my command to endure patiently,
I will also keep you from the hour of trial that
is going to come on the whole world
to test the inhabitants of the earth.
I am coming soon.
Hold on to what you have,
so that no one will take your crown.
The one who is victorious I will make a
pillar in the temple of my God.
Never again will they leave it.
Revelation 3:10-12

PILLARS OF THE CHURCH

The cities of Asia Minor were showcases containing beautiful buildings. The pagans built spectacular temples to pacify and impress the gods. Their thought was that if they pleased a god or goddess, then he or she would richly bless them and their city.

As we discovered on our first stop to Ephesus, followers of Artemis boasted of their splendid physical structures and the elaborate temple constructed for her worship. Artemis's temple was one of the wonders of the ancient world. Its grandeur demonstrated the city's affluence, opulence, and influence.

Jesus reminds the church in Philadelphia and us today, "Let the one who boasts, boast in the Lord" (1 Cor 1:31). The living God is a God who delights in His people, not in lavish temples and monuments.

Unlike handmade idols carved out of wood or molded out of metal, our God is heard and not seen. He speaks to us and invites us to be His temple: "And in him you too are being built together to become a dwelling in which God lives by his Spirit" (Eph 2:22). As unbelievable as it may have seemed to the idolaters of that day and to us today, this is a very simple statement. God is unimpressed by splendid structures and impressive leaders. God finds the most desirable place to dwell is in the hearts of His believers: "Do you not know that your bodies are temples of the Holy Spirit?" (1 Cor 6:19). The living God is a God who desires to dwell in our bodies, not in a "wonder of the world."

Jesus informs the church at Philadelphia that those who overcome will be made pillars of the church. In Galatians 2:9, Paul refers to "James, Peter and John, those reputed to be pillars." To this day, we call someone who is active and influential a "pillar" of that church. These saints in Philadelphia became supporting posts and permanent fixtures in the house of the Lord.

The letter goes on to say that "never again will they leave it" (Rv 3:12). These parishioners lived in fear of an earthquake. They knew the horror of running out into the open to escape falling buildings. They understood the devastation and difficulty of rebuilding from the rubble. They keenly felt the loss of homes, businesses, and loved ones. The reassurance that they would not be forced to leave a person or a place they loved took on a special meaning to them.

Jesus tenderly addresses their specific fears with promises greater than anyone can imagine. He assures them that their reward is worth the price of their endurance.

The pagan believers made sacrifices to the gods to get something in return. What are the challenges of explaining the worship of the true God to these pagans?

What does it mean to be a pillar of the church?

How does it make you feel that God values us so much that He wants us as His Church?

How does this make you want to live differently?

*I will write on them the name of my God
and the name of the city of my God, the new Jerusalem,
which is coming down out of heaven from my God;
and I will also write on them my new name.
Whoever has ears,
let them hear what the Spirit says to the churches.
Revelation 3:12-13*

A NEW NAME

The Asia Minor city of Philadelphia shares its name with one of my favorite cities in the United States. William Penn, governor of the colony of Pennsylvania, chose the site at the confluence of the Schuylkill and Delaware rivers to be his capital city. Through careful design and planning, Penn hoped to avoid many of the problems that plagued cities of the Old World. He envisioned a city with a rural feel that allowed residents to have more room for their homes. This spaciousness was intended to combat the sanitation, public health, overcrowding, and fire issues prevalent in Europe. To this end, he designed the city with five major squares to provide for what we now deem "green space." He made the roads wide and enlarged the size of individual residential plots.

Penn, a religious pacifist, came to America to conduct what he called a "Holy Experiment" to create a city in which people of all faiths and cultures lived together in religious tolerance. He called the city Philadelphia, meaning the City of Brotherly Love, combining the Greek words for love *"phileo"* and brother *"adelphos."* [120]

Over the last few centuries, Philadelphia has evolved into a city known for its rough edge and rabid sports fans. The city's vibe carries very recognizable traits—some more brotherly than others. Here are a few identified by Philly travel and food blogger Alicia Raeburn:

1. Everything you own just happens to be Eagles green. Look, it's not intentional, mostly.
2. You know that there are no heroes, only hoagies.
3. Try walking into any store serving sandwiches in Philadelphia and telling them that you want your sandwich as a "hero" and you're likely to get ignored.
4. In the summer, you go to the shore, not the beach.

5. You can recount exactly where you were and what you were doing the day the Eagles won the Super Bowl. 5. You know that Wawa is the perfect place for every meal and every occasion.

6. You know how to pronounce Schuylkill and Passyunk properly. You say "SKOO-kill" and "PASH-unk."

7. Summer desserts have nothing to do with ice cream and everything to do with water ice.

8. You only eat cheesesteaks when you have non-Philly friends visiting. No one from Philadelphia eats cheesesteaks all the time.[121]

The name of the city of Philadelphia in Revelation evolved also. Its name was changed three times. In the words of Jesus, it received a "new name" two times. He focuses on this theme as one familiar to these residents.

The first name, Philadelphia, commemorates the loyalty of the brothers Attalus II and Eumenes II, the king of Lydia. Attalus served first as his brother's assistant and later as commander of the forces from Pergamum. His love and devotion were renowned throughout the world, and it's for this reason the city was originally named Philadelphia.[122]

In 17 AD, a massive earthquake hit the area, damaging the city of Sardis upon impact. Philadelphia received numerous severe aftershocks causing extensive and repeated damage to homes and buildings and traumatizing city residents. The Roman senator and historian Tacitus wrote that Emperor Tiberius came to Philadelphia's aid by excusing them from paying tribute to Rome for a period of five years and by providing financial aid to the city. In gratitude, the residents renamed their city Neocaesarea, meaning New Caesar.

During the reign of Emperor Vespasian, the founder of the Flavian dynasty, the city was given the great honor to take on the epithet of Flavia. Again, a new name was written for this city. Neocaesarea, which was originally Philadelphia, now had another new name, Flavia. [123]

The city had given itself three names to honor and flatter three men who are now all but forgotten. Their power and impact on the city, its inhabitants, and the world lasted only a short time.

Jesus also promises to write three new names on the faithful. However, his names are powerful. The name of Christ saves. The Bible shows us the eternal strength of His name.

Gospel writer and apostle Matthew tells us that Mary "will give birth to a son, and you are to give him the name Jesus because he will save his people from their sins" (Mt 1:21).

The apostle Paul assures us that "everyone who calls on the name of the Lord will be saved" (Rom 10:13).

Dr. Luke, the author of the history of the early church in Acts, explains, "Salvation is found in no one else, for there is no other name under heaven given to mankind by which we must be saved" (Acts 4:12).

The church at Philadelphia was fragile. The congregation struggled to impact the pagan culture in which they were immersed. They lived in fear of persecution and natural disaster. They did not have the same glowing reputation awarded to other churches, such as Sardis. By human standards, this church was a failure.

However, due to their devoted endurance and loyal obedience, the Lord Jesus Christ wrote His new name on them. He made them pillars in the church of the living God. This underappreciated church earned the highest commendation from the highest source.

How do you think the congregation at Philadelphia received this letter?

Which parts would have been particularly comforting to them?

Have you ever felt underappreciated when doing the Lord's work?

How do Jesus's tender words encourage you?

Out of His love for us, Jesus calls each of us to be his living temple. How does that affect your actions?

Do you feel the call to be that temple?

What is one takeaway and insight from the letter to the church at Philadelphia that resonates with you?

In what way might that insight be calling you into a new way of being and doing?

THE SELF-SUFFICIENT CHURCH IN THE SELF-RELIANT CITY: LAODICEA

L aodicea, located at the eastern end of the Lycus Valley, was one of the most prosperous cities in Asia Minor. The city's wealth derived from its strategic location on a crucial trade route.

Its abundance of commerce was a catalyst for prosperity in other areas. Because of the profusion of money and trading, the city became a major banking center. Black wool, a prized regional commodity, was sold as a raw material. The citizens of Laodicea also used the wool to make fine black woolen cloth and garments that were sold around the world. A medical school specializing in eye treatments was started in the city. A particularly popular treatment was a healing eye salve.

The city's wealth and its resulting pride were legendary. As was true with many of the cities in this area, Laodicea was in an area prone to earthquakes. The buildings and homes there were often damaged and had to be rebuilt. In 60 AD, after a large earthquake destroyed a large portion of the city, Emperor Nero offered the city financial aid to aid the rebuilding process. The self-sufficient Laodiceans refused the assistance. [124]

The city boasted a strong list of assets. However, it had one major liability – water. The lack of a viable source of fresh water was the city's biggest challenge. The rivers were too polluted to provide this precious resource. The closest springs were miles away. Therefore, the city pumped water in terracotta pipes from over four miles away. To prevent infiltration from enemies, these pipes were buried underground.

The water contained large amounts of calcium. Thick deposits of this element built up in the pipes over the years, restricting water flow and requiring frequent repairs to the plumbing.

Laodicea was one of three cities located near each other in the Lycus River Valley. The other two-thirds of the sistership were famous for their exceptional water.

Hierapolis, located six miles away, was a city of hot springs. Its healing waters were ingested for their minerals and soaked in for their medicinal and therapeutic values.

Colosse, the other city of the triumvirate, was known for its cold, refreshing streams and waterfalls. The letter to the Colossians in the Bible was written to the church in this city.

The southern kingdom of Judah fell to the Babylonians, causing many Jews to be deported to Susa. Years later, Antiochus the Great, king of Babylon, sent two thousand Jewish families to Asia Minor. Many of them settled in Laodicea. By the first century, the Jewish population in that city alone had grown to over four thousand families. This number was verified by the amount of their temple apportionment. Jewish men were required to pay a temple tax of half a shekel to Jerusalem each year. When Lucius Valerius Flaccus, governor of Asia, confiscated the offering, it weighed over twenty pounds. With all males paying half a shekel, that equates to over four thousand Jewish men. This large synagogue of Jews coexisted peaceably with the empire. The Roman consul allowed the Jews to worship and observe their holy rituals without interference.

Antiochus II founded the city and named it in honor of his wife and cousin, Laodice. Despite appearances, their relationship was not a close one, and Antiochus divorced her and banished her and their children to Ephesus. Antiochus then married Berenice, daughter of the king of Egypt, for political reasons. When the Egyptian king died four years later, Antiochus divorced Berenice and remarried Laodice. Shortly after their reunion, Laodice poisoned Antiochus. After Antiochus's death, Laodice murdered Berenice and her son.

The church in Laodicea also had relationship issues. It was proud, unsaved, and self-sufficient. At the time of the Revelation letters, this church was probably not undergoing a tremendous amount of persecution. The church members were not extremely different from their pagan persecutors and were, therefore, spared the harassment.

Christ sends two letters with no commendations – one to Sardis and one to Laodicea. However, He did say that Sardis had a few faithful remaining in the congregation. Laodicea does not even seem to have this much going for it. What made this church so distasteful to Jesus?

Let's venture into the last city of our voyage and see what lessons we can learn from this letter.

To the angel of the church in Laodicea write:
These are the words of the Amen,
the faithful and true witness,
the ruler of God's creation.
Revelation 3:14

UNDERESTIMATION

Lonzo Green, the country music great, visited his relatives in Tennessee. His young nephew Jimmy excitedly told his friends about the star who was going to be in their midst. One of Jimmy's friends was particularly excited to meet the celebrity to solicit his help. This friend had an old, out-of-tune guitar with a string as its strap. No one had taken the time to teach him how to tune his instrument. Certain that Lonzo would be willing to help, Jimmy invited his friend to meet his uncle.

When the friend arrived, Jimmy's parents would not allow him inside their home. They deemed him an inferior companion for their son. He was from the "wrong side of the tracks." The star and the wannabe guitarist sat on the curb outside Jimmy's home. Lonzo carefully placed his fingers on the frets, demonstrating how to tune the instrument.

Lonzo, who had also felt the sting of poverty and prejudice in his childhood, saw promise and talent in this young man. He looked beyond the ragged clothes and disheveled hair to see a determined budding musician. The two spent the afternoon singing and strumming together.

Jimmy's parents judged this young man unworthy to enter their home and lives. Had they looked at him through caring eyes, they would have seen a shy, gentle, ambitious boy who needed some guidance and acceptance. Instead, they underestimated him. Jimmy's friend, Elvis Presley, had a brighter future than anything Jimmy's parents could have imagined. [125]

The church in Laodicea was also guilty of underestimating. This congregation was led astray by false teachers from their sister city congregation in Colossae. The teachers claimed that Jesus was not God. Their teaching alleged that He was no better than a created being. The sacrilege regarded Christ as little more than an angel. The apostle Paul realized the importance of acknowledging Christ's deity and wrote a detailed letter to address this issue decisively. This heresy must have traveled down the road to infiltrate the congregation at Laodicea. Paul wanted to verify and validate the holiness of Christ to the Laodiceans as well:

> Give my greetings to the brothers and sisters at Laodicea, and to Nympha and the church in her house. After this letter has been read to you, see that it is also read in the church of the Laodiceans and that you in turn read the letter from Laodicea. (Col 4:16)

Here is what Paul said to both churches and to us today concerning Jesus:

> The Son is the image of the invisible God, the firstborn over all creation. For in him all things were created: things in heaven and on earth, visible and invisible, whether thrones or powers or rulers or authorities; all things have been created through him and for him. He is before all things, and in him all things hold together. And he is the head of the body, the church; he is the beginning and the firstborn from among the dead, so that in everything he might have the supremacy. For God was pleased to have all his fullness dwell in him, and through him to reconcile to himself all things, whether things on earth or things in heaven, by making peace through his blood, shed on the cross. (Col 1:15-20)

Jesus addresses this boldly and clearly from the beginning of this letter. He calls Himself the "Amen." Amen is the Hebrew affirmation meaning "so be it." It validates and supports. It guarantees certainty and veracity.[126] He is communicating that His words are absolute truth. The Bible records Jesus saying "verily, verily" over twenty times when teaching profound lessons. This letter is the only time in the Bible in which "Amen" is used as a formal name. Calling Himself the "Amen" conveys the fact that all Jesus says is true and right and that He, Himself, is truth and sovereignty.[127]

Paul writes that the promises of God are sealed through Jesus further verifying His supreme status: "For no matter how many promises God has made, they are 'Yes' in Christ. And so through Him, the 'Amen' is spoken by us to the glory of God" (2 Cor 1:20).

Jesus assures us that He is the "the faithful and true witness" (Rv 3:14). His words to this church and throughout time will always be exact to the will of the Father.

He goes on to describe himself as the "ruler of God's creation" (Rv 3:14). The word "ruler" connotes that He is the source of God's creation. John describes this in his Gospel:

> Through him all things were made; without him nothing was made that has been made. In him was life, and that life was the light of all mankind. The light shines in the darkness, and the darkness has not overcome it. (Jn 1:3-5)

A correct understanding of the deity of Christ was paramount to these believers as they shaped the early church. It is no less vital to churches and individuals today. Denigrating Jesus lessens the impact and significance of His sacrifice.

Jesus loved us so much that He was willing to leave the glory of heaven to meet us here on earth. He endured suffering and shame and surrendered His life for us. He endured the torture of the cross and, most agonizingly, separation from the Father so that He could pay the price for our sins. He paid a great price to enable us to live in heaven with Him for eternity. To belittle Christ lessens the glory and the hope of His resurrection.

For this reason, Jesus introduces Himself by decisively stating His sovereignty and authority. This was particularly important in cities with tepid faith and doubt in the deity of Christ. Jesus leaves the churches at Colosse and Laodicea no reason to underestimate His power.

Why is it important for the Lord to start this letter stating His sovereignty?

How does this affect the reader's attitude about the contents of the letter?

Christians can err on both sides. Some believers focus on the deity of Christ so much that it is difficult for them to have a relationship with Him.

Others are too casual in their view of the Lord. Where do your beliefs fall on this scale?

Prayerfully consider if you need to adjust your beliefs about Christ's deity.

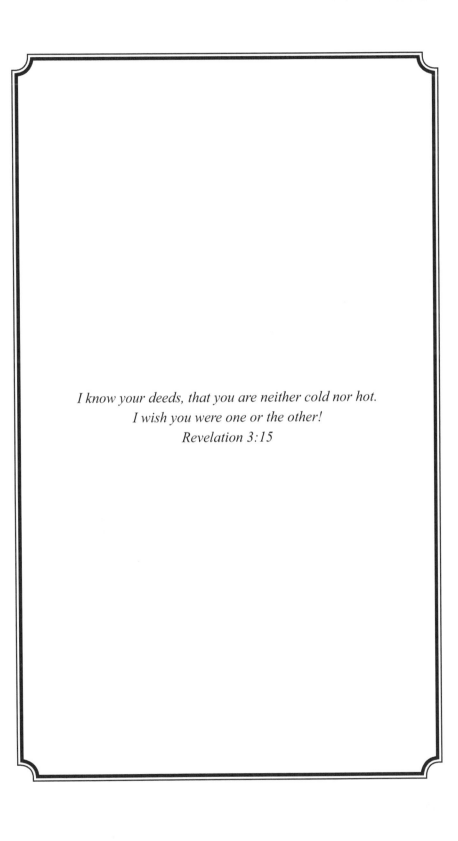

I know your deeds, that you are neither cold nor hot.
I wish you were one or the other!
Revelation 3:15

COLD AND HOT IN THE LYCUS VALLEY

A townsperson returned after a long trip. He asked a fellow church member if they still had the same minister. He recalled, "I remember that he would bang his fist on the pulpit and tell us that if we did not repent, we would go to hell."

"No, that minister has moved on. We have a new minister now. Everyone likes him," his fellow parishioner replied.

"What is his message?" the first man asked.

"He bangs his fist on the pulpit and tells us that if we do not repent, we will go to hell."

"I don't understand. What is different from the former minister?"

The parishioner replied, "When the new minister warns us, he has tears in his eyes."

God did not intend for us to live out our faith life with dry eyes and a lukewarm heart.

The people of Laodicea understood the disappointment of a lukewarm reception. In the Lycus Valley, there were three cities. Hierapolis was famous for its therapeutic springs. Hot sparkling waters rose from deep pools on the city-plateau; they crossed in narrow, raised channels built from calcium carbonate deposits and spilled over the incrustation. The cliff was in full view of Laodicea, six miles away. Its reflections of light and color were unspeakably beautiful. The waters were said to be 95 degrees Fahrenheit. [128]

Colosse boasted cold fresh streams of delicious drinking water. This refreshing water was pure and life-giving.

Laodicea had neither of these assets. The city did not have the benefit of hot therapeutic pools. The city also lacked cold refreshing springs. With its location in a valley, it had a difficult time accessing a healthy supply of drinking water. The city had its water piped in from snow-covered mountain streams located miles away. By the time freshwater reached the Laodiceans, it was "neither cold nor hot." Jesus chose these words specifically for this congregation because He knew that they would instantly identify with the frustration and disappointment of "lukewarm." They knew the situation Jesus was describing and could relate easily to it.

When the Lord was asked the greatest commandment, He replied,

> "'Love the Lord your God with **all** your heart and with **all** your soul and with **all** your mind and with **all** your strength.' The second is this: 'Love your neighbor as yourself.' There is no commandment greater than these." (Mk 12:30-31 italics and bold added) [129]

The Lord commands us to love Him with *all* our heart, soul, mind, and strength. He is not asking for a tepid, half-hearted affection. He does not desire our unenthusiastic devotion. He exhorts us to passionately worship and zealously serve Him. If the greatest commandment is to love the Lord with all our heart, the greatest sin would be to not love Him with this passion.

The opposite of love can be defined as indifference, not hate. If you do not love a person, thing, or idea, in certain situations you may hate it. However, most often, you have little or no emotion for the things you do not love. For example, I do not love sweet potatoes. Neither do I hate them. My feelings are blasé and neutral.

Lukewarm apathy is more damaging than stronger emotions like hate. These strong emotions possess passion and feeling. Apathy lacks energy.

The Lord requires more than indifference from His church. He calls us to a vivacious and active love for Him and our brothers and sisters. He longs for us to sincerely repent of our sins. He yearns for our hearts to ardently seek Him. He desires our genuine concern for others. He requires us to boldly take a stand for the Gospel.

Jesus writes that He knows their deeds, and yet he only has criticism for them. Laodicea is the only congregation where knowing their deeds leads only to condemnation without a single word of praise. This criticism is due to their apathetic, indifferent, tearless, service to Him.

Have you been part of a church or organization that served the Lord in a lethargic manner?
Describe it.

What can you do to make a difference?

Have you been part of something in which the members enthusiastically and passionately worked for the glory of God?
Describe it.

What are the lukewarm areas in your life that could use more energy and vitality?

How can you invigorate them?

So, because you are lukewarm—
neither hot nor cold—
I am about to spit you out of my mouth.
Revelation 3:16

SICKENING COMPROMISE

Paul Harvey tells this story.

> But passengers say the takeoff was already delayed when the
> pilot came on the intercom to announce:
> "There's a warning light for the thermal expander valve on the
> number two engine and I will not fly until it is replaced. Please
> return to the terminal waiting room."
> The passengers were off the plane only ten minutes when they
> were told to get aboard again.
> The passenger from Hartland, Minnesota asked a flight attendant,
> "did they get the new thermal expander valve already?"
> And the attendant said, "My land, no! There's not one of those
> things within a thousand miles. They got us a new pilot."[130]

The new pilot was willing to compromise. He was lukewarm about
safety. His apathy could have fatal results.

Christ was sickened by the compromising, lukewarm church at Laodicea.
The lack of devotion and zeal nauseated Him. The word used for "spit" can
be translated as "vomit." This congregation made Him ill.

One of the reasons Christ was so disgusted and wanted to expel them
was their influence on other followers. When believers see a robber steal
from a bank, they know it is wrong. However, when a believer justifies
wrongfully taking something, other believers could deem that because a
Christian did it, this form of stealing is appropriate. Tepid Christians can
lead others astray by providing excuses for sin.

Christ told this truth. He warned that the punishment for Christians who
cause others to sin by their words or their deeds is severe:

> If anyone causes one of these little ones—those who believe
> in me—to stumble, it would be better for them to have a large

millstone hung around their neck and to be drowned in the depths of the sea. (Mt 18:6)

Christ vehemently disagrees with listless Christianity. He wants His followers to passionately take a stand in one camp or the other.

A story was told of a man in the Civil War who could not decide which side he was on. He wore a gray Confederate jacket and blue Union trousers. He was shot in the heart by a Union sharpshooter and in the backside by a Confederate sniper.

Back when Queen Jezebel and King Ahab ruled God's chosen people in the Northern Tribe of Israel, their devotion to God was lukewarm, similar to the congregation in Laodicea. They half-heartedly served the Lord while also worshiping the idols Baal and Asherah. Now was the time for these people of God to decisively commit to His service. Out of His grace and love for His people, God sent the prophet Elijah to demonstrate the omnipotence of the Lord by committing a spectacular miracle and reminding them of the supremacy of the one true God.

> "Now summon the people from all over Israel to meet me on Mount Carmel. And bring the four hundred and fifty prophets of Baal and the four hundred prophets of Asherah, who eat at Jezebel's table."

> So, Ahab sent word throughout all Israel and assembled the prophets on Mount Carmel. Elijah went before the people and said, "How long will you waver between two opinions? If the Lord is God, follow him; but if Baal is God, follow him."

> But the people said nothing.

> Then Elijah said to them, "I am the only one of the Lord's prophets left, but Baal has four hundred and fifty prophets. Get two bulls for us. Let Baal's prophets choose one for themselves, and let them cut it into pieces and put it on the wood but not set fire to it. I will prepare the other bull and put it on the wood but not set fire to it. Then you call on the name of your god, and I will call on the name of the Lord. The god who answers by fire—he is God."

Then all the people said, "What you say is good."

Elijah said to the prophets of Baal, "Choose one of the bulls and prepare it first, since there are so many of you. Call on the name of your god, but do not light the fire." So, they took the bull given them and prepared it.

Then they called on the name of Baal from morning till noon. "Baal, answer us!" they shouted. But there was no response; no one answered. And they danced around the altar they had made.

At noon Elijah began to taunt them. "Shout louder!" he said. "Surely he is a god! Perhaps he is deep in thought, or busy, or traveling. Maybe he is sleeping and must be awakened." So, they shouted louder and slashed themselves with swords and spears, as was their custom, until their blood flowed. Midday passed, and they continued their frantic prophesying until the time for the evening sacrifice. But there was no response, no one answered, no one paid attention.

Then Elijah said to all the people, "Come here to me." They came to him, and he repaired the altar of the Lord, which had been torn down. Elijah took twelve stones, one for each of the tribes descended from Jacob, to whom the word of the Lord had come, saying, "Your name shall be Israel." With the stones he built an altar in the name of the Lord, and he dug a trench around it large enough to hold two seahs of seed. He arranged the wood, cut the bull into pieces and laid it on the wood. Then he said to them, "Fill four large jars with water and pour it on the offering and on the wood."

"Do it again," he said, and they did it again.

"Do it a third time," he ordered, and they did it the third time. The water ran down around the altar and even filled the trench.

At the time of sacrifice, the prophet Elijah stepped forward and prayed: "Lord, the God of Abraham, Isaac and Israel, let it be known today that you are God in Israel and that I am your servant and have done all these things at your command. Answer me, Lord, answer me, so these people will know that you, Lord, are God, and that you are turning their hearts back again."

Then the fire of the Lord fell and burned up the sacrifice, the wood, the stones and the soil, and also licked up the water in the trench.

When all the people saw this, they fell prostrate and cried, "The Lord—he is God! The Lord—he is God!" (1Kgs 18:19-39)

The Israelites fervently declared their passionate respect and love for the Lord and repented of their tepid dedication. Jesus calls the congregation at Laodicea to this same type of devotion and worship. He wants them to demonstrate the zeal and commitment of the Israelites when they decisively shouted, "The Lord—He is God! The Lord—He is God!"

Why was it so difficult for the Laodicean church to take a stand for Christ?

Information from historians and from the Bible reveals that the church in Laodicea underwent little or no harassment even though neighboring churches endured severe persecution. What was the difference?

What is the spiritual temperature reading for your church?

What is your personal spiritual temperature?

If you need to raise it, what would you do differently?

You say, "I am rich;
I have acquired wealth and do not need a thing."
Revelation 3:17

TOO RICH TO NEED ANYTHING

The following is the prologue to the film *The Path to Nazi Genocide*. The documentary seeks to understand the evolution and unconscionable acceptance of Adolph Hitler's harsh and rogue regime:

> The First World War, from 1914 to 1918, was fought throughout Europe and beyond. It became known as "the war to end all wars." It cast an immense shadow on tens of millions of people. "This is not war," one wounded soldier wrote home. "It is the ending of the world."
>
> Half of all French men aged twenty to thirty-two at the war's outbreak were dead by its conclusion. More than one-third of all German men aged nineteen to twenty-two were killed. Millions of veterans were crippled in body and in spirit. Advances in killing technology included the use of poison gas. Under the pressure of unending carnage, governments toppled and great empires dissolved. It was a cataclysm that darkened the world's view of humanity and its future. Winston Churchill said the war left "a crippled, broken world."
>
> In the aftermath of World War I, Germans struggled to understand their country's uncertain future. Citizens faced poor economic conditions, skyrocketing unemployment, political instability, and profound social change. While downplaying more extreme goals, Adolf Hitler and the Nazi Party offered simple solutions to Germany's problems, exploiting people's fears, frustrations, and hopes to win broad support.[131]

When parents are unable to feed a child, they ask someone to help them. When a population feels oppressed or enslaved, it seeks a liberator.

When people are in need, they search for a savior. This blatant example in Germany illustrates desperation and its consequences. Nazi newsreels boasted of a New Germany where food would be abundant, jobs would be plentiful, new roads would open, and the German military would again be great despite Treaty of Versailles edicts. German citizens were searching. They so urgently desired relief that they were willing to overlook Hitler's radical and extreme ideas to find solutions to their personal problems. They were looking for rescue.

On the contrary, Laodicea was a wealthy city. They did not seek help. The apathy and lack of commitment to Christ in that church was likely triggered by its self-sufficiency. Because of their economic prosperity, the parishioners did not desire a redeemer. They felt as if they had everything they wanted. They did not feel the need for a savior.

In 60 AD the city was destroyed by an earthquake. The Roman Empire offered financial assistance and tax abatement to the cities in the area that suffered damage. All of these accepted the help except Laodicea. Tacitus, the Roman historian, wrote, "Laodicea arose from the ruins by the strength of her own resources, and with no help from us." [132]

Most of the citizens, even the Christians, in Laodicea were lacking in nothing. The economy was booming. Not only were their basic needs met, but they were rich. The city was a banking center, a political center, and an industrial hub. These citizens thought they had it all.

Solomon, with his gift of wisdom from the Lord, understood that extreme economic prosperity and severe financial poverty can hinder a person's relationship with God:

> Two things I ask of you, Lord;
> do not refuse me before I die: Keep falsehood and lies far from me;
> give me neither poverty nor riches, but give me only my daily bread.
> Otherwise, I may have too much and disown you and say, "Who is the Lord?" Or I may become poor and steal,
> and so dishonor the name of my God.
> (Pr 30:7-9)

Solomon's verses describe these two groups. The post-World War I Germans had too little. Because of their extreme poverty and desperation, they acquiesced to a leader who dishonored the name of God. Conversely, the Laodicean congregation had too much. Their riches hindered them from passionately pursuing a relationship with the Lord.

Jesus knew this danger and gave this warning:

> No one can serve two masters. Either you will hate the one and love the other, or you will be devoted to the one and despise the other. You cannot serve both God and money. (Mt 6:24-26)

The church in Laodicea, as with some churches today, hesitated to boldly proclaim the truth of the Gospel for fear of offending people, appearing provincial, or driving out members. The congregation was afraid to take a stand for Biblical truths. Their diluted message was lukewarm.

> Whatever you do, work at it with all your heart, as working for the Lord, not for human masters, since you know that you will receive an inheritance from the Lord as a reward. It is the Lord Christ you are serving. (Col 3:23-24)

There was little difference between Laodicean Christians and the city's heathens. They valued their status in the community and their wealthy lifestyle more than they loved Christ. They were not willing to give up the money and the prestige to serve the Lord. Paul warns Timothy about the dangers of the love of money in his letter:

> But if we have food and clothing, we will be content with that. Those who want to get rich fall into temptation and a trap and into many foolish and harmful desires that plunge people into ruin and destruction. For the love of money is a root of all kinds of evil. Some people, eager for money, have wandered from the faith and pierced themselves with many griefs. (1Tim 16:8-12)

The Germans sought a solution because of their great need. Tragically, they were deceived and misled by an ungodly leader with horrible intentions.

The citizens and church members in Laodicea did not seek any solutions because of their great abundance. They believed they had what they needed. Therefore, they were resistant to fully pursuing a fervent relationship with Christ.

Just as the city of Laodicea was too proud and self-sufficient to accept help from the Roman Empire, the Christians were too self-reliant to put their faith in Christ.

Why is it harder to pursue Christ when situations are favorable?

Have you been involved in a church or organization that experienced great success through worldly measures but was hollow on the inside?

Have you experienced a time when you felt self-sufficient, and your faith faltered?

How can you guard against this?

What other takeaways can you find in the stories of the Germans and the Laodiceans?

But you do not realize that you are wretched,
pitiful, poor, blind, and naked.
I counsel you to buy from me gold refined
in the fire, so you can become rich:
and white clothes to wear,
so you can cover your shameful nakedness;
and salve to put on your eyes, so you can see.
Those whom I love I rebuke and discipline.
So be earnest, and repent.
Revelation 3:17-19

POOR, BLIND, AND NAKED

Laodicea was a proud and ostentatious city. Three main sources of this pride were its banking center, its medical school and eye salve, and its prized black cloth.

Perhaps it was the abundance of money in Laodicea that launched it into becoming a leading banking center. It could also have been its location on the trade route as a place to exchange eastern money into western currency. By 51 BC the city already had a reputation for finance. Ancient texts document that Cicero cashed his bills of credit in that year.[133] The city's coinage portrayed its pretentious attitude by picturing a cornucopia overflowing with corn and fruit. The city boasted some of the wealthiest residents in the ancient world. These flamboyant benefactors underwrote elaborate public works projects using their own personal funds.[134]

The second source of the city's pride was derived from its world-class medical school. The school produced a world-famous eye salve developed from the area's zinc and aluminum. The medical school shipped "Tephra Phrygian," an eye powder, in tablet form throughout the Roman Empire. The tablets were ground and applied to the eyes.[135] Recent research has determined that the compound contained no medicinal value. However, at the time this coveted remedy was pricey and in high demand.

The third celebrated commodity of Laodicea was black wool. Although today we place a negative connotation on the term "black sheep," these animals were renowned throughout the Roman Empire. The Greek geographer Strabo included the cloth woven from this wool as one of the goods listed in the Edict of Emperor Diocletian, in which he limited the maximum price charged for select pieces of valuable merchandise. It was known by the name "Laodicean wool." The tunics produced using this cloth were called "*trimata*." The city, synonymous with these tunics, was sometimes referred to as Trimataria.[136] Interestingly, this area is still known for its clothing industry.

Jesus directly attacks all three of these areas.

He chides the congregation for their spiritual poverty, advising them to buy His gold which has been refined in His fire. In Biblical times and today, purifying gold requires heating the element to over 1000 degrees Celsius. The impurities rise to the top as slag and are scraped off and tossed aside.

The Lord's methods of purification are even more intense. In Proverbs 17:3, the rich and wise Solomon advises, "The crucible for silver and the furnace for gold, but the Lord tests the heart." This verse shows a mature Christian walking with the Lord and enduring His tests. As the trials heat up, impure thoughts, motives, and actions surface. The sincere seeker removes these tainted traits. The hardships are not punitive. They are refining. With each ordeal, the believer grows closer to God.

The believers in Laodicea were not willing to go through the fire to refine and purify their faith. They were content with their present situation. They thought they were rich, but Jesus correctly notes their spiritual poverty.

Next, Jesus tells this group of Christians, in the city famous for its eye salve, that they are blind. The Gospel writer Matthew tells a story of two blind men whose spiritual discernment was as clear as 20/20 vision.

> As Jesus went on from there, two blind men followed him, calling out, "Have mercy on us, Son of David!"
> When he had gone indoors, the blind men came to him, and he asked them, "Do you believe that I am able to do this?"
> "Yes, Lord," they replied.
> Then he touched their eyes and said, "According to your faith let it be done to you"; and their sight was restored. Jesus warned them sternly, "See that no one knows about this." But they went out and spread the news about him all over that region. (Mt 9:27-31)

The blind men were among many with perfect sight. However, they were the only ones who could see that Jesus was Lord. They referred to Him as the "Son of David," a phrase referencing Him as the long-awaited Messiah. Those who were blind were the most able to see.

Unlike the discerning blind men, the Laodiceans were unable to see what was right in front of them. They put their trust in their technology and their advanced learning at places such as the University. Psalmist King David warned that trust should be put in the Creator, not the creation. Victory comes from the Lord, not from implements of battle.

> Now this I know:
> The Lord gives victory to his anointed.
> He answers him from his heavenly sanctuary
> with the victorious power of his right hand.
> Some trust in chariots and some in horses,
> but we trust in the name of the Lord our God.
> They are brought to their knees and fall,
> but we rise up and stand firm.
> Lord, give victory to the king!
> Answer us when we call!
> (Ps 20:6-9)

King David was a great and mighty warrior who had won many battles and conquered numerous foes. He could easily have put his trust in chariots and horses. However, he had a heart for God and knew the wisdom of putting his faith in the eternal, not the temporal.

Finally, to the residents of this city renowned for its black woolen cloth, Christ reveals their nakedness and advises them to wear white garments. The Gospel writer, Mark, describes Christ in His white garments: "His clothes became dazzling white, whiter than anyone in the world could bleach them" (Mk 9:3). Both Christians and pagans wore white garments to represent purity and celebrate festive occasions.

Jesus invites the Christians in Laodicea to come to Him and repent so that He can clothe them in robes of righteousness.

> I delight greatly in the Lord;
> my soul rejoices in my God.
> For he has clothed me with garments of salvation
> and arrayed me in a robe of his righteousness,
> as a bridegroom adorns his head like a priest,
> and as a bride adorns herself with her jewels.

(Is 61:10)

Jesus promises later in the book of Revelation, "they have washed their robes and made them white in the blood of the Lamb" (Rv 7:14). Only through Christ can the Laodiceans truly be rich, see clearly, and be clothed in righteousness.

Christ then exhorts them to "be earnest" and "repent." The phrase "be earnest" can also be translated as "be zealous," again exhorting them to be passionate for the Lord instead of lukewarm. The tense of the verb is present imperative, meaning that it is a continuous action. Christ tells them to keep their enthusiasm and passion for the Lord. The verb "repent" is in the aorist imperative, signifying one-time repentance and pivotal change of heart and attitude.[137]

Jesus shows the Laodicean believers the path to true lasting wealth, clear vision, and robes of righteousness by repenting and continually striving and hungering for a deeper relationship with the Lord.

Have you ever observed an organization or person who is confident in their success but actually deceiving themselves?

Have you ever settled for less and realized later that you missed the true prize?

How would you explain this to a member of the church at Laodicea?

How would you tell someone today of the true riches of Christ?

Here I am!
I stand at the door and knock.
Revelation 3:20

I STAND AT THE DOOR AND KNOCK

According to St. Paul's Cathedral website, William Holman-Hunt's *The Light of the World* is the most-traveled work of art in the world.[138] Holman-Hunt's started the painting at the age of twenty-one. It took him eight years to complete the piece. His goal was to have a "sermon in a frame." He endeavored to teach Biblical truths through his works of art. As the Tate Museum explains, "His new style of symbolic realism was intended to express Christian ideals."[139]

In *The Light of the World,* Jesus is pictured knocking on a door that obviously has not been opened recently. Ivy grows around the door's old and rusty hardware. Notably, the door does not contain a door handle. The symbolism that Holman-Hunt is attempting to convey is that a person must open his or her heart from the inside to let Jesus come in. Christ will never force His way into a person's life. He asks permission to enter and waits patiently for the invitation.

A few years later, Holman-Hunt painted a second version of the same picture with only minor changes. This one can be seen in the Manchester Art Gallery. Fifty years later, Holman-Hunt painted a third and larger version of his popular work. Due to cataracts and failing eyesight, he needed assistance to complete it.

In 1905, this third canvas was taken on a grand tour visiting Canada, South Africa, New Zealand, and Australia. The promoters boasted that four out of five people in Australia viewed the work. The exhibition was seen by millions of people, making it one of the most recognizable paintings of its day. Industrialist Charles Booth purchased the painting and donated it to St Paul's Cathedral in London.[140]

The picture that Jesus paints in the letter to the Laodiceans and that William Holman-Hunt attempted to capture on canvas is a lovely one. The

Creator of the universe is pursuing people. He is knocking on the door of the heart.

In His letter to the church at Philadelphia, He tells us that He holds the key. He has the ability and right to crash open the door. However, Jesus is serenely standing in anticipation of the door being opened to Him. He could use His power and might to force Himself on the Christians at Laodicea and on people today. However, He reserves the gifts of His salvation for those who allow him to come in.

What are the reasons the congregation at Laodicea might not have invited Jesus in?

What motives would cause people to hesitate today?

Have you invited Him to come in?

If not, what is holding you back?

If so, how is your life different because you opened the door?

How can others see evidence of the presence of Jesus in your life?

If anyone hears my voice and opens the door,
I will come in and eat with them,
and he with me.
Revelation 3:21

OPEN THE DOOR, AND COME IN, AND EAT

The saying "the sun never sets on the British Empire" demonstrated the breadth of British holdings around the globe between the eighteenth and twentieth centuries. Approximately 25 percent of the world's landmass was under the care of the British Crown. The saying referred to the fact that the empire covered so many different areas of the world that, at any time, there would be daylight in one of its territories.[141]

With the wealth and prestige of ruling all these different countries and territories came the daunting task of defending them. The British fighting forces were spread thin. One of the most challenging to secure was the American colony across the Atlantic Ocean. The British spent a fortune of money and manpower defending the colonists when the French settlers aided by the Native Americans attacked the British holdings in the French and Indian War. When the war ended, the Crown deemed it necessary to leave troops on the American shores not only defend the colonists but also to keep this rowdy group of subjects subjugated. From the Crown's perspective, the colonists should bear some of the burden for housing these troops.

Thus, the Quartering Act of 1765 was levied on the American colonies. The law mandated that colonies house and feed the British forces stationed in America.

> [Colonial Governors] could hire inns and vacant buildings as quarters for soldiers when regular barracks were unavailable. The law also required colonial governments to furnish the soldiers with firewood, bedding, candles, salt, vinegar, cooking utensils plus a daily ration of beer, cider, or rum. Furthermore, the Quartering Act authorized innkeepers to feed the soldiers at the colonies' expense. Americans saw the Quartering Act of 1765 as an attempt to force the colonists to pay for a standing army that they did not want.[142]

By 1770, most British soldiers were housed in barracks or commercial buildings paid for by the Crown.

When Americans today hear about the Quartering Act of 1765, they see it as an infringement on personal and property rights. They picture slovenly British soldiers bullying their way into innocent people's homes, eating their food, insulting their hosts, and taking advantage of their position. This image is not accurate.[143]

However, it was a true picture at one time in Laodicea. When Sulla was the dictator of Rome in 112-78 BC, Mithridates, the king of Pontus, warred against the Empire. The cities of Asia Minor, including Laodicea, were caught in the middle. Sulla put down the rebellion and pardoned the cities that supported Mithridates.

Plutarch, the Greek biographer, wrote that despite the exoneration, Sulla required five years of taxes paid in one sum, causing great economic strife in these cities. Laodicea, as the point of entry from the east and a regional capital, was also required to provide dinners for the governor's staff, the soldiers, and the empire's guests. The hosts were often compelled to pay a daily sum to the visitors and provide them with clothing. In addition, these hosts had to endure the insults which the "soldiers billeted upon them."[144] The Roman government took advantage of Laodicea's wealth and affluence. Perhaps this explains the city's reluctance to accept any financial assistance from the empire.

This ordeal was engraved in the Laodiceans' minds. Jesus's promise that He will only dine with them if someone hears His voice and welcomes Him sharply contrasts with the brash Roman "guests" who exploited their hosts.

Jesus, who has more power than any ruler or empire, humbly invites the believer to share a meal with Him. In Hebrew culture, hosting a person for a meal is an honor. Abraham hosted three strangers and received a tremendous blessing—the promise of a son.

> The Lord appeared to Abraham near the great trees of Mamre while he was sitting at the entrance to his tent in the heat of the day. Abraham looked up and saw three men standing nearby. When he saw them, he hurried from the entrance of his tent to meet them and bowed low to the ground.

He said, "If I have found favor in your eyes, my lord, do not pass your servant by. Let a little water be brought, and then you may all wash your feet and rest under this tree. Let me get you something to eat, so you can be refreshed and then go on your way—now that you have come to your servant."

"Very well," they answered, "do as you say."

So Abraham hurried into the tent to Sarah. "Quick," he said, "get three seahs of the finest flour and knead it and bake some bread."

(Gn 18:1-6)

In Hebrew culture, eating with a person implied that you were willing to protect him or her. In the twenty-third Psalm, King David of Israel says, "You prepare a table before me in the presence of my enemies" (Ps 23:5). Dining together sealed a bond of friendship and alliance.

The Greek word for "eat" signifies the evening meal. In Greek culture, breakfast was simply bread dipped in wine. Lunch was similarly meager. However, the evening meal, *"deipnon,"* was significant. Diners lingered over their food and drink discussing the day's events, chatting about happenings, and conversing in a relaxed and leisurely manner.[145]

By using this wording, Christ invites the Laodiceans to join Him in an extended, meaningful time together spent conversing and dining. He seeks to connect with them on a deep and profound level. He invites the readers to pursue a lasting relationship with Him.

What would you say to a resident of Laodicea to urge them to accept Christ's invitation?

How do Christ's actions show His great love for us?

Have you opened the door for Jesus to come in and dine with you?

How is Jesus's presence in your life obvious to those around you?

How can you share this message with a world that needs to feel His love?

To him who overcomes,
I will give the right to sit with me on my throne,
just as I overcame
and sat down with my Father on his throne.
He who has an ear,
let him hear what the Spirit says to the churches.
Revelation 3:21-22

THE THRONE OF MY FATHER

The author of Hebrews, under the inspiration of the Spirit, peels back the curtains of Heaven to give us a glimpse of the magnificent glory that believers will behold. Writing to a Jewish audience, he or she makes a case for the preeminence of Christ over the prophets and the angels and describes the glory of God revealed in Jesus.

> In the past God spoke to our ancestors through the prophets at many times and in various ways, but in these last days he has spoken to us by his Son, whom he appointed heir of all things, and through whom also he made the universe. The Son is the radiance of God's glory and the exact representation of his being, sustaining all things by his powerful word. After he had provided purification for sins, he sat down at the right hand of the Majesty in heaven. So he became as much superior to the angels as the name he has inherited is superior to theirs. (Heb 1:1-4)

Jesus provided purification for our sins by sacrificing His life for us on the cross. The atoning blood of His sacrifice would be very familiar to this Hebrew audience who sacrificed animals for the forgiveness of their sins. However, Jesus's sacrifice was different. The Jewish believers continually offered their sacrifice, but Jesus's sacrifice was "once for all" (Heb 9:12).

> But when Christ came as high priest of the good things that are now already here, he went through the greater and more perfect tabernacle that is not made with human hands, that is to say, is not a part of this creation. He did not enter by means of the blood of goats and calves; but he entered the Most Holy Place once for all by his own blood, thus obtaining eternal redemption. (Heb 9:11-12)

When Jesus breathed his last breath on the cross, He told us, "It is finished" (Jn 19:30). He went to heaven and "sat down" because His work was done (Heb 1:3). There were no chairs for priests in the temple. Their work was never done. After one round of sacrifices was offered, they began preparing for the next round. Only Jesus had the power to make the sacrifice "once for all" (Heb 9:12). The battle is over. The victory is won. Jesus sits down.

Another image that would have been familiar to the Jewish mind is that of the High Priest sitting at the right hand of the king. The High Priest was a religious and political figure in their culture. Throughout their history and at the time of the writing of the letters in Revelation, the High Priest was a ruler with governmental jurisdiction and advisory privileges. In the time of King David, the priest Nathan was a trusted counselor and confidante to the king. Therefore, the Hebrews to whom this letter is written could identify with Jesus being deemed the great high priest sitting at the right hand of the king.

> Therefore, since we have a great high priest who has ascended into heaven, Jesus the Son of God, let us hold firmly to the faith we profess. For we do not have a high priest who is unable to empathize with our weaknesses, but we have one who has been tempted in every way, just as we are—yet he did not sin. Let us then approach God's throne of grace with confidence, so that we may receive mercy and find grace to help us in our time of need. (Heb 4:14-16)

In the letter to the Hebrews, the author gives a glimpse of the Father's throne. He closes with the amazing promise that those who invite Him into their lives will have the privilege of approaching the throne to receive mercy and grace.

What did it mean to those in the church of Laodicea to be an "overcomer?"

What does that mean today?

———

Jesus's love for us makes it possible for us to approach the throne of God with the confidence of knowing that we will receive mercy and grace. How does this shape how you live your life today?

How can you take this good news to others?

What is one takeaway and insight from the letter to the church at Laodicea that resonates with you?

In what way might that insight be calling you into a new way of being and doing?

CONCLUSION

What a journey!

We have visited all seven of the congregations to whom Jesus wrote His letters. The backdrop of the cities and their churches adds context. Although this expedition has come to an end, the lessons from the letters will continue to echo in your heart and mind as you journey through life with Christ. Although the epistles to these churches were written thousands of years ago, their message is as relevant to us today as it was to the original recipients.

The writer of Hebrews assures us that "the word of God is alive and active" (Heb 4:12). Therefore, the lessons that caught your attention and resonated with you on this journey may not carry the same meaning when you visit with them again. As you study these same passages in a different phase of your life, the Lord will reveal other truths. The Lord will provide you with exactly what you need.

What resonated with you on this expedition?

When your sandals were clicking down the marble streets of Ephesus, did you question if you had lost the "lovin' feelin'?" While sitting on the pews amid the loyal believers in Smyrna, did you feel the deep love of Christ as He promises the victor's crown to the faithful? Did people or influences in your life which are leading you astray come to mind as you were in Pergamum, "where Satan lives?" Did Jesus's reprimand to the followers of Jezebel convict you while you were in the ordinary town of Thyatira? When you were wearing your fashionable Turkish red clothing in Sardis, did you feel the Spirit moving you to change back into your unsoiled white garment? When you heard the suffering of the believers in Philadelphia and felt the ground quiver under your feet, did you long for the peace and stability of the Lord? Did you ask the merchants in Laodicea to refund your money on that expensive eye salve as your eyes were open to the truths of Jesus?

I am interested to know the lessons which you took away from the letters. Let me hear from you! You can email me at LessonsfromtheLetters@gmail.com or log on to our website, LessonsfromtheLetters.com. If you would like to explore the lessons in a group setting, contact me at the email above.

Remember our journey. Just as you would flip through photos of a vacation, look back over the cities, the churches, and the lessons. Bask in the great love of the One who wrote the letters.

My prayer is that God will reveal the *Lessons from the Letters* and help you to *Live the Abundant Life* to His glory.

May you have the ear to hear His word.

Bon Voyage!

AMEN

BIBLIOGRAPHY

Adams, Charles Frances. *Memoirs of John Quincy Adams: Comprising Portions of His Diary,* Volume 9. Philadelphia: J. B. Lippincott, 1876.

Arnold, Eberhard. *The Early Christians in Their Own Words.* Walden, New York: Plough Publishing House 1997.

Barclay, William. *Letters to the Seven Churches.* New York: Abingdon Press, 1958.

Betenson, Lulu Parker. *Butch Cassidy, My Brother.* Salt Lake City: Brigham Young University Press 1975.

Beaumont, Mike. *The New Lion Bible Encyclopedia.* Oxford: Wilkinson House, 2012.

Black, Martha. *Martha Black.* Whitehorse, Yukon: Wolf Creek Books, 2003.

Bonfante-Warren, Alexandra. *The Louvre.* New York: Barnes and Noble Books, 2003.

Bratt, Bill. "Teddy and Mrs. Thompson." The Power of Encouragement. Retrieved on June 10, 2019. https://achieve.lausd.net/cms/lib/CA01000043/Centricity/domain/625/pdfs/social%20awareness/Article-Power%20of%20Encouragement.pdf.

Caldwell, Zelda. "This Painting of Jesus Knocking at a Door is the Most Traveled Work of Art in History. Aleteia. Accessed July 12, 2019. https://aleteia.org/2019/02/07/this-painting-of-jesus-knocking-at-a-door-is-the-most-traveled-work-of-art-in-history/.

Carlson, Erika K. (October 16, 2017) "Twenty things you didn't know about lasers." *Discover Magazine.* Accessed June 8, 2019. http://discovermagazine.com/2018/nov/20-things-you-didnt-know-about--lasers/.

Chaitkin, Anton. (November 16, 2007) "J Q Adams Promotes Internal Improvements in the American Patriot" ICLC Shiller Institute. Accessed November 10, 2018. https://larouchepub.com/eiw/public/2007/eirv34n45-20071116/70-71_745.pdf.

Chiu, David. (November 18, 1978) "Jonestown: Thirteen Things You Should Know About Cult Massacre." Rolling Stone. Accessed May 20, 2019. https://www.rollingstone.com/culture/culture-features/jonestown-13-things-you-should-know-about-cult-massacre-121974/.

Code and Theory. "How a Little Girl Grew Up to Be an Icon." Morton Salt. Accessed June 25, 2019. ,https://www.mortonsalt.com/heritage-era/littlegirl-grew-upto-icon/.

Collignon, Maxime. *Pergame*. Paris: L. Henry May Publishing, 1898.

Collins, Ace. *Music for your Heart*. Nashville: Abingdon Press, 2013.

Connolly, Peter. *A History of the Jewish People in the Time of Jesus from Herod the Great to Masada*. New York: Peter Bedrick Books 1983.

Constitutional Rights Foundation. (2012) "Quartering of Soldiers in Colonial America: What Really Happened?" CRF. Accessed July 14, 2019. https://www.crf-usa.org/images/pdf/quarteringofsoldiersincolonialaamerica.pdf.

Cosmos Magazine Blog. (September 21, 2017) "Fun Physics Facts about Lasers" Cosmos Magazine. Accessed June 8, 2019. https://cosmosmagazine.com/society/fun-physics-facts-about-lasers.

Culpepper, R. Alan. *John, the Son of Zebedee: The Life of a Legend*. Minneapolis: First Fortress Press, 2000.Daiches, David. *Robert Louis Stevenson*. New York: New Directions Books, 1947.

Douglas, C. N. *Forty Thousand Quotations*. New York: Halcyon House, 1917.

Edmonds, Anna G. *Turkey's Religious Sites*. Turkey: Damko Publications, 1997.

Ellis, Mark. "Missionary Died Thinking He was a Failure 84 Years Later Thriving Churches Found Hidden in the Jungle." Godreports. Accessed July 1, 2019. http://Godreports.com/2014/05/missionary-died-thinking-he-was-a-failure-84-years-later-thriving-churches-found-hidden-in-the-jungle/

Encyclopedia of Greater Philadelphia. "City of 'Brotherly Love' a Duel of Destiny vs. Irony." BBC World Service. Accessed July 1, 2019. https://whyy.org/articles/city-of-brotherly-love-a-duel-of-destiny-vs-irony/

Ewing, Heather. *The Lost World of James Smithson*. New York: Bloomsbury, 2007.

Farquhar, Michael. "James Smithson." Washington Post. Accessed July 2, 2019. https://www.washingtonpost.com/archive/1996/01/10/james-smithson/070c7021-fc44-497d-9010-54f25935aebf/?noredirect=on&utm_term=.59c781cf

Fields, Samantha. (November 9, 2009). "Divided by the Wall-A Family's Tale." ABC News. Accessed June 30, 2019. https://abcnews.go.com/WN/anna-kaminsky-remembers-life-berlin-wall/story?id=9032219.

Faith Bible Baptist Church. "Quotes from Billy Sunday." FBBC. Accessed March 7, 2019 http://www.fbbc.com/messages/billys.htm.

Francis, James Allen, and Kenneth Blanchard. *One Solitary Life*. Nashville: Thomas Nelson Publishing, 2005.

Foster, Herbert Baldwin. *Dio's Rome*. Troy, New York: Pafraets Book Company 1906.

Four Chaplains Memorial Foundation. (2015) "The Story." The saga of the Four Chaplains. Accessed May 19, 2019. http://www.fourchaplains.org/the-saga-of-the-four-chaplains/.

Fox, Margalit. *Conan Doyle for the Defense*. New York: Random House, 2018.

Foxe, John. *Foxe's Book of Martyrs*. London: Frederick Warne and Company, 1869.

Freedman, Russell. *Kids at Work*. New York: Clarion, 1994.

Green, Peter. *Alexander of Macedon, 356-323 B.C.* Berkeley: University of California Press, 1991.

Gregg, Steve. *Revelation: Four Views Revised and Updated.* Nashville: Thomas Nelson Publishing, 2013.

Hamilton, Edith. *Mythology.* Boston: Little, Brown, and Company, 1942.

Hanfmann, George M. A. *From Croesus to Constantine, The Cities of Western Asia Minor and Their Arts in Greek and Roman Times*. Ann Arbor: The University of Michigan Press, 1975.

Harvey, Paul, Jr. *Paul Harvey-For What It's Worth.* New York: Bantam Books, 1991.

Hemer, Colin J. *Letters to the Seven Churches of Asia*. Grand Rapids, MI: Wm. B. Eerdsman Publishing Company, 2001.

Hoerth, Alfred, and McRay, John. *Bible Archeology*. Grand Rapids, MI: Baker Books, 2005.

Hughes, Robert. *The Shock of the New*. New York: Alfred A. Knopf, 2013.

Iza. (October 8, 2018). "Laodicea on the Lycus." Turkey Archeological News. Accessed July 7, 2019. https://turkisharchaeonews.net/site/laodicea-lycus.

Jeremiah, David. *Escape the Coming Night*. Nashville: Thomas Nelson, 2018.

Jilani, Zaid. (March 5, 2011). "Five Things Unions Have Done for All Americans." Think Progress.org. Accessed June 9, 2019. https://thinkprogress.org/report-five-things-unions-have-done-for-all-americans-6379ca1779fe/.

Joshel, Sandra R. *Slavery in the Roman World (Cambridge Introduction to Roman Civilization).* Cambridge: Cambridge University Press, 2010.

Keller, Phillip. *A Shepherd Looks at the Twenty-Third Psalm*. Grand Rapids: Zondervan 1970.

Klara, Robert. (December 1, 2014). "Chances Are, the Clothes You're Wearing Right Now Have Been Washed in Tide." Adweek.com. Accessed March 13, 2019. https://www.adweek.com/brand-marketing/why-clothes-youre-wearing-right-now-have-probably-been-washed-tide-161643/.

LaBella, Laura. *The Nuremberg Trials*. New York: Rosen Publishing, 2015.

Lang, Katie. (February 2, 2018). "Four Chaplains Bring Saving Grace to World War II Ship" DoDLive. Accessed May 19, 2019. http://www.dodlive.mil/2018/02/02/otd-4-chaplains-bring-saving-grace-to-sinking-wwii-ship/.

Luther, Martin. "Martin Luther Quotable Quote" Goodreads. Accessed July 1, 2019. https://www.goodreads.com/quotes/26222-we-are-saved-by-faith-alone-but-the-faith-that

Kinzer, Stephen. (September 14, 1997). "Seeing Pergamon Whole" New York Times. Accessed May 18, 2018. https://www.nytimes.com/1997/09/14/travel/seeing-pergamon-whole.html.

Krznaric, Roman. How Should We Live? Great Ideas from the Past for Everyday Life. Katonah, New York: Blue Bridge Books, 2013.

Maier, Paul L. *In the Fullness of Time, A Historian Looks at Christmas, Easter, and the Early Church.* New York: HarperCollins, 1991.

McGee, J. Vernon. *Thru the Bible.* Nashville: Thomas Nelson, 1983.

McKeown, Niall. *The Invention of Ancient Slavery.* London: Duckworth, 2007.

McMahan, Tammy. *Sword Study 1 Peter: National Bible Bee.* San Antonio, Texas: The Shelby Kennedy Foundation, 2010.

Merriam-Webster. Accessed June 24, 2019. https://www.merriam-webster.com/dictionary.

Miles, C. Austin. "In the Garden." Hymnary. Accessed June 25, 2019. https://hymnary.org/text/i_come_to_the_garden_alone.

Moody, Dwight L. (n.d.). AZQuotes.com. Accessed June 29, 2019. AZQuotes.com Web site: https://www.azquotes.com/quote/662770

Murakami-Fester, Amber. (October 23, 2016) "Counterfeit Cash Gets Harder to Spot: Some Telltale Signs." Nerdwallet. Accessed April 25, 2019. www.usatoday.com/story/money/personalfinance/2016/10/23/counterfeir-money-spot-fake/92080738/.

NBC News. (August 27, 2014) "Severed Snake Heads Can Still Bite and Often Do," Accessed March 7, 2019. https://www.nbcnews.com/science/weird-science/severed-snake-heads-can-still-bite-often-do-n190561.

Nelson, Soraya Sarhaddi. (November 6, 2013) "The Man who Disobeyed His Boss and Opened the Berlin Wall." NPR Parallels. Accessed June 30, 2019. https://www.npr.org/sections/parallels/2014/11/06/361785478/the-man-who-disobeyed-his-boss-and-opened-the-berlin-wall.

Niederkorn, William S. (November 24, 2009). "Missionaries from Congo Confirm Atrocities." Accessed April 12, 2019, https://timestraveler.blogs.nytimes.com/2009/11/24/missionaries-from-congo-confirm-atrocities/?rref=collection%2Fbyline%2Fwilliam-s.-niederkorn&action=click&contentCollection=undefined&regional.

Open Doors. "Christian Persecution Statistics." Accessed May 24, 2019. ,https://www.opendoorsusa.org/christian-persecution/.Perkins, Bill. *Six Battles Every Man Must Win, and the Ancient Secrets You'll Need to Succeed.* Wheaton, Illinois: Tyndale House 2004.

Raeburn, Alicia. (January 15, 2019) "10 Giveaways that You're from Philadelphia." *Matador Network*. Retrieved July 1, 2019. https://matadornetwork.com/read/signs-from-philadelphia/.

Rafferty, John P. (May 22, 2019). "Ermine." Encyclopedia Britannica. Accessed June 28, 2019. https://www.britannica.com/animal/ermine-mammal.

Redwing, Ronald. "Egyptian Gold Processing." *Penn State College of Earth Mineral Sciences*. Accessed May 15, 2019. https://www.e-education.psu.edu/matse81/node/2123.

Reed, Jonathan L. *The HarperCollins Visual Guide to the New Testament*. New York: HarperCollins Publications, 2007.

Reese, Margaret Thompson. (March 2017) "Physiology of Self Renewal." Medical Science Navigator. Accessed June 16, 2019. https://www.medicalsciencenavigator.com/physiology-of-self-renewal/

Robertson, Gordon "The Seat of Satan-Nazi Germany." Christian Broadcast Network. Accessed May 30, 2018. https://www1.cbn.com/700club/seat-satan-nazi-germany.

Rogers, Adrian. *Tapestry: Promises and Prophecy.* Memphis: Love Worth Finding Ministries, Inc., 2010.

Rogers, Adrian. *The Merritt Island Years*. Memphis: Love Worth Finding Ministries, Inc., 2018.

Salt Association, "The History of Salt, Roman Times." Salt Association. Accessed June 18, 2019. https://www.saltassociation.co.uk/education/salt-history/roman-times/.

Sarotte, Mary Elise. *The Collapse, The Accidental Opening of the Berlin Wall*. New York: Basic Books, 2014.

Schreiber, Mordecai. *The Shengold Jewish Encyclopedia.* New York: Shengold Books, 1998.

Schultz, Colin. (December 24, 2014). "There's More to Frankincense and Myrrh Than Meets the Eye." Smithsonian Magazine. Accessed May 18, 2019. www.smithsonianmag.com/smart-news/chemically-theres-lot-more-frankincense-and-myrrh-meets-eye-180953727/#tp6SEQSDMPS342gj.99.

Seneca, Lucius Annaeus. *Anger, Mercy, Revenge-the Complete Works of Seneca translated by Robert A. Kaster and Martha C. Nussbaum*. Chicago: University of Chicago, 2010.

Shields, Sarah. *Turkey.* Washington, DC: National Geographic, 2008.

Simondi, Tom. "The Cobbler Turned Doctor." Fables of Aesop. Accessed July 25, 2019. https://fablesofaesop.com/the-cobbler-turned-doctor.html.

Smithsonian Institute. "Our Museums, Galleries and Zoo." Smithsonian Institute. Accessed March 30, 2019. https://www.si.edu/museums.

Sprague, Michael. *Disaster*. Maitland, Florida: Xulon Press, 2011.

St. Paul's Cathedral. (January 7, 2019). "The Light of the World" St. Paul's Cathedral. Accessed July 13, 2019. https://www.stpauls.co.uk/history-collections/the-collections/collections-highlights/the-light-of-the-world.

Staatliche Museen zu Berlin. "History of the Mussen zu Berlin." Staatliche Mussen zu Berlin. Accessed May 30, 2018. https://www.smb.museum/en/about-us/history.html.

Stanford, Miles J. *Fox's Book of Martyrs*. Grand Rapids: Zondervan, 1967.

Stiles, TJ. *The First Tycoon*. New York: Vintage Books, 2009.

Strassler, Robert B. *The Landmark Herodotus*. New York: Pantheon Books, 2007.

Strong, James. *Strong's Exhaustive Concordance of the Bible*. Peabody, MA: Hendrickson Publishing, 2008.

Sun-tzu and Sawyer, Ralph D. *The Art of War*. New York: Barnes and Noble, 1994.

Swenson, Kyle. (June 18, 2018). "Georgia Woman Kills Rabid Bobcat with Her Bare Hands" Washington Post. Accessed June 20, 2018. https://www.washingtonpost.com/news/morning-mix/wp/2018/06/18/it-was-either-me-or-the-cat-georgia-woman-kills-rabid-bobcat-with-her-bare-hands/?noredirect=on&utm_term=.941f0c2c06e1.

Tate Museum. "William Holman-Hunt." Tate. Accessed July 13, 2019. https://www.tate.org.uk/art/artists/william-holman-hunt-287.

Taylor, Frederick. *The Berlin Wall: A World Divided 1961-1989*. New York: Harper Collins Publishers, 2007.

Tzu, Sun. *The Art of War*. New York: Penguin Group, 2002.

United States Archives and Records Administration. "Constitution Transcript." Accessed April 11, 2019. https://www.archives.gov/founding-docs/constitution-transcript.

United States Holocaust Memorial Museum. Accessed July 11, 2019. https://www.ushmm.org/learn/introduction-to-the-holocaust/path-to-nazi-genocide/chapter-1/aftermath-of-world-war-i-and-the-rise-of-nazism-1918-1933.

United States House of Representatives History, Art & Archives. "State of The Union." Accessed February 8, 2019. https://history.house.gov/Institution/SOTU/State-of-the-Union/.

United States Secret Service. (April 2016). "Know Your Money." United States Secret Service, Department of Homeland Security. Accessed April 25, 2019. https://www.uscurrency.gov/sites/default/files/downloadable-materials/files/KnowYourMoney_062014.pdf.

Utah Travel Industry. (2019) "History of Butch Cassidy" Utah Travel Industry Website. Accessed June 4, 2019. https://utah.com/old-west/butch-cassidy.

Vander Laan, Ray. *Early Church Small Group Edition Discovery Guide.* Grand Rapids: Zondervan 2008.

Vision 180. (July 27, 2019). "Judging by Appearance" Vision 180. Accessed July 27, 2019. https://vision180.org.au/2007/12/11/judging-by-appearances/.

Vozzella, Laura. (December 8, 2006). "It's Johns Hopkins. Johns. Say it again. Johns." The Baltimore Sun. Accessed June 5, 2019. https://www.baltimoresun.com/news/bs-xpm-2006-12-08-0612080220-story.html.

Watson, Thomas. Weigand, David. (February 7, 2014) "Butch Cassidy and the Sundance Kid Separates Fact from Fiction" Houston Chronicle. Accessed June 4, 2019. https://www.houstonchronicle.com/entertainment/tv/article/Butch-Cassidy-the-Sundance-Kid-separates-fact-5215346.php.

Whiston, William. *Josephus the Complete Works.* Nashville: Thomas Nelson Publishers, 1998.

Wigoder, Geoffrey. *The New Standard Jewish Encyclopedia.* New York: Facts on File, 1992.

World Atlas. (May 20, 2018). "What Does the Sun Never Sets on the British Empire Mean?" Accessed July 14, 2019. https://www.worldatlas.com/articles/what-does-the-sun-never-sets-on-the-british-empire-mean.html.

END NOTES

1   English Standard Version Bible (Wheaton:Crossway Bibles, 2001), 1859.

2   Phillip Keller, *A Shepherd Looks at the Twenty-Third Psalm* (Grand Rapids: Zondervan, 1970), 60.

3   R. Alan Culpepper, *John, the Son of Zebedee: The Life of a Legend* (Minneapolis: First Fortress Press, 2000),140.

4   *The Methodist Hymnal* (Nashville:Parthenon,1966), 388.

5   "Constitution Transcript," The United States Archives and Records Administration, accessed April 11, 2019, https://www.archives.gov/founding-docs/constitution-transcript.

6   "State of the Union," United States House of Representatives. History, Art & Archives, accessed February 8, 2019, https://history.house.gov/Institution/SOTU/State-of-the-Union/.

7   Anna G. Edmonds, *Turkey's Religious Sites* (Turkey: Damko Publications 1997), 33.

8   Paul Trebilco, *The Early Churches in Ephesus from Paul* (Tubingen, Germany: Mohu Siebeck 2004), 22.

9   Michael Woods and Mary B. Woods, *Seven Wonders of the Ancient World* (Minneapolis: Twenty-first Century Books, 2009), 64.

10 Ibid.

11 Edith Hamilton, *Mythology* (Boston: Little, Brown and Company, 1942), 44-46.

12 Colin J.Hemer, *Letters to the Seven Churches of Asia* (Grand Rapids, MI: Wm. B. Eerdsman Publishing Company, 2001), 38.

13 Ibid.

14 Michael Sprague, *Disaster* (Maitland, Florida: Xulon Press, 2011), 228.

15 Ibid. 230

16 J. Vernon McGee, Thru the Bible (Nashville: Thomas Nelson, 1983), 901.

17 William Barclay, *Letters to the Seven Churches* (Nashville: Abingdon Press, 1957), 25.

18 Ronald Redwing, "Egyptian Gold Processing." Penn State College of Earth Mineral Sciences. Accessed May 15, 2019. h ttps://www.e-educa-

tion.psu.edu/matse81/node/2123.

19   David Chiu. (November 18, 1978) "Jonestown: Thirteen Things You Should Know About Cult Massacre." Rolling Stone, Accessed May 20, 2019. https://www.rollingstone.com/culture/culture-features/jonestown-13-things-you-should-know-about-cult-massacre-121974/.

20   Pierre Berton, *The Klondike Fever,* The Life and Death of the Last Great Gold Rush (New York: Alfred A Knopf, 1958), 433.

21   Donna Walsh Shepherd, *The Klondike Gold Rush* (New York, Grolier Publishing, 1998), 18.

22   Burton, *The Klondike Fever*, 430.

23   Tom Simondi, "The Cobbler Turned Doctor." *Fables of Aesop*, accessed July 25, 2019, https://fablesofaesop.com/the-cobbler-turned-doctor.html.

24   Barclay, *Letters to the Seven Churches*, 27.

25   Amber Murakami-Fester, (October 23, 2016) "Counterfeit Cash Gets Harder to Spot: Some Telltale Signs." *Nerdwallet*, accessed April 25, 2019, www.usatoday.com/story/money/personalfinance/2016/10/23/counter-feir-money-spot-fake/92080738/.

26   United States Secret Service. (April 2016) "Know Your Money." United States Secret Service, Department of Homeland Security, accessed April 25, 2019, https://www.uscurrency.gov/sites/default/files/downloadable-materials/files/KnowYourMoney_062014.pdf.

27   Niall McKeown, The Invention of Ancient Slavery, (London: Duckworth, 2007), 116.

28   Ibid.

29   Seneca, *Anger, Mercy, Revenge-the Complete Works of Seneca translated by Robert A. Kaster and Martha C. Nussbaum* (Chicago: University of Chicago, 2010), 172.

30   Barclay, *Letters to the Seven Churches,* 84.

31   J. Vernon McGee, *Thru the Bible* (Nashville: Thomas Nelson, 1983), 903.

32   Hemer, *Letters to the Seven Churches of Asia*, 59.

33   Ibid, 57.

34   Foundation of the Four Chaplains, "The Story" http://www.fourchaplains.org/the-saga-of-the-four-chaplains/.

35   Katie Lang, "Four Chaplains Bring Saving Grace to World War II Ship" http://www.dodlive.mil/2018/02/02/otd-4-chaplains-bring-saving-grace-to-sinking-wwii-ship/

36   Foundations of the Four Chaplains.

37   Katie Lang.

38 Peter Green, Alexander of Macedon, 356-323 BC (Berkeley: University of California Press, 1991), 188.

39 Barclay, *Letters to Seven Churches*, 34.

40 Paul L. Maier, In the Fullness of Time, A Historian Looks at Christmas, Easter, and the Early Church (New York: HarperCollins 1991), 66.

41 Colin Schultz, "There's More to Frankincense and Myrrh Than Meets the Eye," https://www.smithsonianmag.com/smart-news/chemically-theres-lot-more-frankincense-and-myrrh-meets-eye-180953727/#t-p6SEQSDMPS342gj.99.

42 McGee, *Thru the Bible*, 494.

43 Maier, *In the Fullness of Time, A Historian Looks at Christmas, Easter, and the Early Church,* 66.

44 Ibid.

45 James Allen Francis and Kenneth Blanchard, *One Solitary Life*. Nashville:Thomas Nelson Publishing 2005.

46 Faith Bible Baptist Church. "Quotes from Billy Sunday." FBBC, accessed March 7, 2019, http://www.fbbc.com/messages/billys.htm.

47 Open Doors. "Christian Persecution Statistics," accessed May 24, 2019, https://www.opendoorsusa.org/christian-persecution/.

48 Arnold Eberhard. *The Early Christians in Their Own Words* (Walden, New York:Plough Publishing House, 1997), 133.

49 John Foxe, *Foxe's Book of Martyrs,* (London, Frederick Warne and Company, 1869), 27.

50 Foxe, *Foxe's Book of Martyrs,* 29.

51 Kyle Swenson, (June 18, 2018) "Georgia Woman Kills Rabid Bobcat With Her Bare Hands" Washington Post, accessed June 20, 2018, https://www.washingtonpost.com/news/morning-mix/wp/2018/06/18/it-was-either-me-or-the-cat-georgia-woman-kills-rabid-bobcat-with-her-bare-hands/?noredirect=on&utm_term=.941f0c2c06e1.

52 Ibid.

53 James Strong, *Strong's Exhaustive Concordance of the Bible* (Peabody, MA, Hendrickson Publishing, 2008), 1515.

54 Strong, *Strong's Exhaustive Concordance of the Bible*, 1656

55 https://www.biblestudytools.com/lexicons/greek/nas/diadema.html.

56 Barclay, *Letters to the Seven Churches*, 38.

57 Alexandra Bonfante-Warren, *The Louvre* (New York: Barnes and Noble Books 2003), 25.

58 George M. A. Hanfmann, *From Croesus to Constantine, The Cities of Western Asia Minor and their Arts in Greek and Roman Times* (Ann Arbor: The University of Michigan Press, 1975), 29.

59 Herbert Baldwin Foster, *Dio's Rome* (Troy, New York: Pafraets Book Company, 1906), 172.

60 Stephen Kinzcr, "Seeing Pergamon Whole" *New York Times*,accessed May 18, 2018, https://www.nytimes.com/1997/09/14/travel/seeing-pergamon-whole.html.

61 "History of the Mussen zu Berlin." Staatliche Mussen zu Berlin, accessed May 30, 2018, https://www.smb.museum/en/about-us/history.html.

62 Robert Hughes, *The Shock of the New* (New York: Alfred A. Knopf, 2013), 63.

63 LaBella, Laura. *The Nuremburg Trials* (New York: Rosen Publishing, 2015), 15.

64 Ray Vander Laan, *Early Church Small Group Edition Discovery Guide* (Grand Rapids: Zondervan, 2008), 84.

65 Goodreads, 2019, "Blaise Pascal Quotes," accessed July 25, https://www.goodreads.com/quotes/801132-there-is-a-god-shaped-vacuum-in-the-heart-of-each.

66 Sun Tzu, *The Art of War* (New York: Penguin Group, 2002), 19.

67 Barclay, *Letters to the Seven Churches,* 23.

68 J. Vernon McGee, *Thru the Bible*, 903.

69 Ibid, 903.

70 Barclay, *Letters to the Seven Churches*, 52.

71 LauraVozzella, (December 8, 2006), " It's Johns Hopkins. Johns. Say it again. Johns" The Baltimore Sun, accessed June 5, 2019, https://www.baltimoresun.com/news/bs-xpm-2006-12-08-0612080220-story.html.

72 Hemer, *Letters to the Seven Churches of Asia,* 107.

73 Margalit Fox, Conan Doyle for the Defense (New York, Random House, 2018), xv.

74 Carlson, Erika K. (October 16, 2017) "Twenty things you didn't know about lasers." Discover Magazine, accessed June 8, 2019, http://discovermagazine.com/2018/nov/20-things-you-didnt-know-about--lasers/.

75 Adrian Rogers, *Tapestry: Promises and Prophecy* (Memphis: Love Worth Finding Ministries, Inc., 2010), 37.

76 Ibid.

77 Bill Bratt, "Teddy and Mrs. Thompson" accessed https://achieve.lausd.net/cms/lib/CA01000043/Centricity/domain/625/pdfs/social%20awareness/

Article-Power%20of%20Encouragement.pdf

78   Freedman, Russell. Kids at Work (New York: Clarion, 1994), 1-2.

79   Ibid.

80   Zaid Jilani https://thinkprogress.org/report-five-things-unions-have-done-for-all-americans-6379ca1779fe/.

81   Barclay, *Letters to the Seven Churches,* 84.

82   Ewing, Heather. *The Lost World of James Smithson* (New York: Blooms-bury 2007) 16.

83   Ewing, The Lost World of James Smithson, 298.

84   Smithsonian Institute. "Our Museums, Galleries and Zoo." Smithsonian Institute, accessed March 30, 2019, https://www.si.edu/museums.

85   Ace Collins, *Music for your Heart* (Nashville: Abingdon Press 2013), 26.

86   Reese, Margaret Thompson. (March 2017) "Physiology of Self Renewal." Medical Science Navigator, accessed https://www.medicalsciencenavigator.com/physiology-of-self-renewal/

87   Rogers, Tapestry, Promises and Prophecy, 39

88   Charles Frances Adams, *Memoirs of John Quincy Adams: Comprising Portions of His Diary, Volume 9* (Philadelphia: J. B. Lippincott, 1876), 29, 31.

89   Chaitkin, Anton. (November 16, 2007) "J Q Adams Promotes Internal Improvements in the American Patriot" *ICLC Shiller Institute*, accessed November 10, 2018, https://larouchepub.com/eiw/public/2007/eir-v34n45-20071116/70-71_745.pdf.

90   TJ Styles, *The First Tycoon* (New York: Vintage Books, 2009), 124.

91   Code and Theory. "How a Little Girl Grew Up to Be an Icon." Morton Salt, accessed June 25, 2019, https://www.mortonsalt.com/heritage-era/littlegirl-grew-upto-icon/.

92   Salt Association "The History of Salt, Roman Times." Salt Association, accessed June 18, 2019ll. https://www.saltassociation.co.uk/education/salt-history/roman-times/.

93   Ray Vander Laan, *Early Church Small Group Edition Discovery Guide,* (Grand Rapids: Zondervan, 2008), 48.

94   Ibid, 51.

95   Ibid, 50.

96   Accessed June 23, 2019. http://thomaswatsonquotes.com/when-the-world-gets-into-the-heart/.

97   Robert B. Strassler, *The Landmark Herodotus,* (New York, Pantheon

Books, 2007),48.

98   John P. Rafferty. (May 22, 2019) "Ermine." *Encyclopedia Britannica.* Accessed June 28, 2019. https://www.britannica.com/animal/ermine-mammal.

99   Bill Perkins. Six Battles Every Man Must Win, (Wheaton, Illinois, Tyndale House, 2004), 52.

100   Dwight L. Moody. (n.d.). AZQuotes.com. Accessed June 29, 2019. AZQuotes.com Web site: https://www.azquotes.com/quote/662770.

101   GodTube Staff (2019) "In the Garden," *GodTube.* Accessed June 29, 2019. https://www.godtube.com/popular-hymns/in-the-garden/.

102   Austin C. Miles, "In the Garden." Hymnary. Accessed June 25, 2019. https://hymnary.org/text/i_come_to_the_garden_alone.

103   Henry Ford. (n.d.). AZQuotes.com. Accessed June 29, 2019. AZQuotes.com Web site: https://www.azquotes.com/quote/481726.

104   Klara, Robert. (December 1, 2014) "Chances Are, the Clothes You're Wearing Right Now Have Been Washed in Tide." Adweek.com. Accessed March 13, 2019. https://www.adweek.com/brand-marketing/why-clothes-youre-wearing-right-now-have-probably-been-washed-tide-161643/.

105   Ibid.

106   Roman Krznaric, *How Should We Live? Great Ideas from the Past for Everyday Life* (Katonah, New York: Blue Bridge Books 2013), 7.

107   Alfred Hoerth and John McRay,John, *Bible Archeology* (Grand Rapids, MI: Baker Books 2005), 234.

108   Edith Hamilton, Mythology (Boston: Little, Brown and Company 1942), 73,67-68.

109   Martin Luther (n.d.) "Martin Luther Quotable Quote" *Goodreads.* Retrieved on July 1, 2019 from https://www.goodreads.com/quotes/26222-we-are-saved-by-faith-alone-but-the-faith-that.

110   Peter Wyden, Wall, the Inside Story of Divided Berlin, (New York, Simon and Schuster, 1989), 21.

111   Samantha Fields. (November 9, 2009) "Divided by the Wall- a Family's Tale" ABC News. Retrieved on June 30, 2019 from https://abcnews.go.com/WN/anna-kaminsky-remembers-life-berlin-wall/story?id=9032219.

112   Mary Elise Sarotte, The Collapse, The Accidental Opening of the Berlin Wall, (New York, Basic Books, 2014) 115.

113   Ibid,144.

114   Ibid,147.

115 Soraya Sarhaddi Nelson. (November 6, 2013) "The Man who Dis-
     obeyed His Boss and Opened the Berlin Wall." NPR Parallels.
     Retrieved on June 30, 2019 from https://www.npr.org/sections/
     parallels/2014/11/06/361785478/the-man-who-disobeyed-his-boss-and-
     opened-the-berlin-wall.

116 Mark Ellis (May 19, 2014). "Missionary Died Thinking He was a Failure
     84 Years Later Thriving Churches Found Hidden in the Jungle." Godre-
     ports. Retrieved on July 1, 2019 from http://godreports.com/2014/05/mis-
     sionary-died-thinking-he-was-a-failure-84-years-later-thriving-churches-
     found-hidden-in-the-jungle/.

117 Ibid.

118 William S. Niederkorn (November 24, 2009). "Missionaries From Congo
     Confirm Atrocities" *NY Times*.Retrieved from https://timestraveler.blogs.
     nytimes.com/2009/11/24/missionaries-from-congo-confirm-atrocities/?r-
     ref=collection%2Fbyline%2Fwilliam-s.-niederkorn&action=click&con-
     tentCollection=undefined&regional.

119 Tammy McMahan, *Sword Study 1 Peter: National Bible Bee,* (San Anto-
     nio, Texas: The Shelby Kennedy Foundation 2010), 66-69.

120 Encyclopedia of Greater Philadelphia.(n.d.) "' City of Brotherly Love' a
     Duel of Destiny vs. Irony." *BBC World Service.* Retrieved on July 1, 2019.
     https://whyy.org/articles/city-of-brotherly-love-a-duel-of-destiny-vs-irony/.

121 Alicia Raeburn. (January 15, 2019) "10 Giveaways that You're from Phila-
     delphia." *Matador Network.* Retrieved July 1, 2019 from https://matador-
     network.com/read/signs-from-philadelphia/.

122 Hemer, *Letters to the Seven Churches of Asia,* 107.

123 Ibid, 157-158.

124 Iza, (October 8,2018) "Laodicea on the Lycus." *Turkey Archeological
     News.* Retrieved from https://turkisharchaeonews.net/site/laodicea-lycus.

125 "Judging by Appearance" *Vision 180* Retrieved on July 27, 2019 from
     https://vision180.org.au/2007/12/11/judging-by-appearances/.

126 Steve Gregg, Revelation-Four Views. 113.

127 Barclay, *Letters to the Seven Churches,* 84.

128 Hemer, *Letters to the Seven Churches of Asia,* 107.

129 Ibid, 189.

130 Paul Harvey, Jr. *Paul Harvey-For What It's Worth.* (New York: Bantam
     Books 1991), 25.

131 United States Holocaust Memorial Museum. Retrieved on July 11, 2019
     from https://www.ushmm.org/learn/introduction-to-the-holocaust/path-
     to-nazi-genocide/chapter-1/aftermath-of-world-war-i-and-the-rise-of-na-

zism-1918-1933.

132 William Barclay, *Letters to the Seven Churches*, 81.

133 Hemer, *Letters to the Seven Churches of Asia,* 85.

134 Hemer, *Letters to the Seven Churches of Asia,* 80.

135 Barclay, *Letters to the Seven Churches*, 82.

136 Iza, Laodicea on the Lycus, 74.

137 Barclay, *Letters to the Seven Churches*, 87.

138 St. Paul's Cathedral. (January 7, 2019) "The Light of the World" St. Paul's Cathedral. Retrieved on July 13, 2019 from https://www.stpauls.co.uk/history-collections/the-collections/collections-highlights/the-light-of-the-world.

139 Tate Museum. (n.d.) "William Holman-Hunt." Tate. Retrieved on July 13, 2019 from https://www.tate.org.uk/art/artists/william-holman-hunt-287.

140 St. Paul's Cathedral.

141 World Atlas. (May 20, 2018). "What Does the Sun Never Sets on the British Empire Mean?" Retrived on July 14, 2019 from https://www.worldatlas.com/articles/what-does-the-sun-never-sets-on-the-british-empire-mean.html.

142 Constitutional Rights Foundation. (2012) "Quartering of Soldiers in Colonial America: What Really Happened?" CRF Retrieved on July 14, 2019 from https://www.crf-usa.org/images/pdf/quarteringofsoldiersincolonialaamerica.pdf.

143 "Parliament Passes the Quartering Act," *History.com,* last updated July 17, 2019 retrieved on July 23, 2019 from https://www.history.com/this-day-in-history/parliament-passes-the-quartering-act.

144 Hemer, *Letters to the Seven Churches of Asia,* 202.

145 Barclay, *Letters to the Seven Churches,* 88.

Made in the USA
Columbia, SC
12 September 2024

41618842R00205